Catholic Environmentalism

Catholic Environmentalism

From Stewardship to Love in Laudato Si'

Mark E. Graham

t&tclark

NEW YORK · LONDON · OXFORD · NEW DELHI · SYDNEY

T&T CLARK
Bloomsbury Publishing Inc, 1359 Broadway, New York, NY 10018, USA
Bloomsbury Publishing Plc, 50 Bedford Square, London, WC1B 3DP, UK
Bloomsbury Publishing Ireland, 29 Earlsfort Terrace, Dublin 2, D02 AY28, Ireland

BLOOMSBURY, T&T CLARK and the T&T Clark logo are trademarks of Bloomsbury Publishing Plc

First published in the United States of America 2026

Cover design: Diana Nuhn
Cover image: iStock.com/mrwyano

Library of Congress Cataloging-in-Publication Data

Names: Graham, Mark E. author
Title: Catholic environmentalism : from stewardship to love in Laudato si' / by
Mark E. Graham, Ph.D.
Description: New York : T&T Clark, 2026. | Includes bibliographical references and index. |
Summary: "This work challenges traditional Catholic environmental thought, advocating for a
theocentric approach-one that sees all of creation as a manifestation of divine love. Engaging,
urgent, and deeply theological, Graham offers a transformative vision and a moral imperative that
places biodiversity and creation's intrinsic value at the center of Catholic ethics"– Provided by
publisher.
Identifiers: LCCN 2025044602 (print) | LCCN 2025044603 (ebook) | ISBN 9780567726025 HB
| ISBN 9780567725981 PB | ISBN 9780567725998 ePDF | ISBN 9780567726001 eBook
Subjects: LCSH: Catholic Church. Pope (2013- : Francis). Laudato sì. | Human ecology–Religious
aspects–Catholic Church | Environmentalism–Religious aspects–Catholic Church | Ecotheology–
Catholic Church | Catholic Church–Doctrines
Classification: LCC BX1795.H82 G725 2026 (print) | LCC BX1795.H82 (ebook)
LC record available at https://lccn.loc.gov/2025044602
LC ebook record available at https://lccn.loc.gov/2025044603

ISBN: HB: 978-0-567-72602-5
          PB: 978-0-567-72598-1
          ePDF: 978-0-567-72599-8
          eBook: 978-0-567-72600-1

Typeset by Integra Software Services Pvt. Ltd.
Printed and bound in the United States of America

For product safety related questions contact productsafety@bloomsbury.com.

To find out more about our authors and books visit www.bloomsbury.com
and sign up for our newsletters.

Contents

Acknowledgments

My life has been bathed in divine grace from the very beginning and as a result I have a lot of gratitude to express. My parents, Mike (RIP) and Laurie Graham, provided me with constant love, affection, patience, and freedom during every phase of my life. I cannot imagine a better pair of parents and I am awfully lucky to have been raised and nurtured by these two. Even at 80+ years of age, my mom still continues to parent me well by serving up heaping doses of humility when she consistently beats me on the golf course. Thanks, Mom, for never letting me forget the importance of being humble!

My two children, Peter and Hannah, are easily the best things to happen to me and I have cherished every moment we have spent together. They are incredibly talented and generous and I look forward to seeing the many lives they will touch as they graduate from college and start their adult lives. They are enormous gifts to the universe and I thank God every day that I was chosen to be their dad.

My sister and brother-in-law, Angie and Steve Koop, are models of hospitality and charity and they make my family's all-too-infrequent trips to their farm in Iowa to be cherished adventures. When my son, Pete, was tasked with writing an essay on "My Favorite Place in the World" in the fourth grade, he wrote eloquently on the grandiosity of the Koop farm. If he were tasked to write an essay on the same topic today, I am sure the subject would still be the Koop farm. Thanks, Angie and Steve, for all the pleasant memories.

I have been fortunate to enjoy the friendship of many animals whose kindness and companionship have been treasured. They were play partners and protectors when I was young, forgiving and nonjudgmental buddies during my awkward teenage years, enthusiastic outdoor adventurers who relished days afield with me as an adult, and one in particular saved my life. So my heartfelt thanks go to all these wonderful friends who have given me so much: Whiskers, Ajax, Heidi, Dan, Mick, Morgan, Max, Jake, Roxy, Swishy, Buddy Boy, Molly, and Angelica.

I have been educated by a number of esteemed theologians, whose fertile minds and generous spirits have challenged and clarified what I understand about God and our bountiful universe. In the sphere of Catholic theological ethics, I owe an enormous debt of gratitude to Philip Keane, S.S. (RIP), Edward Vacek, S.J., Lisa Cahill, David Hollenbach, S.J., and James Keenan, S.J., who each provided a model for skillful inquiry and intellectual generosity. James Keenan, in particular, has read and commented upon a great deal of my work over the years and I have internalized his penchant for charitable criticism, so Jim's presence sculpted this book surreptitiously. If you happen to find the following pages illuminating or interesting, most of the credit goes to Jim, for he has been my mental interlocutor throughout.

Present and former colleagues at Villanova University have blessed me beyond measure with their insights, camaraderie, and support. Tim Brunk, Peter Spitaler, Chris Barnett, Jennifer Jackson, Massimo Faggioli, Jonathan Yates, Timothy Hanchin, Christy Lang-Hearlson, Ilia Delio, Edward Hastings, Joanna Scholz, Stephanie Wong, Jerry Beyer, Joe Loya, Bernard Prusak, Anthony Godzieba, Sue Toton, and Bill Werpehowski— thanks so much for everything you have given me.

Teaching extraordinarily bright and talented students for over two decades has been a unique privilege and I am grateful for those students who have shared their thoughts freely, helped me expand my theological imagination, and openly displayed an infectious enthusiasm for studying theological ethics. Mat Verghese, Ceire Kealty, Jacques Linder, Sharon Gutkowski, Bill Kuncken, Joe Evans, Fr. Ha Nguyen, Sam Odidi, Holden Ackerman, Dane Litchfield, Jeff Ruffin, John Edwards, Sandra Hassink, Brandon Joa, Bill Collins, Gabby Southworth, Dan Griffin, Scott Grapin, Ezra Doyle, Allison Baroni, Catherine Wang, Chris Haw, Andrew Keagy, Mary Catherine O'Reilly-Gindhardt, Mike Santos, Jeff Mayer, and Pete O'Connell— thanks for your love of theological ethics and for your many contributions to academia and the Church. To my students at SCI Phoenix, my heartfelt thanks for your warm welcome and consistent gestures of gratitude. To Brandon Ambrosino, I treasure our friendship and admire the depth of your compassion and love. My life would not be the same without you.

A great deal of this book was written during a sabbatical sponsored by the College of Liberal Arts and Sciences at Villanova University. My thanks to Dean Adele Lindenmeyr for granting me the sabbatical.

Introduction

Contemporary Catholic environmentalism is at a critical juncture theologically and politically. Outside of a few passing references in papal encyclicals in the first half of the twentieth century, scant attention was paid to environmentalism in Catholic circles[1] until Pope John Paul II's New Year's Day address in 1990,[2] which later became known as "The Ecological Crisis." Pope John Paul II's terse admonitions and prescient predictions about emerging large-scale environmental issues roused the Catholic theological world into action and within a span of two years scores of regional bishops' statements were published that documented local environmental issues begging for timely and sustained attention. So by the mid-1990s, Catholic environmentalism had not only become a distinct area of theological inquiry, but also a nascent political movement that had gained the allegiance of critical components of the Catholic hierarchy as well as lay Catholics worldwide.

While Pope John Paul II managed to place environmentalism front and center on the Catholic moral radar screen, he was far less successful at gaining allegiance to the stewardship paradigm, which functioned as the theological foundation for his version of Catholic environmentalism, from the theological community. While his successor, Pope Benedict XVI, enthusiastically embraced the stewardship paradigm in his writings on environmentalism, many Catholic voices from the publication of "The Ecological Crisis" until the eve of Pope Francis's encyclical on Catholic environmentalism, *Laudato Si'* (2015),[3] expressed a host of misgivings about the stewardship paradigm. Some believed that the stewardship paradigm offered vague and indeterminate practical advice, due to its equally fuzzy theological foundations; others criticized the anthropocentrism inherent in the stewardship paradigm and wished to expand moral considerations and God's love beyond humans and our limited interests; others objected to the idea of one strand of scripture having such a formative influence over an entire body of environmental thought, when the entirety of scripture is littered with ideas and concepts that potentially bear upon our relation to God and creation; and others either simply wished to sidestep contentious theological debates or found the stewardship paradigm to be so hopelessly irredeemable that they largely ignored the stewardship paradigm in their analyses. So while papal environmentalism confidently coalesced around the stewardship paradigm as the theological foundation for Catholic environmentalism from the early 1990s until the publication of *Laudato Si'*, other strands of Catholic environmentalism were openly critical of it and desired an alternative theological foundation.

The publication of Pope Francis's *Laudato Si'* was a watershed moment for the Catholic Church, and is, I think, the most important religious document to be published since the Protestant reformation. This was the first papal encyclical devoted exclusively to environmental issues, and Pope Francis both affirmed the instincts of Popes John Paul II and Benedict XVI that environmental matters are both theologically meaningful as well as soteriologically and practically significant, as well as expressed significant misgivings about our naïve and self-sabotaging technophilia and entrenched and often unwitting anthropocentrism. *Laudato Si'* is a siren call from the highest office in the Catholic Church that our planet is being ravaged by out-of-control humans and that a dismal future awaits all life on Earth if we do not embrace a collective ecological conversion and embark upon a far more benign path environmentally. According to Pope Francis, we have constructed a "world system" that is unquestionably damaging and unsustainable, which has greatly "disappointed God's expectations" for us.[4]

Pope Francis's theological inclinations in *Laudato Si'* are fundamentally laudable and have potentially seismic implications for Catholic environmentalism.[5] Perhaps his most notable theological achievement is to place love at the heart of creation. For Pope Francis, each creature is not only created out of divine love, but everything in creation is a manifestation of divine love, from stars to trees to rivers to humans to insects. Our response to creation, then, is to become lovers, to gaze on our fellow creatures, as St. Francis of Assisi did, as brothers and sisters, and to habituate ourselves to expand the scope of our love beyond our native anthropocentrism to include a broader range of creatures than ever before.

By doing so, we transcend our normal human limitations and begin to understand and cherish everything in creation as God does and to love all creatures as God does.

The purpose of this book is to advance the agenda begun by Francis in *Laudato Si'*, partially by deconstructing the stewardship paradigm that has been a mainstay in Catholic environmentalism, but also by demonstrating the many ways in which a more theocentric (or if you prefer, less anthropocentric) Catholic environmentalism is far more preferable theologically. In turn, this theocentric shift generates a determinate trajectory by which Catholics can not only begin to make better sense of our place and purpose in creation, but also to renovate our lifestyles and practical behavior to make them more conformable to a new understanding of God's action in creation to construct a universe replete with life and love.

More specifically, Chapter 1 documents the widespread discontent with the stewardship paradigm and develops several theological currents contributing to this dissatisfaction. Beginning with early American environmentalism and Lynn White Jr.'s searing critique of anthropocentrism in his famous "The Historical Roots of Our Ecological Crisis" (1967), this chapter then moves into the early theological components of the stewardship paradigm, which have their beginnings in papal encyclicals from the late 1800s through the late 1900s. Then there is an extended discussion of Pope John Paul II's seminal "The Ecological Crisis," which solidified the stewardship paradigm theologically and made it virtually impossible not to be some shade of green if one is Catholic. The interim period between "The Ecological Crisis" and *Laudato Si'* was marked by a period of feverish theological activity and significant reservations about the adequacy of the stewardship paradigm, which are developed at length. The lesson to be learned in Chapter 1 is that Catholic environmentalism is very much a contested theological tradition, with a great deal of its theological foundations in the process of internal change and renovation.

Chapter 2 develops the thought of Thomas Berry, who as a Passionist priest was highly sympathetic to Catholic theology but also equally critical of the anthropocentrism at the heart of the Catholic theological enterprise. Perhaps more than anyone else in Catholic environmental circles, Berry's thought represents a clear and distinct alternative to the stewardship paradigm, as he not only rejects anthropocentrism, but he also consistently reminds his readers that our universe has a good, which always transcends—and should be given priority over—our good as a species or individuals. If Catholics are to love creation as God loves creation, this means that our moral landscape must be sculpted by the larger good of planet Earth and the prodigious amount of biodiversity it has produced, which makes our home the crown jewel of creation, insofar as it is the only place in the known universe where God's relationality can be satisfied and divine love can be given and received consciously.

Chapter 3 documents Pope Francis's reservations about anthropocentrism in *Laudato Si'* and his conscious attempt to construct a non-anthropocentric Catholic environmentalism. In the end, however, the temptation of anthropocentrism proves to be too seductive even for Pope Francis to transcend, and he reverts to the familiar pattern consistently found in prior papal documents of feigning a theoretically chastened anthropocentrism while embracing an unreserved practical anthropocentrism. In other words, while disavowing anthropocentrism on a theoretical level, Pope Francis consistently considers only human desires and goods when he considers practical environmental policy. Fortunately, there are a number of elements in *Laudato Si'* that can be developed to construct a non-anthropocentric Catholic environmentalism, and the bulk of this chapter is spent outlining the lineaments of this strand of thought, which coalesces around the position that biodiversity on Earth is the paramount moral objective for humans to pursue, which in turn leads Catholics to embrace the 50/50 principle. The 50/50 principle has two components: first, a psychological one that habituates us to realize that we must share our planet with other creatures and that their interests must be included in our moral decision-making processes; and second, a normative component that requires us to sculpt lifestyles and behavioral patterns consistent with the fact that our planet must be shared with other species.

Chapter 4 treats our dominant mental habituation toward the natural sphere and the principal obstacle to embracing and acting upon the 50/50 principle. In our post-Baconian era, nature is regarded as something needing to be controlled, revamped, changed, and transformed into something else (usually a consumer product) in order for it to become valuable to humans and thereby worthy of our attention. In other words, we are consistently taught, albeit often unwittingly, that nature is not a fitting object of love or affection, unless it does something beneficial for us. Of course, none of us were born with this emotionally barren response to nature. Indeed, children are perhaps the most unabashed lovers of nature, finding it almost endlessly fascinating to dig in dirt, explore creeks and wood lots, catch butterflies and bugs, and play with animals. Over time, this native inquisitiveness and love for creation eventually subsides under the pressure of the socially mandatory Baconian indifference to the natural world. Yet if Catholics are to undergo the ecological conversion described in *Laudato Si'* and to start acting consistently with the 50/50 principle, the surest way to achieve these goals is to find an effective strategy for resurrecting our native affection for nature, to make it loveable again. For children, this means figuring out a way to foster their native biophilia and to allow that love for nature to flourish without impediment. A large portion of Chapter 4 offers parents and caretakers a practical strategy for stoking the fires of love for creation in children, which is precisely what is needed if a long-term and effective ecological conversion is to take hold and create a Catholic Church replete with nature lovers for generations to come.

Foundational to the Catholic moral identity is protection of the weak, the vulnerable, those who are voiceless, defenseless, and easily exploited, marginalized, and made invisible. As relayed in the final judgment scene in the Parable of the Sheep and Goats, just as we do to the least of our brothers and sisters, so we do to Jesus (Matt. 25:40). Chapter 5 documents how the most vulnerable humans among us are being savaged by environmental toxicants, even before they are born. The world of environmental toxicants is dark and disturbing and is getting increasingly disorienting as more scientific data emerge that show precisely how environmental toxicants are getting into the bodies of fetuses during all stages of development and wreaking havoc on vital organ systems, consigning children to lives of underperformance, struggle, hardship, and sometimes lifelong debilitating injuries. This represents perhaps the most glaring illustration of widespread unnecessary harm imaginable, and if the sentiment expressed in the Parable of the Sheep and Goats is accurate, it also represents a grave moral failure of those who remain indifferent to the plight of babies and children affected by environmental toxicants. Very few know about this vexing and maddening world, but those who do can take productive strides toward protecting their own babies and children from these insidious contaminants and encourage public policy that creates a safer and more nurturing world for the most vulnerable and defenseless among us.

Notes

1. Notable exceptions were John Carmody, *Ecology and Religion: Toward a New Christian Theology of* Nature (New York: Paulist Press, 1983); Sean McDonagh, *To Care for the Earth: A Call to a New Theology* (Santa Fe: Bear & Co., 1987); Matthew Fox, *Original Blessing: A Primer in Creation Spirituality* (Sante Fe: Bear & Co., 1983); and Thomas Berry, *The Dream of the Earth* (San Francisco: Sierra Club Books, 1988).
2. Pope John Paul II, "Message of His Holiness Pope John Paul II For the Celebration of the World Day of Peace," January 1, 1990, https://www.vatican.va/content/john-paul-ii/en/messages/peace/documents/hf_jp-ii_mes_19891208_xxiii-world-day-for-peace.html (accessed November 27, 2025). This document will be referred to as "The Ecological Crisis" in this book.
3. Pope Francis, *Laudato Si'*, May 24, 2015, https://www.vatican.va/content/francesco/en/encyclicals/documents/papa-francesco_20150524_enciclica-laudato-si.html (accessed November 27, 2025).
4. Pope Francis, *Laudato Si'*, #61.
5. For a more detailed critique of *Laudato Si'*, see Mark Graham, "Pope Francis's *Laudato Si'*: A Critical Response," *Minding Nature* 10 (2) (2017): 57–64.

1

Contemporary Catholic Environmentalism:

Anthropocentrism, the Stewardship Paradigm, and Its Discontents

Early Environmentalism in the United States

Long before Pope John Paul II inaugurated Catholic environmentalism as a distinct branch of theology, which subsequently blossomed into one of the most popular areas of theological inquiry—and arguably one of the most relevant to the future of life on our planet—the environmental movement in the United States had become a highly organized and potent political force and environmental considerations were often displayed prominently in our national media. John Muir's (1838-1914) adventures in the Sierra Nevada and subsequent founding of the Sierra Club, coupled with the overt religiosity of his nature writing, earned him the moniker of patron saint of the American conservation movement.[1] Aldo Leopold (1887-1948), whose *A Sand County Almanac* (1949) sold over two million copies, was an influential voice for wilderness conservation and a pivotal figure in the development of American environmental ethics. Theodore

Roosevelt (1858-1919), who became known as the conservation president, protected over 230 million acres during his tenure as the twenty-sixth American president by creating the United States Forest Service and signing the American Antiquities Act (1906), which proved to be one of the most potent conservation tools in American history. Rachel Carson (1907-1964) of *Silent Spring* (1962) fame became an international leader on the effects of pesticides on animal populations and ushered in a new awareness of the interconnectedness of all life on Earth. Edward Abbey (1927-1989), whose iconic *Desert Solitaire* (1968) became a staple within American environmental literature, was among the first to promote eco-sabotage as a way to resist encroaching development and became something of a cult figure among more radical elements of the American environmental movement.

In addition to these popular figures in American environmentalism, during this time period a number of academics were sounding alarm bells about emerging environmental problems. Paul Ehrlich, author of *The Population Bomb* (1968), argued that anticipated population growth would result in worldwide famine and significant geopolitical strife. Barry Commoner, one of the first popularizers of the concept of sustainability, argued that economics ought to be organized around the laws of biology in his best-selling *The Closing Circle* (1971). Garrett Hardin's (1915-2003) popular piece "The Tragedy of the Commons" in *Science* (1968) introduced the concept of lifeboat ethics and claimed that nothing short of mutually agreed upon coercion would be an effective bulwark against a burgeoning world population. Frances Moore Lappé, author of nineteen books including the three million copy selling *Diet for a Small Planet* (1971), put agriculture, the Green Revolution, and the future of food front and center on the American moral radar screen.

By the mid to late 1900s, American environmentalism had produced towering figures in the conservation movement, government agencies intended to protect our environment, an internationally renowned system of national parks and public lands, leading academics whose voices are still influential today, and considerable public awareness about the fragile state of our planet and the necessity of disallowing the forces of industrialism, capitalism, and development to lay waste to our treasured natural assets. Yet amidst this panoply of ideas, concepts, iconoclastic figures, and movements represented by American environmentalism, one stands out as having seminal influence on the trajectory of Christian environmental ethics: the American professor of medieval history, Lynn White, Jr. White was neither a conservationist, nor a connoisseur of nature experiences, nor a nature writer; his academic interest was principally medieval technology, especially technologies that promoted social and political change, and he had only a tangential interest in the environmental effects of those technologies. As part of his research, however, the question "Why was European medieval technology so successful?" kept cropping up, and as part of his answer he wrote the famous piece "The Historical Roots of Our Ecological Crisis," which was published in *Science* in 1967.[2] In it White claimed that the most prodigious episode of technological innovation occurred during the medieval period in which Europe, which White characterizes as a continent of "small, mutually hostile nations," emerged as the technologically dominant world power that was able to "spill out over all the rest of the world, conquering, looting, and colonizing."[3] Europeans were able to do this by bringing together the heretofore conceptually disparate areas of science, which was the purview of academics and universities and was intended for the acquisition of knowledge alone, with technology, which was the field of artisans and craftsmen and focused on the creation of practical tools and implements. When coupled with the aggressive creed of using technological prowess to control, manipulate, and subdue nature for the benefit of humankind, this melding of science and technology and the momentous achievements for which it is responsible represent "the greatest event in human history since the invention of agriculture."[4] From the thirteenth century onward, according to White, global scientific leadership lay squarely in the West, along with all the advantages that accrue from possessing superior technologies.[5]

According to White, this period of feverish technological innovation did not happen by accident, and the creed that provided the impulse to attain such new technological heights was Christianity, more specifically the creation stories in Genesis,[6] which portray a loving and powerful God gradually constructing an organized and hospitable world from chaos and darkness and giving humans dominion over creation, as we are the only creatures made in the image of God, which grants us an exalted status in the universe. Phrased a little differently, the Christian creation stories provide meaning to the universe—it exists to serve us. As White writes, "God planned all of this explicitly for man's benefit and rule: no item in the physical creation had any purpose save to serve man's purposes."[7]

As a consequence, Christianity spawned a robustly aggressive attitude toward creation and regarded it as a repository of resources to be used and managed for human benefit, and after dispelling the remaining vestiges of pagan animism that understood the universe as sacred and effectively functioned as a limiting force on human interference, Christianity proceeded to march virtually unimpeded across large swaths of our planet, bringing more ecosystems under human control via the use of increasingly complex and powerful technologies.

Furthermore, in White's estimation, Christianity is the "most anthropocentric religion the world has seen,"[8] and the particular type of anthropocentrism it has spawned is one of the worst: "We are superior to nature, contemptuous of it, and willing to use it for our slightest whim."[9] As a result of this potent triad of anthropocentrism, advanced technologies, and increasing control over nature, Christianity "bears a huge burden of guilt" for the historically unprecedented amount of environmental destruction it has caused, and White claims that frequent pleas for better science and technology to counteract this destruction miss the point completely and are an exercise in futility. The environmental devastation occurring in the West is a religious problem, and the only way to solve this problem is by changing Christian beliefs and understanding our place in the universe differently.[10]

White's article reverberated like a bombshell in Christian circles, and over the next decade there was an avalanche of responses both in academic journals and in popular periodicals to White's theses.[11] Some were laudatory and grateful, many were skeptical of his claims and chided his undifferentiated presentation of Christianity, and some were overtly hostile to the assertion that Christianity is responsible for the bulk of the environmental destruction in the West. Regardless of one's opinion about the veracity of White's assertions, however, there is no doubt that his "The Historical Roots of Our Ecological Crisis" represented a watershed moment for Christian environmentalism, not only in the sense that it was a jarring public charge of widespread moral turpitude on the part of Christians, but also because his piece established the working assumptions for the emerging field of Christian environmentalism, which fall along the following lines: behavior is inextricably (and directly?) linked to an underlying set of cosmological and anthropological beliefs; the first two creation stories in the book of Genesis provide this underlying belief system; one significant part of this belief system is anthropocentrism, or the belief that humans are superior to everything else in creation; that God created the universe with human beings in mind, and it is our mission to use and control nature to improve the lot of humans; and that the result of this mentality has been widespread environmental devastation.

For better or worse, the Lynn White episode popularized and solidified this cluster of propositions to the extent that it became almost automatic that mainstream Christian environmentalism, whether Catholic or Protestant, would have to reckon with White's thesis in some way, and easily the most popular approach was to accept White's theses with one major caveat. For Christians of virtually any theological persuasion, the idea that the Bible—a revelation of God—could contain something so profoundly erroneous as to lead to worldwide environmental destruction and a declining quality of life for billions of people is preposterous, which means that something has to be amiss with the way in which Christians have understood the Genesis creation stories. Commentators in the post-White period zeroed in on the term "dominion" as the culprit fostering this misunderstanding, claiming that a better hermeneutic would understand the term as calling humans to good stewardship of our planet, and not to an aggressive subjugation of nature. In other words, properly understood, the cosmology of Genesis implies a benign presence for humans on Earth. This became the explicit approach of Catholic bishops all over the world as they began publishing statements on environmentalism in the 1990s, and although many of the practical issues they addressed represented local concerns, the theological framework and assumptions from which they worked followed Lynn White's template closely, albeit with a different interpretation of the Genesis creation stories that warranted a gentler attitude toward nature.[12]

Yet a growing—and influential—body of theologians wanted little to do with this creative reinterpretation of Genesis, as they found any version of anthropocentrism to be distasteful at best, and at worst a serious theological mistake that has occasioned not only an unappetizing psychology of entitlement but also a corresponding pattern of myopic behavior that is at the heart of ecological destruction. Their approach was to directly challenge the belief that humans are the apex of creation, the apogee of God's creative power, or the raison d'être for the universe.

James Gustafson, one of the most influential English-speaking Christian ethicists of the twentieth century, devotes a large portion of his magnum opus, *Ethics from a Theocentric Perspective*, to deconstructing anthropocentrism and its many pitfalls, and consistently reminding his readers that God's ways and human well-being are not necessarily synonymous.[13] Rosemary Radford Ruether, a leading Catholic feminist theologian, warned that anthropocentrism is one of the most pernicious threats to the sustainability of life on Earth.[14] Noted ecofeminist and liberationist Catholic nun Ivone Gebara documents the many ways in which anthropocentrism infects every level of the theological endeavor and decries its propensity to exclude any non-human interest as irrelevant to ethical deliberation.[15] Added to these esteemed scholars are a number of other contemporary voices who have articulated various deficiencies with anthropocentrism.[16]

By the time of Pope John Paul II's papacy (1978-2005), then, there was widespread agreement among Christian theologians that the levels of environmental deterioration were historically unprecedented and that something was fundamentally wrong about our Western lifestyle, and despite the growing chorus of influential theological voices pointing a finger at the anthropocentrism at the heart of the Christian story, the dominant method for Catholic environmentalism at this point readily embraced Lynn White's template, although it had not, and still has not, come to a reflective consensus on the status of anthropocentrism.

Papal Anthropocentrism and the Stewardship Paradigm

There are two seminal moments in the history of Catholic environmentalism. The first was Pope John Paul II's "The Ecological Crisis" (1990) which called attention to and chided the massive amount of environmental degradation occurring in the Western world, established Catholic environmentalism as a distinct sphere of theological reflection, and also prompted a series of statements from regional bishops' conferences in the ensuing decade that explored a number of local environmental issues and gave regional flavor to the emerging stewardship paradigm.[17] "The Ecological Crisis" took an issue that was often the subject of indifference or outright scorn in popular Catholic circles and placed it front and center in the Catholic moral imagination. From this point forward, Catholic environmentalism would garner the attention of some of the finest theological minds and it would be difficult to identify as a Catholic without being some shade of green.

The second moment was Pope Francis's *Laudato Si'* (2015), which as the first papal encyclical on environmental matters was easily the most comprehensive treatment of Catholic environmentalism to this point. While few would accuse Pope Francis of being terribly innovative doctrinally during his papacy (although pastorally he has certainly been highly creative), *Laudato Si'* represents a quixotic mixture of deference to the received stewardship paradigm coupled with a sincere yearning for theological innovation that calls into question key elements of that stewardship paradigm, while simultaneously having great difficulty in actually breaking out of deeply ingrained and often unconscious anthropocentric mental habits and theological categories. Tradition can be both freeing and limiting, and the latter is clearly the case in *Laudato Si'* as Pope Francis clearly yearns to break new ground in his encyclical but in the end is unable to extricate himself from the tenets of the stewardship paradigm. Since I believe that Pope Francis has laid the incipient foundation for a significant theological renovation of Catholic environmentalism that represents a marked improvement over business as usual, part of my agenda in a later chapter is to develop a Catholic environmentalism, from theological foundations to practical behavior, that breaks free from the reigning anthropocentricism.

The Theological Antecedents

While Pope John Paul II's "The Ecological Crisis" represents a watershed moment as being the first major official statement on environmental matters in the Catholic Church, the building blocks for the theological framework employed by John Paul II began over 100 years earlier with Pope Leo XIII's *Rerum Novarum* (1891), which addressed economic systems, the deplorable working conditions that industrialism had spawned, and the widespread abuse of workers. Pope Leo XIII's theological anthropology, which borrows heavily from Thomas Aquinas, is decidedly anthropocentric, and this anthropocentrism is propounded and defended in a number of different ways.

Thomas Aquinas, who was declared by Pope Leo XIII in *Aeterni Patris* (1879) as "the special bulwark and glory of the Catholic faith"[18] is renowned for his hierarchical universe in which animals (and the rest of creation, for that matter) exist for the sake of humans, based on the qualitative difference in capabilities. While both humans and animals possess an animal nature that impels each toward certain goods such as reproduction and nutrition and the preservation of one's life, animals have nothing beyond these brute instincts to guide and direct them. They simply experience an instinct and immediately pursue the object indicated by the instinct. Humans, on the other hand, have reason, which affords us the ability to select means and ends, the ability to discriminate between different courses of action, and the ability to ponder larger existential questions like the nature of God and the meaning of life. This capacity for reason creates freedom from our animalistic instincts, insofar as it simultaneously creates the ability to deliberate about whether the promptings of our instincts are actually leading us to the good, but it also creates freedom to deliberate among the various ways in which instincts can be followed and acted upon.

In *Rerum Novarum*, Pope Leo XIII adopted this qualitative distinction between humans and animals based on the rationality of humans:

> This is one of the chief points of distinction between man and the animal creation, for the brute has no power of self direction, but is governed by two main instincts, which keep his powers on the alert, impel him to develop them in a fitting manner, and stimulate and determine him to action without any power of choice …. But with man it is wholly different. He possesses, on the one hand, the full perfection of the animal being, and hence enjoys at least as much as the rest of the animal kind, the fruition of things material. But animal nature, however perfect, is far from representing the human being in its completeness, and is in truth but humanity's humble handmaid, made to serve and to obey. It is the mind, or reason, which is the predominant element in us who are human creatures; it is this which renders a human being human, and distinguishes him essentially from the brute.[19]

For Pope Leo XIII, the fact that God created human beings as rational agents who are the "master[s] of [our] own acts"[20] not only leads to an ontological distinction between humans and the rest of creation, but to the superiority of humans in the created sphere, which in turn has led God to turn over the creation to us. As Pope Leo XIII writes, "God has given the earth for the use and enjoyment of the whole human race"[21] and therefore "Man is commanded to rule the creatures below him and to use the earth and the ocean for his profit and advantage. 'Fill the earth and subdue it, and rule over the fishes of the sea, and the fowls of the air, and all living creatures that move upon the earth.'"[22]

Despite our exalted status in the created universe and the unique privileges granted to our species, however, Pope Leo XIII is quick to point out that our terrestrial existence is neither ultimate nor permanent and that our entire created existence—our bodies and our planet—is transitory and perishable. As a result, even though we hold pride of place in the order of creation, we must regard our world as "a place of exile" and our true home to be in heaven with God.[23]

A half century later, Pope John XXIII (1958-1963), who a mere three months into his papacy stunned the Catholic world by calling for a Second Vatican Council, intensifies Pope Leo XIII's anthropocentrism and develops two additional themes that will become staple fare in Catholic environmentalism in two papal encyclicals, *Mater et Magistra* (1961) and *Pacem in Terris* (1963). Pope John XXIII cites the usual passages in Genesis to the effect that humans are made in the image and likeness of God[24] and because of our superior status within creation that we are called to "Fill the earth, and subdue it."[25] Then he engages in a bit of rhetorical flourish to impress upon his readers the grandiosity of humans within the order of creation, citing the Psalms that humans are just a little less than angels, that God has crowned us with "glory and honor," and that all things have been placed under our feet.[26] As if being just a little less than angels is inadequate to capture the revered place of humans in creation, he then relies on a common Christological title to describe us, stating that God has appointed us "lord of creation"![27]

As commentators have noted, this historical period witnessed a number of technological successes ranging from the Green Revolution that precipitated spectacular increases in food production in the post–Second World War era, a space race between the United States and the Soviet Union that put a man on the moon, and the fruits of the industrialization process that provided an abundance of consumer products for less money than ever before, and this spirit of technological optimism was not lost on Pope John XXIII, who called for the increasing use of science and technology to extend our dominion over the world. Indeed, he intimates that our wonderful gift of reason, which allows us to understand natural processes especially through the tools of modern science, was given to us by God precisely to exploit the "well-nigh inexhaustible" collection of natural resources on our planet to improve human well-being, and he calls for a "renewed technical and scientific effort" to bring more natural processes under our control.[28]

Finally, Pope John XXIII maintains that creation is suffuse with an order implanted by God in us, other creatures, natural processes, and laws of nature, which makes creation stable, constant, and intelligible.[29] This clear nod to natural theology or natural law has been a predominant theme in Catholic theology for millennia, although it has fallen into disrepute in the post-*Humanae Vitae* period. The concept of nature as a conduit for the divine does two important things: (1) it makes creation a visible revelation of the divine, which can give us important information about God and God's purposes in creation; and (2) if these purposes can be ascertained, then it becomes morally obligatory for humans to cooperate with God in trying to bring these purposes to fruition. In other words, nature is the bearer of moral normativity in some way.

The final document deserving mention as the theological context for Pope John Paul II's seminal "The Ecological Crisis" is the Second Vatican Council's *Gaudium et Spes* (1965), which does not introduce anything new theologically, but certainly bristles with confidence about the exalted place of humans in creation and reaffirms the robust anthropocentrism already prominent in papal teaching. After giving obligatory homage to the passages in Genesis concerning humans being made in the image and likeness of God, the council fathers write, "According to the almost unanimous opinion of believers and unbelievers alike, all things on earth should be related to man as their center and crown"[30] and that "God intended the earth with everything contained in it" for human use.[31] We are not only the "master of all earthly creatures" and are called to subdue them and to use them for God's glory,[32] but Christ himself is actively working to make creation submit to us in order that we may increasingly humanize our planet and transform it for human benefit.[33] For the council fathers, our control over our world must be exercised with "justice and holiness,"[34] but the raison d'être of creation in *Gaudium et Spes* could not be clearer or simpler: God created the world for humans, and we ought to place our entire planet under our control in order to benefit us.

Pope John Paul II (1978–2005)

By the beginning of Pope John Paul II's papacy, a theological anthropology and cosmology had coalesced in papal encyclicals and conciliar documents that was remarkably similar to the one identified by Lynn White, Jr. in his famous 1967 piece in *Science*, which has the following four components: (1) that humans are qualitatively different from, and superior to, everything else in creation, based either on the Thomistic distinction between humans and animals, or on humans being the only species made in the "image and likeness" of God (Gen. 1:26); (2) that because of our privileged status, God has given humans the task of "subduing" the earth and exercising "dominion" over all creation (Gen. 1:26-28); (3) that this dominion requires humans to be "stewards" or "caretakers" or "managers" of creation and to cultivate and renovate creation for the betterment of humans; (4) and that this stewardship is circumscribed by God's wishes for creation, which are expressed either in Scripture or the moral order inscribed by God in creation. This last point is important for Christian anthropocentrists, as they will quickly point out that human dominion over creation is always exercised in the context of God's purposes for creation. In other words, the goal of human stewardship is first and foremost to mold creation into something fitting to God, and not simply to use it to satisfy human interests. So even though humans have a pivotal role to play in managing creation, there are definite limits to what humans are allowed to do to creation—at least in theory.

Pope John Paul II follows this pattern closely in his earlier works. He begins his analysis with the first creation account in Genesis, in which humans are made in the image and likeness of God,[35] which according to Pope John Paul II not only establishes the superiority of humans over other creatures,[36] but also grounds human dignity as the proximate norm for morality.[37] As a result of humans' special place in the order of creation, the first words that God speaks to humans (Gen. 1:28) is the mandate to subdue creation and to have dominion over it.[38] Pope John Paul II is quick to point out, however, that neither subduing nor exercising dominion over creation entails any absolute right of disposal over it, and he uses both garden metaphors and adjectives qualifying human dominion in order to specify further the type of limitations God has placed on humans. So he writes that Adam and Eve were placed in the Garden of Eden with "the duty of cultivating and watching over it," so there is no indication of any "indiscriminate possession of created things."[39] Likewise, God imposes limits on human dominion over creation:

> The dominion granted to man [*sic*] by the Creator is not an absolute power, nor can one speak of a freedom to 'use and misuse,' or to dispose of things as one pleases. The limitation imposed from the beginning by the Creator himself and expressed symbolically by the prohibition not to 'eat of the fruit of the tree' (cf. Gen. 2:16-17) shows clearly enough that, when it comes to the natural world, we are subject not only to biological laws but also to moral ones, which cannot be violated with impunity.[40]

In Pope John Paul II's later works, he follows the same structural pattern established in his earlier writings, with a few notable shifts in his presentation of the stewardship paradigm. He adduces other biblical evidence to bolster the legitimacy of human dominion over creation, citing passages from Wisdom and the Psalms to illustrate the glory and honor bestowed on humans by God.[41] He also becomes more direct and forceful about the privileged place of humans in the order of creation, writing that Genesis "places man at the summit of God's creative activity, as its crown, at the culmination of a process which leads from indistinct chaos to the most perfect of creatures. Everything in creation is ordered to man and everything is made subject to him."[42] Yet in spite of this exalted place of humans in the created order, Pope John Paul II is quick to assert that the dominion granted to humans is qualified and must be exercised by humans with "wisdom and love."[43]

The introduction of qualifiers to the concept of dominion typically proves to be the critical hermeneutical move for Pope John Paul II and other proponents of the stewardship paradigm, even though the term dominion, by itself, tells the reader little about how he or she ought to exercise this power. Unfortunately, qualifiers such as wisdom and love do not lend a lot of clarity to the discussion. Presumably, wisdom refers to how the object ought to be managed, and love refers to the disposition of the manager (although neither is stated explicitly). Yet even given these assumptions, there are still a number of management possibilities. If someone is going to manage a small plot of land "wisely," for instance, does this mean as efficiently as possible (how is this measured?), or using only locally available inputs, or using nature as a guide (commonly called biomimicry), or using only solar power and no fossil fuels, or maintaining it in a way that is sustainable, and the possibilities go on and on. Likewise with "love": Does this refer to the internal disposition of the manager? If so, does this have any connection to the particular way in which the ecosystem is managed (are there loving and unloving ways to manage particular ecosystems)? Or is the love directed toward someone or something outside the ecosystem, for whom or which the ecosystem is managed, such as the manager's children, extended family, or local community? Cryptic qualifiers do little to render clarity to the concept of dominion, and absent some fuller context, simply telling someone to manage something wisely or lovingly is unintelligible.

Ironically, despite Pope John Paul II's attempt to dull the sharp edge of dominion language via softer and kinder adjectives, the bulk of the evidence suggests that such a move is actually contrary to the Priestly author's intentions in Genesis 1. Here is the verse that Pope John Paul II wants to qualify: "God blessed them, and God said to them, 'Be fruitful and multiply, and fill the earth and subdue it; and have dominion over the fish of the sea and over the birds of the air and over every living thing that moves upon the earth'" (Gen. 1:28).[44] While Pope John Paul II zeroes in on the term dominion, this passage also includes the mandate to subdue the earth, which likely refers to agricultural land[45] and in other biblical contexts means to engage in "hostile action" such as conquering enemies or raping,[46] which implies an aggressive, forceful posture. According to another commentator, subduing means "trampling under one's feet, and it connotes absolute subjugation."[47] The object of "dominion," on the other hand, is animals and according to one biblical scholar, the expressions for the exercise of this dominion "are remarkably strong," which include treading, trampling, and stamping.[48] Others note that exercising dominion is comparable to "ruling over reluctant subjects"[49] and is often compared in other Old Testament literature to subduing or treading the wine press.[50] The overriding impression gleaned from the exegetical literature on the Priestly account of creation in Genesis 1 is that creation is often recalcitrant and stubborn in the face of attempts to being ordered and controlled and that it takes a firm hand, a resolute spirit, and sometimes considerable cajoling and force to make it comply.

This aggressive and domineering posture, it should be noted, is quite understandable in its respective context. The Hebrews at this time had recently transitioned from semi-nomadism to settled agriculture; their agricultural technologies were rudimentary and highly labor-intensive, the dry and hot climate created harsh and often unpredictable conditions in which to grow crops, and the threats of widespread crop loss and potential hunger and starvation were always looming on the horizon.[51] Given the myriad difficulties facing food production for the ancient Hebrews and the high stakes in getting settled agriculture right, it is no wonder that the Priestly author endorsed such an antagonistic relationship to the land.

While Pope John Paul II's attempt to soften the language of Genesis 1:28, then, is questionable hermeneutically, the more important point is that Pope John Paul II's notion of dominion, which he claims must be exercised wisely and lovingly, suffers from a foundational vacuity that offers little substantive guidance for any Catholic who wants to implement the stewardship paradigm in his or her life, although his corpus of writings does provide a number of clues about the good that the management regime is intended to realize. Pope John Paul II writes that the overarching context for moral decision-making is respecting human dignity: *"the dignity of the human person … is the ultimate guiding norm for any sound economic, industrial or scientific progress."*[52]

On the issue of the principle of the common good, which is a mainstay of Catholic social thought, the pope makes it clear that God is only interested in an equitable distribution of Earth's goods among humans: "God destined the earth and everything it contains for the use of every individual and all peoples."[53] The pope articulates a new right to a "safe environment" and recommends that this right be enshrined in the United Nations' Charter of Human Rights, which means that this right applies only to humans.[54] His discussion of poverty is concerned only with the deprivations and injustices suffered by humans.[55] When affirming the sanctity of life and prohibiting unjust aggression against it, his singular concern is the life of humans, not any non-human life.[56] When he turns to the issue of war, it is clear that the "survivors" of which he speaks and the social unrest they have to endure are humans.[57] The pope's discussion of a "new solidarity" clearly refers to a solidarity among humans for the sake of humans.[58] When he moves into an analysis of poverty and the environment, he is singularly interested in the way in which environmental degradation affects humans, especially poor humans.[59] Finally, in discussing the aesthetic value of creation, the pope notes the "deep restorative power" and the "peace and serenity" that are engendered by contemplating nature in all its grandeur, yet it is obvious that the pope is extolling nature's beauty as perceived by humans for the sake of human enjoyment.[60]

So while Pope John Paul II is keen to point out that anthropocentrism must be limited theoretically by the moral order instituted by God, there is nothing in any of his writings to indicate that any tangible limits exist, nor anything to indicate that anything other than human interests factor into the process of moral deliberation and judgment. Quite clearly, for Pope John Paul II, the exercise of dominion is explicitly for the sake of human well-being, and no other interest factors into his analyses at either the policy level or concrete situations. Thus, what begins as a qualified anthropocentrism in its theological foundations eventually culminates in a virtually unrestricted anthropocentrism in practice, which focuses exclusively on human interests and regards the material world as a natural resource base that gets meaning and value from satisfying human needs and desires.

"The Ecological Crisis" (1990)

Leaving aside for a moment the anthropocentrism underlying Pope John Paul II's environmentalism, as the first major statement on environmental matters that birthed Catholic environmentalism as a distinct branch of theological inquiry and concern, "The Ecological Crisis" represents a fledgling attempt to go beyond the theological anthropology and cosmology already concretized in prior papal encyclicals and to extend the stewardship paradigm into the spheres of politics, policy, culture, and most importantly, practical ethics. This attempt to expand the sphere of Catholic environmentalism into something more comprehensive and concrete was insightful, prescient, and prophetic while also being a bit confounding, intellectually puzzling, and practically inconclusive. Let me develop the main contours of "The Ecological Crisis" and explain why.

First, the insightful, prescient, and prophetic elements. Pope John Paul II begins "The Ecological Crisis" with a litany of environmental ills, and like Lynn White, Jr., not only decries all the destruction occurring in the Western world but also maintains that a day of reckoning is coming quickly and that a new *ecological awareness*"[61] is emerging that needs to be nurtured and welcomed. In particular, he mentions two issues of concern: global climate change and environmental pollution, which in my opinion today two of the most insidious threats to life and the well-being of all lifeforms on our planet, albeit for different reasons—yet this was years before the first Conference of Parties (COP) meeting for the United Nations that dealt with global climate change, and research on environmental toxicants was nascent at best. Pope John Paul II was not only clearly well-informed about the latest information emerging from secular environmental circles, but he was also able to distinguish between the trivial and momentous, as he identified very early for the Catholic Church two issues that would require long-term engagement and coordinated action—and I suspect that if Catholics had heeded his dire warnings in 1990, it is quite likely that neither would be such a formidable threat today.

While Catholic moral theology often focuses on discrete, individual actions as the locus of moral evaluation,[62] Pope John Paul II recognizes that systems, and especially natural systems, have an enormous impact on the well-being of all lifeforms. As he mentions, creatures within these natural systems are connected, so that the behavior of one will inevitably affect many others, but creatures within different systems also reciprocally condition and influence their behavior and living conditions. This inextricable independence of all life forms on Earth leads Pope John Paul II to claim that "ecological balance"[63] is a key indicator of overall system health and ought to be a moral criterion for human behavior, as without this balance diverse ecosystems are likely to be in a state of stress or decline. The Pope's singular concern with ecological balance is sustainability, and especially the concern that our consumptive behavior today does not undermine natural resource bases for future generations, as God has destined creation for the use of all people at all times. What is most important about Pope John Paul II's notion of ecological balance, however, is that he makes systems an object of moral concern, which means that a staple part of Catholic environmentalism is asking the following questions: What is the purpose of a system? How does a system flourish? What must I do individually to support the smooth functioning of systems vital to life on Earth?

In addition to drawing on Scripture for his analysis, in a nod to natural theology Pope John Paul II also claims that God has endowed creation with its own integrity, which must be observed: "Theology, philosophy and science all speak of a harmonious universe, of a 'cosmos' endowed with its own integrity, its own internal, dynamic balance. *This order must be respected*. The human race is called to explore this order, to examine it with due care and to make use of it while safeguarding its integrity."[64] Once again, the pope connects this order inherent in creation to the ability of all people at all times to be able to able to use the bounty of creation and to lead healthy, fulfilling lives, but his main purpose in citing this order is to castigate those whose rapacious consumption levels wittingly or unwittingly deprive those of less economic means the ability to enjoy the bounty of creation adequately, writing that "It is manifestly unjust that a privileged few should continue to accumulate excess goods, squandering available resources, while masses of people are living in conditions of misery at the very lowest level of subsistence."[65] In consequence, this order requires that greed and selfishness be discouraged individually and collectively, but it also mandates that questions of justice and a fair distribution of resources are a necessary part of the process of assessing this order.

In a move that draws upon the rights tradition within Catholic social thought, Pope John Paul II declares a new right in "The Ecological Crisis," namely, the right to a safe environment,[66] which he states ought to be included in an updated Charter of Human Rights. There are usually two genres of rights: negative rights, which limit governmental intrusion and create a zone of freedom in which individuals may make choices and sculpt their lives; and positive rights, which typically involve some positive claim and an attendant obligation on some entity, usually the state, to provide the good indicated by that right. While John Paul II does not go to great lengths to specify the content of the right to a safe environment or whether the right is a positive or negative one, the mere fact that he uses rights language is significant, as rights claims tend to be the most rigorous moral language employed in the Catholic social thought tradition.

The last point to be commended in "The Ecological Crisis" is that Pope John Paul II counteracts the contemporary tendency to place faith in technological improvements and increasing efficiency to extricate ourselves from the environmental pickles that we have created, which in turn will allow us to continue the same patterns of consumption while experiencing less and less environmental destruction associated with those patterns. Pope John Paul II is quite blunt, however, that intentional austerity measures from each individual are necessary to reverse negative environmental trends: "Modern society will find no solution to the ecological problem unless it *takes a serious look at its life style*."[67] In Pope John Paul II's mind, the ecological crisis is a moral crisis, not a technical one, so each person must be honest about his or her contribution to large-scale environmental ills, counteract a culture of instant gratification and consumerism, and be willing to muster the self-discipline necessary to implement a regimen of personal restraint.

In summary, there is a great deal to commend in "The Ecological Crisis." As the first major official statement on Catholic environmentalism, it provides a cosmology and theological anthropology that situates our place in the universe and identifies the broad-based duties and responsibilities incumbent upon Catholics. It correctly identifies environmental issues that have become large-scale threats to life on Earth, and it attempts to impress upon its readers not only their urgency but the enormous scale of the response necessary for mitigation efforts to be successful. It is candid and outspoken that environmental problems cannot be solved by technical improvements or managerial prowess alone, but only by a moral conversion that involves an abrupt change in priorities. Finally, he offers a practical trajectory to his theological deliberations via an environmental virtue ethic for Catholics, which focuses on restraint and self-control in order to consume and pollute less.

Yet there are a number of elements in "The Ecological Crisis" that are unclear, intellectually puzzling, or at cross purposes with other elements of his brand of environmentalism. As I wrote above, it is abundantly clear that Pope John Paul II is an unrepentant anthropocentrist who believes that creation was intended for humans and that its purpose is to satisfy human needs and desires. Yet he must also reckon with several strands of Scripture which either indicate that creation has a purpose independent of humans or that God's salvific action encompasses all of creation. So, Pope John Paul II mentions that creation is called to praise God,[68] that the death and resurrection of Christ reconciled "*all things*" to God,[69] and that in the fullness of time "*all things*" will be united through Christ.[70] If God's salvific intent and action are directed to everything in creation, one would suspect that this means that non-human creation is beloved by God, that God cares for it, and that regardless of its utility for humans it has enormous value to God. Yet, oddly enough, these considerations are never raised by Pope John Paul II, who gives exclusive preference to the stewardship paradigm as the foundation for practical normative ethics. So while universal salvation might have a solid Scriptural warrant and significant theoretical value, for Pope John Paul II it remains suspended in theological ether and the moral implications of universal salvation remain opaque. Like an idea that gets stuck in one's head and never gets put into practice, universal salvation remains purely a concept, even though its practical implications beg to be explored.

A significant theme of "The Ecological Crisis" is that a robust ecological education is needed to convey the knowledge and impart the habits necessary to curb our destructive consumerist appetites. According to Pope John Paul II, it is incumbent upon Catholic parents to educate their children from a young age in this ecological education: "The first educator, however, is the family, where the child learns to respect his neighbour and to love nature."[71] This passage is remarkable for two reasons. First, it shows that Pope John Paul II has little practical experience with children, as a love for nature does not need to be taught to them. Biophilia and love for nature are innate in children and part of their genetic ancestry, and their fascination with animals and the natural world is apparent almost from birth. Nature is like a wonderland for children, full of mystery, intrigue, joy, and happiness, and all that needs to be done in order to witness this wonder and awe is to let children explore nature freely: to wade creeks, to chase butterflies, to dig in the dirt for grubs, to touch tree bark, to watch birds flitting about, to play with their pets, to hike through the woods, to taste fresh berries picked from the bush. Even when not actively exploring nature directly, young children are fascinated by stories about animals, children's books are dominated by stories about animals, and many children have a collection of stuffed animals for comfort and play. Even some older children and teenagers have a favorite stuffed animal or two that gets cuddled regularly at night. Kids are robustly inclined to love nature and to immerse themselves in nature—it is their formal and informal education that both restrains and kills their native biophilia by limiting their contact with nature, in addition to telling them that nature is an unimportant backdrop for the far more important realm of human activity and no more than a repository of resources to satisfy human desires and needs.

Yet perhaps more importantly, in the passage quoted above, Pope John Paul II says straightforwardly that nature ought to be an object of love. This has potentially seismic implications for Catholic environmentalism. Love in Christian theology is typically a highly exclusive club, with God and humans being the only legitimate objects of love. Nor does the idea of loving nature sit well with the stewardship paradigm, which depends on a bifurcated moral universe consisting of humans, whom we are called to love as ourselves, and the rest of creation, which we are called to manage and control in order to secure human well-being. Of course, proponents of the stewardship paradigm might retort that creation ought to be loved for the beneficial services it provides; yet this instrumental love is a far cry from the love that we are enjoined to feel and express toward our fellow human beings, regardless of any benefits or advantages that accrue from it. So, very much like Pope John Paul II's notion of universal salvation remains in theological ether, bereft of any practical import, so too his statement about loving nature might have some rhetorical value, but certainly does little to challenge the stewardship paradigm's relegation of nature to the status of a repository of resources for humans to manage and use.

Another irksome issue raised by Pope John Paul II's analysis is the link between environmental destruction and sin. In "The Ecological Crisis," the pope uses the sins of Adam and Eve to typify sin as an action performed deliberately that thwarts the divine plan for creation.[72] The problem with locating sin in intentional individual acts is twofold: large-scale, long-term environmental problems almost never occur because of an individual act; and rarely do people intend to cause environmental destruction.[73] Most environmental problems are caused by large groups of people engaging in certain patterns of behavior done week after week, month after month, and year after year, and over time the unintended side-effect of those patterns is the emergence of significant environmental problems. Indeed, as Thomas Berry notes, environmental destruction is usually the result of people acting according to revered religious and cultural traditions:

> The difficulty is that the assault on the natural world has been carried out by good persons for the best of purposes, the betterment of life for this generation and especially for our children. It was not bad people, it was the good people acting for good purposes within the ethical perspectives of our cultural traditions that have brought such ruin on this continent and on the entire planet.[74]

So unless sin is used to describe the behavioral patterns that many in the Western world consider part and parcel of our everyday lives and necessary to live the "good life," it really fails to identify and condemn the actual causes of large-scale environmental destruction.

Finally, Pope John Paul II's nod to "the created order" as a revelation of God's intentions opens the door to natural theology and to the natural law tradition that has been a mainstay of Catholic theology for centuries. The problem with Pope John Paul II's notion of the created order, however, as Willis Jenkins argues convincingly,[75] is that he always interprets the moral normativity generated by the created order as consistent with the stewardship paradigm, the foundational basis of which is the creation stories in Genesis. This theological strategy of attributing moral import to the natural order but specifying the contents of that moral normativity via Scripture rather than the natural order itself strips this attempt at natural theology from any kind of normativity or from any epistemic clarity outside of Scripture. So until it can be explained how moral meaning can be derived from the created order independently of Scripture, the attempt at natural theology remains vacuous and Scripture remains the only functional conduit for ascertaining God's intentions.

Despite these reservations, Pope John Paul II's "The Ecological Crisis" was a watershed moment in the Catholic Church, which not only prompted a number of regional Catholic bishops' conferences to issue statements on the environment but also made it impossible not to be some shade of green if one is Catholic. Pope John Paul II further solidified the stewardship paradigm as the theological foundation for Catholic environmentalism, despite Lynn White Jr.'s incisive critique of it in "The Historical Roots of Our Ecological Crisis" and growing hostility to the stewardship paradigm among influential secular environmental groups worldwide. Yet in the interim period between "The Ecological Crisis" and the second watershed moment in Catholic environmentalism, which was the publication of the first papal encyclical on environmentalism, Pope Francis's *Laudato Si'*, there were a number of documents that maintained a very uneasy alliance with the stewardship paradigm. One would suspect that with the anthropology developed in the social encyclicals from the time of Pope Leo XIII's *Rerum Novarum* (1891) until after the Second Vatican Council, the stewardship paradigm at this point would be resting on a solid foundation, and the significant task for the authors of these documents would be applying the stewardship paradigm in their unique circumstances. Yet in document after document during this interim period, despite professing allegiance to the stewardship paradigm, each in its own way searches for different theological foundations and better explanations for the purpose of creation. Some question what it means for creation to be a "revelation" of

God and what practical implications this has. Some want to extend moral consideration beyond humans and draw a wider zone of intimacy with the natural world. Some want to resacralize the universe and consider creation as one big sacrament. There is nary a hint in these documents that the stewardship paradigm as a foundation for Catholic environmentalism is theologically sufficient, and still less an inclination simply to apply the stewardship paradigm to local circumstances. These documents wrestle with the stewardship paradigm, yearn for a richer theology of creation, and frequently seek to transcend the anthropocentric assumptions undergirding Catholic environmentalism. Phrased a bit differently, this interim period shows a remarkable degree of theological inquisitiveness and development and represents a tradition that is consciously struggling with itself and is a bit unsure about where it wants to go or the practical implications of its theological commitments.

The Interim Period (1990–2015)

United States Conference of Catholic Bishops, "Renewing the Earth" (1991)

Published less than two years on the heels of Pope John Paul II's "The Ecological Crisis," one would suspect that the first major official statement from the United States Conference of Catholic Bishops (USCCB) on the environment would show significant points of convergence with "The Ecological Crisis," and yet this is precisely not the case on certain critical points. While there is an overt triumphalist edge to Pope John Paul II's anthropocentrism, in which humans are the "crown" of creation, the "summit of God's creative activity," and "the most perfect of creatures,"[76] the USCCB in "Renewing the Earth"[77] shies away from such grandiose assertions and softens the anthropocentric language considerably. Whether this stems from sensitivity to Lynn White Jr.'s critique of anthropocentrism or a desire not to offend potential constructive partnerships with secular environmental organizations in the United States is anyone's guess. What is clear, though, is that the USCCB is clearly uncomfortable with Pope John Paul II's anthropocentrism even though, in the end, there is little practical difference between the two.

The bishops in "Renewing the Earth" are so allergic to the received anthropocentrism that they avoid almost entirely the Priestly account of creation (Gen. 1–2:4), which is the first of two creation accounts in Genesis. One mention of this creation account occurs when the bishops describe humans as "made in the image and likeness of God," without actually referencing the source of this passage.[78] The only other mention is the end of the first creation account, where the Priestly author writes that God looked at creation and declared everything that God had made to be "very good" (Gen. 1:31).[79] So despite the first creation account being the biblical foundation for Pope John Paul II's environmentalism, the topic of intense exegetical skirmishes among Bible scholars, extensive debate among theologians, and an excoriating piece by Lynn White, Jr., the Catholic bishops simply sidestep these thorny conceptual issues and largely ignore the first creation account.

Instead, the organizing schema for "Renewing the Earth" is a set of principles from Catholic social thought, which occupies the bulk of the document's space, so the Catholic bishops are more interested in developing the finer lineaments of these principles than in discussing substantively the biblical or theological materials underlying their particular brand of Catholic environmentalism. So in rather cursory fashion, the Catholic bishops discuss Christian responsibility for the environment as based on God's affirmation of the entirety of creation as being "very good" (Gen. 1:31), that creation ought to be understood as a divine gift to every creature, and that everything in creation—mountains, seas, rivers, birds, wild beasts—is invited to join humans in praising God's goodness.[80] Then the Catholic bishops offer their version of the stewardship paradigm:

> People share the earth with other creatures. But humans, made in the image and likeness of God, are called in a special way to 'cultivate and care for it' (Gn 2:15). Men and women, therefore, bear a unique responsibility under God: to safeguard the created world and by their creative labor even to enhance it. Safeguarding creation requires us to live responsibly within it, rather than manage creation as though we are outside it. The human family is charged with preserving the beauty, diversity, and integrity of nature, as well as with fostering its productivity.[81]

This description of the stewardship paradigm suffers from the same kind of opaqueness that was discussed above with Pope John Paul II's environmentalism, insofar as certain words and phrases (safeguarding, living responsibly, cultivating and caring) give little indication about the kinds of behavior consistent with these or for whom or what creation is being managed. In the absence of any determinate and well-defined meaning or trajectory, the typical default position within Catholic environmentalism is to assume that humans are the raison d'être for creation and that creation is to be managed for the benefit of humans.

Yet the quote above ends with a rather tantalizing sentence. One of the most revered figures in American environmentalism, Aldo Leopold, whose *A Sand County Almanac* was one of the best-selling environmental books in American history, was famous for his anti-anthropocentric sentiments, which are encapsulated in the following statement: "A thing is right when it tends to preserve the integrity, beauty, and stability of the biotic community. It is wrong when it tends otherwise."[82] For Leopold, the good of ecosystems is prior ethically to the good of any constituent part, which means that human well-being (or the well-being of any particular species or individual, for the matter) is always secondary to and dependent upon the flourishing of the larger ecosystem.

There is an unmistakable similarity between the triad presented in "Renewing the Earth" (beauty, diversity, and integrity) and Leopold's triad (integrity, beauty, and stability), and it is quite possible that the one difference between the two triads, namely the Catholic bishops' replacement of Leopold's "stability" with "diversity" could very well correspond to the decline of steady state systems thought in biology circles that was prevalent during the early to mid-twentieth century. Whether true or not, the fact that one of the best-known phrases of one of the most famous American environmentalists appears almost verbatim in a major statement on the environment by the American Catholic bishops is yet another clear sign that the American bishops are uncomfortable with anthropocentrism and wish to develop a broader and more inclusive environmental ethic in which non-human interests are given consideration.

Several other lines of inquiry in "Renewing the Earth" bolster this contention. The Catholic bishops develop the idea of creation as a sacrament conveying the divine presence. They state, "Throughout history, people have continued to meet the Creator on mountaintops, in vast deserts, and alongside waterfalls and gently flowing springs. In storms and earthquakes, they found expressions of divine power."[83] This creates a prima facie case for environmental preservation as these natural artifacts make God's presence manifest in their present form, but as soon as the mountaintops disappear due to strip mining operations or the waterfalls run dry due to water being diverted for agricultural fields, the ability of these natural artifacts ceases to be a conduit for the divine presence in the universe.

The bishops also maintain that other species, ecosystems, and distinctive landscapes have value independent of their usefulness to humans and, in their own unique way, give glory to God. As evidence for this value, the Catholic bishops cite God's statement after the Great Flood in Genesis to the effect that God has established a covenant with "every living creature,"[84] not just with human beings. Moreover, in addition to individual creatures and natural artifacts giving glory to God, the entire assemblage of individuals and the enormous amount of variability and diversity within creation better represent the goodness of God. Citing Thomas Aquinas, the Catholic bishops write, God "produced many and diverse creatures, so that what was wanting to one in representation of the divine goodness might be supplied by another … hence the whole universe together participates in the divine goodness more perfectly, and represents it better than any single creature whatever."[85]

Furthermore, using St. Francis of Assisi as an exemplar, who is the patron saint of ecology in the Catholic Church, the bishops nervously claim that creation is a proper object of our love, albeit with certain qualifications:

> An ordered love for creation, therefore, is ecological without being ecocentric. We can and must care for the earth without mistaking it for the ultimate object of our devotion. A Christian love of the natural world, as St. Francis showed us, can restrain grasping and wanton human behavior and help mightily to preserve and nurture all that God has made. We believe that faith in a good and loving God is a compelling source of passionate and enduring care for all creation.[86]

The significant reservation for the Catholic bishops is that the love due to creation and non-human creatures must always be understood as secondary to our love for our human neighbors, especially the poor among us who have immediate unmet needs. So the Catholic bishops have a clear priority of loves: first, actually existing humans, especially the weakest and most vulnerable; and second, future generations of humans and the rest of non-human creation.

While the Catholic bishops are clearly nervous about traditional anthropocentrism and want to extend theological and ethical consideration beyond human interests to a love and respect that encompasses the entirety of creation, this inclination to greater heights of theoretical inclusivity hits a proverbial brick wall when it comes to the practical implications of this broader vision. So, for instance, when the Catholic bishops discuss the universal purpose of created things, their notion of "universal" extends to all humans, while leaving out everything else: "God has given the fruit of the earth to sustain the entire human family 'without excluding or favoring anyone.'"[87] The bishops exhort Catholics to cultivate the virtue of solidarity as a means of securing the universal common good, which includes sacrificing one's own self-interest for the good of "others," with these others clearly being humans.[88] The preferential option for the poor refers not to vulnerable animals, species, or ecosystems, but only to vulnerable humans.[89] The concept of "authentic development" is explicitly concerned only with the way in which the pursuit of purported progress affects humans and favors certain human groups over others, while remaining silent about the effects on non-human creation.[90] In perhaps one of the most egregious instances of forgetfulness, the Catholic bishops praise the National Catholic Rural Life Conference's work on sustainability, promoting farming methods that minimize topsoil erosion, and fighting for a living wage for farmers, all of which concern human well-being,[91] while remaining silent on the millions of animals suffering unspeakable horrors in factory farms, which are little more than organized torture systems that care about nothing other than inexpensive food for humans.[92]

So while trying to part ways with Pope John Paul II's triumphal anthropocentrism by developing several theological strands of thought that cast a wider net of moral consideration and encouraging us to expand our sphere of love and concern and care—sometimes very eloquently and with a great deal of emotional fervor—the Catholic bishops fail to show how this gentler and kinder version of Catholic environmentalism makes any practical difference. The danger in this strategy of constructing a theology that confers greater consideration to non-human interests while disallowing it from having any practical import is twofold. On one level, the divorce between theological foundations and actual practice invites rampant greenwashing, insofar as it allows for the legitimation of certain environmentally destructive practices simply by redescribing them theologically in more appealing and culturally acceptable terms. But more importantly, it makes theology irrelevant by creating theological concepts that are either so broad and vague or so indeterminate in meaning that virtually any practice can fall under the umbrella of good stewardship, or caring for creation, or loving God's earth. Just as a father's practice of beating his kids out of anger cannot be described as loving behavior, so too things like factory farming cannot be described as loving creation or respecting animals. Of course, I readily concede the possibility that anthropocentrism is so ingrained in the Catholic theological tradition that the bishops are either unaware that their attempt to create a kinder and gentler version of Catholic environmentalism is mostly a theological rhetorical flourish bereft of practical content, or that they simply cannot fathom how to construct a practical non-anthropocentric ethic.

Regardless of the real reason for this divorce between theory and practice, it is clear that the Catholic bishops are striving to sculpt a kinder and gentler version of Catholic environmentalism that includes a broader array of interests and expands the scope of moral consideration, while simultaneously being either unwilling or unable to articulate the kinds of patterns of behavior and the types of institutions that are consistent with this new Catholic environmentalism. So despite obviously good intentions and a fair bit of theological innovation, the Catholic bishops are a divided house in "Renewing the Earth" who strive assiduously to strike a new chord in Catholic environmentalism while unwittingly spinning their wheels and surreptitiously affirming the same old anthropocentrism in practice that they sought to leave behind.

United Methodist and Roman Catholic Statement on the Eucharist and Ecology, "Heaven and Earth are Full of Your Glory" (2008)

For the signatories to "Heaven and Earth are Full of Your Glory" (2008), which was a joint statement of Methodist and Roman Catholic theologians, Christian environmentalism is cast as the "ecological stewardship of God's earth," but unlike the typical format of developing the stewardship paradigm from the first two creation stories in Genesis, they begin their document with a theology of creation as a gift: "Creation is God's *first* gift. Creation is the first sign of God's glory and God's love. For humans, the world is not simply a stage for human action; our relation to the world, to creation, is constitutive of our very identity as persons."[93] Since everything that exists comes from God, the entire universe is sacred and everything within it—from the complex and marvelous to the simple and pedestrian—is to be regarded as "signs of God among us."[94] Therefore, when Christians think about "creation" the first thing to jump into our heads should not be trees, creeks, animals, ecosystems, or other natural artifacts, but God's love which all these objects represent and embody.

Given that creation is a gift of God's love, the "fundamental posture" of a Christian ought to be gratitude, or gratefulness, which arises from the "awe and wonder" that we exist and are cherished by the Creator of our universe—two phenomena that are replete with "transcendental depth" which has captivated the imagination of "poets, artists, philosophers" and other major world religions. So according to "Heaven and Earth are Full of Your Glory," Christians ought to embody a "grateful receptivity"[95] to everything that exists in the universe, from those things we enjoy and hold dear to those things strange and antithetical to human life to everything in between, as the entirety of creation should be understood as a sacramental encounter with God: "This means that the world, humans, and all creatures great and small, are signs of God among us."[96]

Two notable insights follow from this theology of creation. First, while Jesus became incarnate in human form and achieved salvation for all humans, God's redemptive purpose extends to the entirety of creation. Citing St. Paul's oft-quoted phrase that the whole creation waits with eager longing to be liberated from the futility of bondage to decay (Romans 8:18-25), the signatories claim that we must resist our usual anthropocentric assumptions that limit the soteriological import of God's salvific activity and affirm the genuine universal scope of salvation.[97]

Second, while human distinctiveness has often been used in the theological tradition to undergird claims to superiority and or to greater importance to God, the authors assiduously want to avoid such conclusions. To be sure, humans possess many distinctive characteristics; but so too do many other creatures. Indeed, every creature has its own unique voice, its own set of relationships, its own value to its respective ecosystem, and intrinsic value as a creature loved by God. Thus, our human task is not to allow our uniqueness unwittingly to lead to a knee-jerk anthropocentrism that regards other creatures as subservient to our needs and desires, but to use our unique human capacities to "celebrate other creatures' joy in their own being"[98] and to treasure the distinctive ways in which they express the grandiosity of God.

Catholic Bishops of the Northwest Region, "The Columbia River Watershed" (2001)

Out of three documents surveyed during this interim period, "The Columbia River Watershed" represents the clearest test case of the malleability of the stewardship paradigm and the potential for a non-anthropocentric Catholic environmentalism. Written by bishops and archbishops in The Columbia River Watershed, an enormous geographical area that spans over 259,000 square miles, which includes the Canadian province of British Columbia and four states (Washington, Oregon, Idaho, Montana), the regional bishops represent an area that is indebted to a few industries (forestry, fishing, and farming) that are the lifeblood of the region but which also and have a number of direct environmental impacts on the health of ecosystems within the watershed. In many ways, this situation represents the classic case of human economic interests versus environmental considerations, although the bishops are well aware that human economic interests are in no way divorced from the larger health and sustainability of ecosystems. In this context, it is almost impossible for the Catholic bishops not to offer some practical policy recommendations and to show concretely how their version of the stewardship paradigm gets embodied.

The Catholic bishops are also extremely allergic to the robustly anthropocentric elements of the stewardship paradigm and follow a strategy similar to that of the USCCB in "Renewing the Earth" of entirely glossing over key terms in Genesis 1 that they find problematic, unlike Pope John Paul II who made these the centerpiece of his theological anthropology. While the Catholic bishops make extensive use of the image of God metaphor, nowhere in "The Columbia River Watershed" do they mention the almost necessary corollary that humans are granted dominion over animals and are called to subdue the earth. Instead, their preferred implication of the image of God metaphor is that humans are called to be caring stewards, who use our unique gifts and talents to "celebrate, develop, and care for creation":[99]

> Stewardship is the traditional Christian expression of the role of people in relation to creation. Stewards, as caretakers for the things of God, are called to use wisely and distribute justly the goods of God's earth to meet the needs of God's children. They are to care for the earth as their home and as a beautiful revelation of the creativity, goodness and love of God.[100]

Coupled with this theological anthropology that centers on humans caring for creation is a persistent attempt to establish theologically that divine concern and love transcend humans to embrace all of creation. To be sure, the Catholic bishops maintain that humans have unique qualities that make us highly qualified to manage ecosystems across our planet, but "The Columbia River Watershed" is replete with statements that God's love and concern—and thus our management efforts and goals—must extend beyond mere human interests. Here is a list of the various ways the Catholic bishops extend moral consideration:

1 God "is lovingly concerned" about all of creation.[101]
2 God cares for all creatures.[102]
3 God loves the entire community of life.[103]
4 Creation has inherent value, independent of its usefulness to humans.[104]
5 All living beings have dignity.[105]
6 A number of biblical passages testify to this broadening of moral consideration beyond human interests:

   a Genesis 9:12-13: God establishes a covenant "with every living creature" and with "the earth."
   b Wisdom 11:24: God loves everything that exists.
   c Job 38-41: God's providence extends to all creatures.
   d Sirach 42:23-25: God has made nothing in vain, and everything that God has created is good.
   e Luke 12:24-28: Jesus cares for the flowers of the fields and the birds of the air.
   f Colossians 1:20: Christ has reconciled all things to the Father.[106]

The Catholic bishops also point out several times that creation, as a visible effect of God's loving and nurturing activity, ought to be regarded as a revelation of the divine, and that to gaze upon and to experience creation is to encounter many signs of God. Therefore, good stewardship must prioritize environmental preservation as an overarching goal, as any renovation or destruction of creation obscures the grandiosity of creation and dims the divine presence in the universe.

So what does this expanded sense of moral consideration and of God's love for creation entail practically? Perhaps the most pressing environmental issue in the Columbia River watershed region is the plummeting numbers of spawning salmon. Counts in the early 1800s estimate between 16 and 20 million salmon would return up the Columbia River annually to spawn; that number has dropped to 1–2 million today, and the vast majority of these salmon are hatchery raised, so significant human inputs and resources are required for even this historically low number of salmon.[107] Today salmon are extinct from nearly 40 percent of the streams in which they once spawned, and salmon populations are at risk of extinction in 44 percent of the streams where they remain.[108] In terms of genetic diversity, scientists estimate that 27 percent of the genetic diversity of Pacific salmon in the western United States has vanished.[109] A number of factors are responsible for this historical demise, among which are factory fishing, the construction of dams, and the destruction of habitat due to logging and mining.

Salmon spawns are vital to the health of forests in the Northwest and to the many species who inhabit these forests. Described as "a veritable conveyor belt for nutrients,"[110] salmon spawns release copious amounts of nitrogen, phosphorus, and a number of other nutrients to plants in a watershed as salmon are consumed by a wide array of animals and their remnants spread throughout adjacent forests. Biologists estimate that as much as 70 percent of nitrogen absorbed by trees in northwestern riparian zones comes from the bodies of salmon, and researchers have discovered that trees in areas that still have salmon runs grow three times faster than trees in areas where salmon runs no longer exist.[111] In the Columbia River watershed and elsewhere, salmon runs are arguably the most vital element for healthy forests and thriving ecosystems.

Given the importance of large numbers of spawning salmon to the health of the forests in the Northwest and to the many animals that call these forests home, it is not unreasonable to expect the Northwest Catholic bishops to take a strong position on protecting existing salmon populations and perhaps even recommending tangible steps to increase salmon numbers or to restore salmon spawning areas and the creeks that create access to them. Yet beyond some broad ethical principles and the articulation of some ideal scenarios, they fail to make any practical policy recommendation dealing with the preservation or enhancement of salmon numbers or habitats. The northwest bishops mention authentic stewardship, the just treatment of all peoples, living wages, the integration of communities into their environments, the responsible use of creation's goods, careful conservation of regional goods, recycling resources, wise management of forests, responsible timber harvesting, efficient energy usage, ecological integrity, regional sustainability, organic crops, clean water and air, and abundant fish populations that allow opportunities for commercial, recreational, and private fishing.[112] In addition, they endorse the common good as an organizing principle for ethical deliberation: "the common goal is the well-being of the entire community of life and the promotion of the common good." They also draw on Isaiah's peaceable kingdom as their idealized vision for the Columbia River watershed: "The wolf lives with the lamb, the panther lies down with the kid, calf and lion cub feed together with a little child to lead them" (Isaiah 11:6).[113]

The methodology of the Northwest bishops is to identify values, to propose general moral principles, and to articulate idealized visions (ecological, spiritual, economic, etc.), but they assiduously avoid making any practical ethical recommendations or endorsing any policy directive, especially when there are perceived competing interests at stake. So when it comes to giving preference to increasing salmon numbers in the Pacific Northwest, the Catholic bishops certainly wax eloquently about desiring abundant fish populations, but they neither propose any policy designed to bring these about such as the breaching dams, nor do they endorse anything approaching moral normativity to curb behavior that exacerbates the conditions negatively affecting wild salmon populations such as commercial fishing or logging.

"The Columbia River Watershed" is a document replete with idealized visions, statements, and desires, and while the Catholic moral life certainly needs moral ideals to fire our imagination and to inspire us to ever greater heights of love for and service to God, ideals without practical steps to realize these ideals is tantamount to little more than wishful thinking. Just as the ideal of having a happy, nurturing marriage involves a number of building blocks such as open communication, learning a partner's love language, intentional acts of kindness, an appreciation for one's partner, and ongoing love, support, and compassion toward a beloved, so too an idealized vision for the Columbia River watershed is little more than a mental fantasy unless the practical components of this vision are identified and ordered, and the conditions undermining these components are restrained.

While "The Columbia River Watershed" represents a landmark document insofar as it intentionally departs from the dominant anthropocentrism that began with the social encyclicals of Pope Leo XIII and culminated in the triumphalist anthropocentrism of Pope John Paul II, the practical implications of this more non-anthropocentric Catholic environmentalism remain unclear, as without some more precise delineation of the direction in which this version of Catholic environmentalism heads, it is impossible to ascertain whether there is any meaningful difference between these two different commitments at the foundation of Catholic environmentalism.

Pope Benedict XVI (2005–2013)

Pope Benedict XVI was dubbed "the green pope" for making the Vatican the first sovereign state to become carbon neutral through tree planting initiatives,[114] having 2400 solar panels installed on the roof of the Paul VI Audience Hall, and using a hybrid popemobile on his travels.[115] Theologically, his environmentalism closely follows that of his successor, Pope John Paul II, as he casts Catholic environmentalism in terms of responsible stewardship. Benedict XVI regards creation as a gift from God,[116] which contains a moral order that must be followed by humans, and as the only creatures made in the image and likeness of God it is our job to have dominion over creation[117] and to act as stewards over the entirety of creation. Pope Benedict XVI's theological anthropology is tinged with the same triumphalist anthropocentrism that we have seen before in Pope John Paul II and other papal predecessors, as he maintains that humans are "the apex of God's creation," "the heart of the marvel of creation," and crowned with "glory and honor."[118] Yet Pope Benedict XVI explains that despite our exalted status within creation and the fact that the entirety of creation has been entrusted to humans,[119] God's bestowal of dominion upon us should not simply be understood as being given authority over creation, but to function as "God's co-worker" in managing creation, which precludes anything akin to "absolute domination"[120] or a "total technical dominion over nature."[121] Pope Benedict XVI writes,

> The created world, structured in an intelligent way by God, is entrusted to our responsibility and though we are able to analyze it and transform it we cannot consider ourselves creation's absolute master. We are called, rather, to exercise responsible stewardship of creation, in order to protect it, to enjoy its fruits, and to cultivate it, finding the resources necessary for everyone to live with dignity. Through the help of nature itself and through hard work and creativity, humanity is indeed capable of carrying out its grave duty to hand on the earth to future generations so that they too, in turn, will be able to inhabit it worthily and continue to cultivate it. For this to happen, it is essential to develop 'that covenant between human beings and the environment, which should mirror the creative love of God,' recognizing that we all come from God and that we are all journeying toward him.[122]

We have seen a typical pattern among proponents of the stewardship paradigm of feigning a chastened anthropocentrism on the theoretical level while maintaining an unchecked anthropocentrism on the practical level, which knows virtually no limits to the degree to which humans are favored and the interests of all other creatures are relegated to secondary status, and Pope Benedict XVI is no different. Notice the many ways in which he attempts to qualify the notion of stewardship in the block quote above: It must be responsible, not absolute, protective, with an eye to cultivating creation with the same creative love that God has modeled for us so that future generations may enjoy similar fruits. Yet when Pope Benedict XVI's corpus is surveyed for any way in which this chastened anthropocentrism gets embodied practically either in policies or actions, so that human interests and well-being are not the sole and exclusive determinants of morality, there is nary a hint of evidence to suggest that the stewardship paradigm protects anything but human interests.

For instance, in delineating our relationship to the natural world, the pope writes that we have a "responsibility towards the poor, towards future generations and towards humanity as a whole," without averring to any non-human source of moral responsibility.[123] The oft cited principle of the universal destination of creation's goods refers to humans alone.[124] Pope Benedict XVI's treatment of Christian love clearly indicates that love is to be directed to God and to one's human neighbor, but he remains silent on whether anything else in the created order is a proper object of love.[125] The pope also says nothing on the issue of whether the Church's charitable activity should be directed to any non-human part of creation.[126] The pope uses the phrase "natural resources," which entails understanding the goods of creation as raw materials to be transformed and used by humans.[127] When the pope addresses practical considerations (drinking water, energy use, rural development, climate change) there is never any hint that anything beyond human interests is given importance in his analyses.[128] If there is any lingering doubt about Pope Benedict's anthropocentrism, he goes on to chide proponents of "ecocentrism and biocentrism" for "abolishing the distinctiveness and superior role of human beings."[129] Much like Pope John Paul II, Pope Benedict XVI may feign some theoretical chastening of his anthropocentrism, but there is no tangible evidence that anything other than human interests fall under the umbrella of moral consideration where practical matters are concerned.

Conclusion

While the stewardship paradigm has clearly won the day as the theological foundation for Catholic environmentalism, this survey of recent Catholic figures and documents ought to impress upon the reader that this is a contested theological tradition very much in the process of internal renovation and change. The confident, swaggering, even haughty anthropocentrism that was resoundingly criticized by Lynn White Jr. in his seminal "The Historical Roots of Our Ecological Crisis" (1967) has found a secure foothold in papal documents from Pope Leo XIII to Pope Benedict XVI, yet recent documents coming from different Catholic corners show a distinct aversion to this pretentious anthropocentrism, ranging from a mild allergy to a complete rejection, even while retaining the theological superstructure of the stewardship paradigm. So while anthropocentrism remains a highly divisive issue theologically for Catholic environmentalism, similar misgivings do not exist about the stewardship paradigm.

Yet Catholics ought to have reservations about the stewardship paradigm. The famous anthropologist Claude Lévi-Strauss, who coined the phrase "floating signifiers" to denote terms and concepts that are "void of meaning and thus apt to receive any meaning,"[130] could have just as easily been describing the stewardship paradigm, as it is sufficiently opaque and indeterminate in its practical trajectory to mean many different things to many different persons. To be sure, several popes try to rectify this obscurity by listing a litany of adverbs and adjectives that quality stewardship, from "responsible" stewardship, to exercising stewardship "lovingly" and "wisely," to being "caretakers" for creation, to condemnations of manipulating nature "indiscriminately." As Lévi-Strauss would retort, however, these attempts to specify the content of stewardship are as ambiguous as the concept they are trying to clarify. As a result, the stewardship paradigm, while garnering almost universal allegiance in Catholic circles as the theological foundation for Catholic environmentalism, suffers from a level of unclarity as to render it almost functionally useless.

In addition, when faced with such intractable opacity, the almost universal tendency when transitioning from the theoretical concept of stewardship to more practical considerations is unwittingly to smuggle into the ethical deliberations a bevy of anthropocentric assumptions so that practical reasoning becomes bereft of anything other than a calculation of benefit to human beings from certain policies or courses of action. So despite protestations to the contrary and predictable theological maneuvers intended to include a broader array of interests, the stewardship paradigm invariably induces something akin to theological amnesia, in which verbal commitments to greater consideration of non-human interests are readily forgotten and practical ethics take on a highly predictable and one-dimensional anthropocentric character.

Yet perhaps the most intellectually suspect aspect of the stewardship paradigm—and one that is rarely discussed in theological circles—is that it is theologically thin and captures very little of the Catholic moral identity. The papal documents discussed above are largely content to generate an environmentalism based on the first two creation accounts in Genesis, with a focus on a few key terms (subduing, dominion, and image and likeness of God) that are qualified in different ways. While the non-papal documents discussed above stay within the confines of the stewardship paradigm, they all want to construct notions of God, creation, and humans that go far beyond that contained in the first couple chapters of Genesis. The authors of "Heaven and Earth are Full of Your Glory" want to situate environmentalism in the context of creation as a gift of God's love, and then to explore our response to the giftedness of creation via our response of gratitude, which comprises our foundational moral identity.

The American Catholic bishops in "Renewing the Earth" virtually ignore most of Genesis, flirt with Aldo Leopold's land ethic, claim that there is intrinsic value to creation regardless of benefit to humans, extol the virtue of biodiversity from a Thomistic perspective, and use St. Francis of Assisi as a model for making the claim that creation is a proper object of our love. While these two documents clearly are striving to transcend the theological limitations of the stewardship paradigm and to develop a more robust cosmology and anthropology, the clear winner in the category of theological expansiveness goes to the Northwest Catholic bishops in "The Columbia River Watershed," who not only draw upon a vast array of biblical sources (the Genesis account of the Great Flood and subsequent covenant; wisdom literature (Wisdom and Sirach); the book of Job; the Gospels; and Pauline literature), but who also spend considerable time developing a notion of God whose love is both represented by creation and who cares deeply for all creatures and the entire community of life, which in turn vests all creatures with inherent dignity and value. Although all three documents accept stewardship as an organizing principle for Catholic environmentalism, each in its own way strives to transcend the limited theological foundations for the stewardship paradigm in Genesis 1-2 that are found in the papal documents, and each seeks to bolster and expand the theological considerations that are deemed necessary to constructing an intellectually credible Catholic environmentalism. In many ways, given the degree to which these documents clearly want to depart from the reigning papal anthropocentrism, I am beyond puzzled as to why they still want to retain allegiance to the stewardship paradigm.

Notes

1. Steven Holmes, *The Young John Muir: An Environmental Biography* (Madison: University of Wisconsin Press, 1999).
2. Lynn White, Jr., "The Historical Roots of Our Ecological Crisis," *Science* 155 (3767) (March 10, 1967): 1203-7.
3. White, "The Historical Roots," 1204.
4. White, "The Historical Roots," 1203.
5. White, "The Historical Roots," 1204.
6. In "The Historical Roots," White blends the two creation stories in Genesis and writes about them as if they were coupled naturally, even

though they were written by different authors for different purposes, and accordingly the represent very distinct strands of theological and anthropological thought.

7. White, "The Historical Roots," 1205.

8. White, "The Historical Roots," 1205.

9. White, "The Historical Roots," 1206.

10. White, "The Historical Roots," 1207.

11. Thomas Derr, "Religion's Responsibility for 'The Ecological Crisis': An Argument Run Amok," *Worldview* 18 (1) (1975): 39-45; Reznseat M. Darnell, "Morality and 'The Ecological Crisis'," *BioScience* 17 (10) (Oct. 1967): 685-6; Robert L. Schuller, "Ecology—The New Religion?" *America* 122 (11) (March 21, 1970): 292-5; Kenneth Cauthen, "The Churches and the Future: A Utopian Proposal," *Zygon* 6 (4) (Dec. 1971): 311-29; Eric Doyle, "Ecology and the Canticle of Brother Sun," *New Blackfriars* 55 (262) (Sept. 1974): 292-402; Phyllis Trible, "Ancient Priests and Modern Polluters," *Foundations* 17 (2) (Apr.—June 1974): 158-63; James C. Livingston, "The Ecological Challenge to Christian Ethics," *The Christian Century* 88 (48) (Dec. 1, 1971): 1409-12; H. Paul Santmire, "Reflections on the Alleged Ecological Bankruptcy of Western Theology," *Anglican Theological Review* 57 (2) (April 1975): 131-52; John Macquarrie, "Creation and Environment," *Expository Times* 83 (1) (Oct. 1971): 4-9; and Richard McCormick, "Notes on Moral Theology," *Theological Studies* 32 (1) (Mar. 1971): 97-107.

12. For an illustrative collection of bishops' statements following this pattern, see United States Catholic Conference, *And God Saw That It Was Good: Catholic Theology and the Environment*, eds. Drew Christiansen and Walter Grazer (Washington, DC: United States Catholic Conference, 1996), 223-320.

13. James Gustafson, *Ethics from a Theocentric Perspective*, vol. 1, *Theology and Ethics* (Chicago: The University of Chicago, 1981), 86-113.

14. Rosemary Radford Ruether, "The Politics of God in the Christian Tradition," *Feminist Theology* 17 (3) (2009): 329-38.

15. Ivone Gebara, *Longing for Running Water: Ecofeminism and Liberation* (Minneapolis: Augsburg Fortress, 1999), 27.

16. Andrew J. Hoffman and Lloyd E. Sandelands, "Getting Right with Nature: Anthropocentrism, Ecocentricm, and Theocentrism," *Organization and Environment* 18 (2) (June 2005): 141-62; Eileen Crist and Helen Kopnina, "Unsettling Anthropocentrism," *Dialectical Anthropology* 38 (2014): 387-96; Noel E. Boulting, "Between Anthropocentrism and Ecocentrism," *Philosophy in the*

Contemporary World 2 (4) (Winter 1995): 1–8; J. Baird Callicott,
"Non-Anthropocentric Value Theory and Environmental Ethics,"
American Philosophical Quarterly 21 (4) (Oct. 1984): 299–309; William
Grey, "Environmental Value and Anthropocentrism," *Ethics and
the Environment* 3 (1) (1998): 97–103; Andrew K. Gabriel, "Beyond
Anthropocentrism in Barth's Doctrine of Creation: Searching for a
Theology of Nature," *Religious Studies and Theology* 28 (2) (2009):
175–87; Paul Haught, "Hume's Knave and Nonanthropocentric Virtues,"
Journal of Agricultural and Environmental Ethics 23 (2010): 129–43;
Holmes Rolston III, *Environmental Ethics: Duties to and Values in the
Natural World* (Philadelphia: Temple University Press, 1988); Paul W.
Taylor, *Respect for Nature: A Theory of Environmental Ethics* (Princeton:
Princeton University Press, 1986); Katie McShane, "Anthropocentrism
vs. Nonanthropocentrism: Why Should We Care?" *Environmental
Values* 16 (2007): 169–85; and John Nolt, "Anthropocentrism and
Egoism," *Environmental Values* 22 (2013): 441–59.

17. For a collection of these regional bishops' statements, see Drew
   Christiansen and Grazer, *And God Saw That It Was Good.*
18. Pope Leo XIII, *Aeterni Patris* (August 4, 1879), #17, https://www.
   vatican.va/content/leo-xiii/en/encyclicals/documents/hf_l-xiii_
   enc_04081879_aeterni-patris.html (accessed November 27, 2025).
19. Pope Leo XIII, *Rerum Novarum* (May 15, 1891), #6, https://www.
   vatican.va/content/leo-xiii/en/encyclicals/documents/hf_l-xiii_
   enc_15051891_rerum-novarum.pdf (accessed November 27, 2025).
20. Pope Leo XIII, *Rerum Novarum*, #7.
21. Pope Leo XIII, *Rerum Novarum*, #8.
22. Pope Leo XIII, *Rerum Novarum*, #40, quoting Genesis 1:28.
23. Pope Leo XIII, *Rerum Novarum*, #21.
24. Pope John XXIII, *Pacem in Terris* (April 11, 1963), #3, https://www.
   vatican.va/content/john-xxiii/en/encyclicals/documents/hf_j-xxiii_
   enc_11041963_pacem.html (accessed November 27, 2025).
25. Pope John XXIII, *Mater et Magistra* (May 15, 1961), #196, https://www.
   vatican.va/content/john-xxiii/en/encyclicals/documents/hf_j-xxiii_
   enc_15051961_mater.html (accessed November 27, 2025).
26. Pope John XXIII, *Pacem in Terris*, #3, referencing Psalms 8:5–6.
27. Pope John XXIII, *Pacem in Terris*, #3.
28. Pope John XXIII, *Mater et Magistra*, #189.
29. Pope John XXIII, *Pacem in Terris*, #2.
30. Second Vatican Council, *Gaudium et Spes* (December 7, 1965), #12,
   https://www.vatican.va/archive/hist_councils/ii_vatican_council/

documents/vat-ii_const_19651207_gaudium-et-spes_en.html (accessed November 27, 2025).

31. Second Vatican Council, *Gaudium et Spes*, #69.

32. Second Vatican Council, *Gaudium et Spes*, #12.

33. Second Vatican Council, *Gaudium et Spes*, #38.

34. Second Vatican Council, *Gaudium et Spes*, #34.

35. Pope John Paul II, *Laborem Exercens* (Sept. 14, 1981), #4, http://www.vatican.va/content/john-paul-ii/en/encyclicals/documents/hf_jp-ii_enc_14091981_laborem-exercens.html (accessed November 27, 2025).; Pope John Paul II, *Sollicitudo Rei Socialis* (Dec. 30, 1987), #29, http://www.vatican.va/content/john-paul-ii/en/encyclicals/documents/hf_jp-ii_enc_30121987_sollicitudo-rei-socialis.html (accessed November 27, 2025).

36. Pope John Paul II, *Sollicitudo Rei Socialis*, #29.

37. Pope John Paul II, *Redemptor Hominis* (Mar. 4, 1979), #14, http://www.vatican.va/content/john-paul-ii/en/encyclicals/documents/hf_jp-ii_enc_04031979_redemptor-hominis.html (accessed November 27, 2025).

38. Pope John Paul II, *Redemptor Hominis*, #16.

39. Pope John Paul II, *Sollicitudo Rei Socialis*, #29.

40. Pope John Paul II, *Sollicitudo Rei Socialis*, #34.

41. Wisdom 9:1, 2-3 and Psalms 8:6-8.

42. Pope John Paul II, *Evangelium Vitae* (Mar. 25, 1995), #34.

43. Pope John Paul II, "The Ecological Crisis," #3.

44. This passage is from the New Revised Standard Version.

45. Richard Bauckham, "Humans, Animals, and the Environment in Genesis 1-3," in *Genesis and Christian Theology*, eds. Nathan MacDonald, Mark W. Elliott, and Grant Macaskill (Grand Rapids, MI: William B. Eerdmans Publishing Company, 2012), 180.

46. James McKeown, *Genesis* (Grand Rapids, MI: William B. Eerdmans Publishing Company, 2008), 27.

47. Bruce Vawter, *On Genesis: A New Reading* (Garden City, NY: Doubleday & Company, 1977), 60.

48. Gerhard von Rad, *Genesis: A Commentary*, rev. ed. (Philadelphia: Westminster Press, 1972), 60.

49. McKeown, *Genesis*, 27.

50. Claus Westermann, *Genesis 1-11*, trans. John J. Scullion S.J. (Minneapolis: Fortress Press, 1994), 158.

51. David C. Hopkins, *The Highlands of Canaan: Agricultural Life in the Early Iron Age* (Decatur, Georgia: The Almond Press, 1985); and Patricia

K. Tull, *Inhabiting Eden: Christians, the Bible, and "The Ecological Crisis"* (Louisville: Westminster John Knox Press, 2013), 24.

52. Pope John Paul II, "The Ecological Crisis," #7.

53. Pope John Paul II, "The Ecological Crisis," #8, quoting the Second Vatican Council's *Gaudium et Spes*, #69.

54. Pope John Paul II, "The Ecological Crisis," #9.

55. Pope John Paul II, *Laborem Exercens*, #2; Pope John Paul II, *Sollicitudo Rei Socialis*, #42; Pope John Paul II, "The Ecological Crisis," #11.

56. Pope John Paul, *Evangelium Vitae*, #52-67.

57. Pope John Paul II, *Redemptor Hominis*, #16; Pope John Paul II, "The Ecological Crisis," #12.

58. Pope John Paul II, "The Ecological Crisis," #10.

59. Pope John Paul II, "The Ecological Crisis," #11.

60. Pope John Paul II, "The Ecological Crisis," #14.

61. Pope John Paul II, "The Ecological Crisis," #1, italics in original.

62. Mark Graham, "Catholic Act Analysis and Unintended Side Effects: Time for a New Tradition," *Studies in Christian Ethics* 18 (2) (2005): 67-88.

63. Pope John Paul II, "The Ecological Crisis," #7.

64. Pope John Paul II, "The Ecological Crisis," #8.

65. Pope John Paul II, "The Ecological Crisis," #8.

66. Pope John Paul II, "The Ecological Crisis," #9.

67. Pope John Paul II, "The Ecological Crisis," #13.

68. Pope John Paul II, "The Ecological Crisis," #16, citing Psalm 148:96.

69. Pope John Paul II, "The Ecological Crisis," #4, italics in original, citing Colossians 1:19-20.

70. Pope John Paul II, "The Ecological Crisis," #4, italics in original, citing Ephesians 1:9-10.

71. Pope John Paul II, "The Ecological Crisis," #13.

72. Pope John Paul II, "The Ecological Crisis," #3.

73. Graham, "Catholic Act Analysis and Unintended Side Effects," 67-88.

74. Thomas Berry, "Ethics and Ecology," in *Educating for Humanity: Rethinking the Purposes of Education*, ed. Mike Seymour (New York: Routledge, 2004), 150.

75. Willis Jenkins, *Ecologies of Grace: Environmental Ethics and Christian Theology* (New York: Oxford University Press, 2008), 82-4.

76. Pope John Paul II, *Evangelium Vitae* (Mar. 25, 1995), #34.

77. United States Conference of Catholic Bishops, "Renewing the Earth: An Invitation to Reflection and Action on Environment in Light of Catholic

Social Teaching," (Nov. 14, 1991), https://www.usccb.org/resources/renewing-earth (accessed November 27, 2025).

78. USCCB, "Renewing the Earth," "II. The Biblical Vision of God's Good Earth," "A. The Witness of the Hebrew Scriptures."

79. USCCB, "Renewing the Earth," "II. The Biblical Vision of God's Good Earth," "A. The Witness of the Hebrew Scriptures."

80. USCCB, "Renewing the Earth," "II. The Biblical Vision of God's Good Earth," "A. The Witness of the Hebrew Scriptures."

81. USCCB, "Renewing the Earth," "II. The Biblical Vision of God's Good Earth," "A. The Witness of the Hebrew Scriptures."

82. Aldo Leopold, *A Sand County Almanac* (New York: Oxford University Press, 1949), 224.

83. USCCB, "Renewing the Earth," "III. Catholic Social Teaching and Environmental Ethics," "A. A Sacramental Universe."

84. USCCB, "Renewing the Earth," "III. Catholic Social Teaching and Environmental Ethics," B. Respect for Life."

85. USCCB, "Renewing the Earth," "III. Catholic Social Teaching and Environmental Ethics," B. Respect for Life," citing Thomas Aquinas's *Summa Theologica*, Prima Pars, ques. 48, ad 2.

86. USCCB, "Renewing the Earth," "IV. Theological and Pastoral Concerns," "The Creator and Creation."

87. USCCB, "Renewing the Earth," "III. Catholic Social Teaching and Environmental Ethics," "E. Universal Purpose of Created Things." Quoting Pope John Paul II.

88. USCCB, "Renewing the Earth," "V. God's Stewards and Co-Creators," "B. New Actions."

89. USCCB, "Renewing the Earth," "III. Catholic Social Teaching and Environmental Ethics," "F. Option for the Poor."

90. USCCB, "Renewing the Earth," "III. Catholic Social Teaching and Environmental Ethics," "G. Authentic Development."

91. USCCB, "Renewing the Earth," "I. Signs of the Times," "C. Catholic Responses."

92. For an informative exposé on factory farming, see Matthew Scully, *Dominion: The Power of Man, the Suffering of Animals, and the Call to Mercy* (New York: St. Martin's Griffin, 2002).

93. William S. Skylstad, Timothy Whitaker, et al., "Heaven and Earth are Full of Your Glory," A United Methodist and Roman Catholic Statement on the Eucharist and Ecology (2008), #8, accessed at https://www.usccb.org/resources/heaven-and-earth-are-full-your-glory-united-methodist-and-roman-catholic-statement (accessed November 27, 2025).

94. Skylstad and Whitaker, et al., "Heaven and Earth are Full of Your Glory," #9.

95. Skylstad and Whitaker, et al., "Heaven and Earth are Full of Your Glory," #14.

96. Skylstad and Whitaker, et al., "Heaven and Earth are Full of Your Glory," #9.

97. Skylstad and Whitaker, et al., "Heaven and Earth are Full of Your Glory," #28.

98. Skylstad and Whitaker, et al., "Heaven and Earth are Full of Your Glory," #18.

99. Catholic Bishops of the Columbia River Watershed Region, "The Columbia River Watershed: Caring for Creation and the Common Good," (Jan. 8, 2001), 9, https://www.wacatholics.org/stay-informed/the-columbia-river-watershed-caring-for-creation-and-the-common-good (accessed November 27, 2025).

100. Catholic Bishops of the Columbia River Watershed Region, "The Columbia River Watershed," 9.

101. Catholic Bishops of the Columbia River Watershed Region, "The Columbia River Watershed," 7.

102. Catholic Bishops of the Columbia River Watershed Region, "The Columbia River Watershed," 9.

103. Catholic Bishops of the Columbia River Watershed Region, "The Columbia River Watershed," 16.

104. Catholic Bishops of the Columbia River Watershed Region, "The Columbia River Watershed," 14.

105. Catholic Bishops of the Columbia River Watershed Region, "The Columbia River Watershed," 14.

106. Catholic Bishops of the Columbia River Watershed Region, "The Columbia River Watershed," 9.

107. US Fish and Wildlife Service, "Salmon: A Pacific Northwest Icon," https://www.fws.gov/story/2022-06/salmona-pacific-northwest-icon#:~:text=Through%20the%2019th%20and,habitat%20in%20rivers%20and%20streams (accessed November 27, 2025).

108. Northwest Power and Conservation Council, "Extinction," https://www.nwcouncil.org/reports/columbia-river-history/extinction (accessed November 27, 2025).

109. Liz Osborn, "Hundreds of Pacific Salmon Populations Now Extinct," https://www.currentresults.com/Wildlife/Endangered-Species/Endangered-Fish/hundreds-801101.php (accessed November 27, 2025).

110. Anne Post, "Why Fish Need Trees and Trees Need Fish," https://www.
adfg.alaska.gov/index.cfm?adfg=wildlifenews.view_article&articles_
id=407 (accessed November 27, 2025).

111. Post, "Why Fish Need Trees and Trees Need Fish."

112. Catholic Bishops of the Columbia River Watershed Region, "The
Columbia River Watershed," 13–15.

113. Catholic Bishops of the Columbia River Watershed Region, "The
Columbia River Watershed," 15.

114. Brian Roewe, "The first green pope: How Benedict's eco-theology
paved the way for Francis," (January 4, 2023), https://www.ncronline.
org/news/first-green-pope-how-benedicts-eco-theology-paved-way-
francis (accessed December 24, 2025).

115. Brian Roewe, "The first green pope: How Benedict's eco-theology
paved the way for Francis," *National Catholic Reporter* (Jan. 4, 2023),
https://www.ncronline.org/earthbeat/faith/first-green-pope-how-
benedicts-eco-theology-paved-way-francis (accessed November 27,
2025).

116. Pope Benedict XVI, "Message for the Celebration of the World
Day of Peace," (January 1, 2010), #2, https://www.vatican.va/
content/benedict-xvi/en/messages/peace/documents/hf_ben-xvi_
mes_20091208_xliii-world-day-peace.html (accessed November 27,
2025).

117. Pope Benedict XVI, "Message for the Celebration of the World Day of
Peace," #6.

118. Pope Benedict XVI, "Address at the Welcoming Celebration by
the Young People, Apostolic Journey to Sydney (Australia) on the
Occasion of the Twenty-third World Youth Day, Barangaroo, Sydney
Harbor," in *The Garden of God: Toward a Human Ecology*, ed. Maria
Milvia Morciano (Washington, DC: The Catholic University Press of
America, 2014), 22–3.

119. Pope Benedict XVI, "Message for the Celebration of the World Day of
Peace," #6.

120. Pope Benedict XVI, "Message for the Celebration of the World Day of
Peace," #6.

121. Pope Benedict XVI, *Caritas et Veritate* (June 29, 2009), #48, http://
www.vatican.va/content/benedict-xvi/en/encyclicals/documents/hf_
ben-xvi_enc_20090629_caritas-in-veritate.html (accessed November
27, 2025), #6.

122. Pope Benedict XVI, "General Audience, August 26, 2009," in *The
Garden of God: Toward a Human Ecology*, ed. Maria Milvia Morciano

(Washington, DC: The Catholic University Press of America, 2014), 34.

123. Pope Benedict XVI, *Caritas et Veritate,* #48.

124. Pope Benedict XVI, "Message for the Celebration of the World Day of Peace," #7.

125. Pope Benedict XVI, *Deus Caritas Est* (Dec. 25, 2005), #18, https://www.vatican.va/content/benedict-xvi/en/encyclicals/documents/hf_ben-xvi_enc_20051225_deus-caritas-est.html (accessed November 27, 2025).

126. Pope Benedict XVI, *Deus Caritas Est*, #19–39.

127. Pope Benedict XVI, *Caritas et Veritate*, #49–50.

128. Pope Benedict XVI, "Message for the Celebration of the World Day of Peace," #10-12.

129. Pope Benedict XVI, "Message for the Celebration of the World Day of Peace," #13.

130. Claude Lévi-Strauss, *Introduction to Marcel Mauss*, trans. Felicity Baker (London: Routledge, 1987), 63-4.

2

Thomas Berry's Critique of Anthropocentrism and the Stewardship Paradigm

The New Story

Thomas Berry is a uniquely valuable interlocutor for Catholic proponents of the stewardship paradigm, especially in its more anthropocentric iterations. As a Passionist priest, Berry was sympathetic to Catholic doctrine and attentive to papal theological developments, yet for several decades he championed an environmentalism substantively different from that propounded by the popes. Indeed, Berry was not only critical of many of the foundational theological elements of Catholic environmentalism, but he also eschewed the common strategy of reforming the tradition from within by recovering and developing neglected elements of the tradition. Although Berry found nothing inherently problematic with reconstructionist proclivities, he thought that the dominant Catholic environmentalism had become so fundamentally misguided at its core that the best approach would be to develop a new metanarrative, based on a different cosmology, which in turn would lead to an alternative anthropology and ethics. Otherwise, according to Berry, such a reconstruction would amount to nothing more than ineffectual tinkering around the periphery while leaving the more problematic core intact. Such a venture, in Berry's mind, was an exercise in futility that was likely to waste precious time while the planet was being ravaged by a number of pernicious large-scale environmental problems.

According to Berry, in order to construct a more credible Catholic environmentalism, we must situate ourselves in the context of the universe, what God is attempting to do with the universe, and our role and function within this larger pattern of divine activity. The key to understanding the universe is to grasp that it is evolving and in perpetual motion. At one time, according to Berry, we understood the universe as "cosmos," which consisted of a series of recurrent events that were largely cyclical in nature, which also tended to make us understand the universe as a fixed system in which events were infinitely repeatable.[1] Today, however, we understand the universe as constituted by the twin phenomena of necessity and chance, the combination of which provides stability and constancy but also novelty and newness at every level, which in turn create a universe that is constantly evolving and changing.[2]

Berry calls this evolutionary dynamic at the heart of the universe the Cosmogenetic Principle, and he claims that because of three characteristics found everywhere in the universe that all of creation is forever in flux, changing, becoming something else, and generating newness in the universe. The first is communion, which means that everything in the universe exists only in relationship and it is possible to understand something only in the context of those relationships. The second is autopoesis, which refers to the self-organizing tendency that exists in all reality, from the largest systems to the smallest components. The third, and perhaps most important, characteristic is differentiation, or the tendency of all reality to become something new and different and unique. These tendencies culminate in a universe that is stupendously creative, forever generating newness and continually exploring different avenues for lifeforms and relationships. As he writes,

> When we examine the entire display [of the universe] we find, pervasive with being, an insistence to create anew …. At the heart of the universe is an outrageous bias for the novel, for the unfurling of surprise in prodigious dimensions throughout the vast range of existence. The creativity of each time and place differs from that of every other time and place. The universe comes to us, each being and each moment announcing its thrilling news: I am fresh.[3]

As this evolutionary dynamic has progressed on Earth, it has spawned a virtual explosion of biodiversity, with each species occupying a particular ecological niche and expressing characteristics beneficial to that species, and, in turn, providing a platform for further evolutionary explorations to occur. Like a grand experiment, new avenues are taken, some are beneficial and others are failures, and the cumulative, long-term effect of this experiment is an astonishing creativity and diversity. Berry estimates that upward of 20 million different species existed on Earth during the height of the Cenozoic period (66 million years ago—present), which represents almost unimaginable biological novelty.[4]

For Berry, it is important to recognize that the good of the universe, and from our perspective, the good of planet Earth, is primary, and any other good is derivative.[5] The reason is that every species or individual or other potential locus of value (a stream, mountain, ocean, etc.), whether human or not, cannot emerge or be sustained without the larger whole on which it depends for virtually everything. So, for instance, there is no way for my individual good to be realized without the network of larger goods in place that make my life and flourishing possible. While this in no way denies or denigrates the value on lower levels, it does, however, necessitate that larger goods such as the good of planet Earth be given priority over derivative goods, and that our meaning as individuals be located first and foremost in the fostering of the good of planet Earth, and only secondarily in our own good as individuals or as a species.[6]

Stated a bit differently, God has created a universe that is creative and exploratory, and in our little corner of the universe on planet Earth, this inherent creativity has resulted not only in life—something so rare and unique that it is currently found nowhere else in the universe—but an explosion of life, all originating from primitive one-celled organisms. This trend toward increasing biodiversity on Earth represents God's ordering and creative activity, and as such ought to be one of the paramount ethical goods which should guide our lives.[7] Thus far, it has been the fate of any one particular species to emerge, gain a foothold in specific ecosystems, flourish for a while, and then undergo a decline and go extinct. Indeed, over 99 percent of all species that have ever existed have gone extinct.[8] So God has created a universe in which particular species, from the simplest to the most complex, emerge, flourish, and then disappear forever, but the underlying biodiversity remains to provide a stable base from which the universe's creativity continues to explore new possibilities and to generate new and different forms of life.

If this is the narrative by which Catholics understand the human place in the universe, then anthropocentrism becomes quite untenable. If, as a species, we will at some point either go extinct or will evolve into some other species and the universe will continue on without *Homo sapiens* for as long as planet Earth continues to exist, it is hard to sustain all the typical beliefs that support anthropocentrism, such as humans having a "special" place in creation, or that we are the apex of creation, or that the universe has been intentionally engineered to guarantee our emergence (commonly called the anthropic principle). Instead, we ought to embrace the fact that we are simply one species among many, blessed to have emerged in such a delightful universe, and content to be part of an enormously creative process that has given us the opportunity to enjoy the bountiful creation and to work for the larger goods that God has been fostering on planet Earth, such as biodiversity, for billions of years.

Moreover, this narrative also relativizes the managerial ethic commonly associated with the stewardship paradigm. If our role as humans is to understand ourselves as a moment in the larger sweep of evolution, and our task is to participate in God's ongoing project of increasing biodiversity on planet Earth, then our principal ethical imperative ought to be to conduct our lives in ways that promote biodiversity, and at the very least do not undermine it. To the extent, then, that biodiversity is enhanced by increasing human management of planet Earth, then we ought to assume such a managerial posture. But if increasing human control decreases biodiversity, then we ought to restrict our influence. Thus, the type of posture assumed by humans is contingent upon our actual effectiveness in promoting biodiversity.

On the issue of environmental degradation, Thomas Berry and the aforementioned popes unanimously agree that contemporary humans are first-class malefactors. Pope John Paul II writes that we are guilty of "plundering natural resources" and causing "a progressive decline in the quality of life" and by our consumptive habits have precipitated a "widespread destruction of the environment."[9] Pope Benedict XVI notes that humans are currently experiencing a moral crisis, the symptoms of which are witnessed through our extensive abuse of nature.[10] Pope Francis[11] and Thomas Berry are even more pointed. Pope Francis states that we are quickly reducing our beloved planet to "an immense pile of filth"[12] and that we are leaving to our ancestors an environment filled with debris and desolation.[13] Thomas Berry claims that we are quickly reducing planet Earth to a "Wasteworld"[14] and have become destroyers of creation, pitting ourselves directly in opposition to God's creative handiwork on Earth.[15]

This unanimity unravels, however, when solutions to the environmentally nefarious behavior of humans are contemplated. Proponents of the stewardship paradigm are ideologically committed to a robust interventionist posture by humans, as humans are the designated managers and caretakers of creation, so their typical response is to claim some type of flaw with the management regime currently in place—and this is precisely what Pope John Paul II and Pope Benedict XVI do. Both popes recommend a two-pronged strategy. First, to refashion human desires, which have become rapacious and environmentally damaging to satisfy. Second, to institute a more extensive and coordinated system of international management, in order to prevent the inefficient, wasteful, or unjust use of natural resources. Pope Francis agrees that human desires need to be refashioned and tempered, but he is skeptical of international organizations and thinks that they are often simply coercive tools of the world's economic elite designed to benefit the rich and powerful few at the expense of the many, so he parts ways with Popes John Paul II and Benedict XVI and refuses to endorse the creation of an international management regime. But Francis is also not willing simply to endorse local groups as effective environmental managers, as he realizes that a significant amount of environmental degradation is attributed to these groups as well. As a result, Francis tends to avoid proposing solutions, and his discussions of particular environmental problems, while sometimes highly informative and insightful, are very indeterminate when it comes to practical initiatives.

Both positions are attempts to deal with one of the stewardship paradigm's glaring internal inconsistencies, and neither one is very successful. The stewardship paradigm is built on the belief that humans have a divine mandate to manage planet Earth for God. If it were the case that humans were highly effective at this task, then this planet-wide managerial role would have been a good choice by God. Yet part of the Genesis narrative also conveys that original sin has warped humans in significant ways and has diminished our ability to choose what is right, and as all the popes agree, the effects of original sin are seen every day in the environmentally damaging policies, institutions, and behavior that are the products of human choices. Absent some way to minimize original sin's effects on humans, this seems like an almost perfect recipe for environmental disaster: A worldwide management regime administered by a group of beings who are constitutionally unable to make good decisions or to exercise the necessary self-control to halt ongoing environmental degradation.

In contradistinction to the stewardship paradigm, Berry claims that if we understand our place within the broad sweep of Earth's evolutionary history, we will understand ourselves as simply one species among many,[16] which in turn will foster a self-identity focused on limits. One aspect of this recognition of limits is that, as humans, our epistemic obstacles are formidable, and we should always stand humble and awed before the complexity of creation as it will often be too complicated for us to understand fully. As Berry writes,

> As humans we need to recognize the limitations in our capacity to deal with these comprehensive issues of the earth's functioning. So long as we are under the illusion that we know best what is good for the earth and for ourselves, then we will continue our present course, with its devastating consequences on the entire earth community.[17]

According to Berry, until the emergence of modern humans, each species functioned within a system of competition and pressures that curtailed the expansion and influence of each species. Principally through our development and use of increasingly sophisticated technologies, however, humans have circumvented these formerly natural limitations and have expanded the human influence literally to every part of the planet—which has been an unmitigated disaster for planet Earth. One of our principal tasks, then, Berry writes, is to accept clear limits on our ecological footprint, both individually and communally:

> We must first accept life within the limitations presented to us by the natural world. We must lower the human presence on the planet, accept the human condition, and not think that we can outdo the natural world …. The basic biological law is that every life form should have opposed life forms or conditions that limit each life form so that no one life form or group of them would overwhelm the others. Technology enables us to get around these limiting conditions. We can overpopulate; we can tear the earth to pieces in a devastating manner; we can overcome the opposition of gravity by building automobiles and riding up a mountain.[18]

According to Berry, this insistence on limitations should not be interpreted as a rejection of modern technology, as technological development can sometimes lead to a more beneficial human presence on Earth. What is important is that we realize that the good of the Earth and the promotion of biodiversity are always the broader contexts in which we have to seek our own good, both individually and as a species, and to the extent that we need to self-limit in order to achieve those larger ethical goals, then we are obligated to do so.

Before moving on to a comparative assessment of the stewardship paradigm and Berry's New Story, I want to address one important issue that Berry raises regarding the justification of anthropocentrism. As we have already seen, the common strategy of the popes is to establish the validity of the stewardship paradigm by appealing directly to biblical authority via the first creation account in Genesis. Yet another strategy commonly found in papal documents to justify anthropocentrism is what Andrew Linzey calls "uniqueness spotting,"[19] which involves the identification of some characteristic or cluster of characteristics possessed by humans alone, which in turn supposedly establishes our superiority over all creation. So, for instance, Pope John Paul II claims that the conferral of dominion is based on "those abilities and gifts which distinguish the human being from all other creatures."[20] Pope Francis makes a similar claim, but he goes even further and identifies the specific characteristics that set humans apart from other creatures, which are the "unique abilities of knowledge, will, freedom and responsibility."[21] Indeed, Pope Francis believes that these characteristics are so novel in the created order that only a direct divine intervention, and not the usual vehicles of natural forces that are responsible for the emergence and sculpting of all other creatures, would be necessary to fashion a personal being with such rare attributes.[22]

Attempting to establish anthropocentrism on the basis of unique characteristics is problematic in a number of different ways. First, this strategy relies on factual claims of uniqueness, and the more ethologists study animals in their own environments and catalog a growing list of behaviors and characteristics, the more so-called unique human traits are found in other animals, too. In other words, we humans are not as unique as we like to think.[23] Moreover, from an evolutionary perspective, this should be expected. Each species has emerged from other species, and will share a considerable number of similar characteristics, and thus it is much more likely to witness small, incremental differences and a great deal of continuity in the characteristics of closely related species rather than qualitative novelty and newness.

Second, even if humans possess some unique characteristic or cluster of characteristics, it is not always an easy task to assign moral relevance to such facts, as the connection between facts and moral consideration is often unclear. Indeed, few today would argue that the facts of a certain skin color, gender, height, IQ, mathematical aptitude, or spatial recognition, among many other possible characteristics or skills, either make someone superior or are a sufficient basis for treating someone with those characteristics differently than someone without them, even though historically some of these facts have been used as a basis for claims of superiority and corresponding discriminatory treatment. As contemporary ethicists have argued, over time the number of facts that have been deemed morally relevant has shrunk markedly and the scope of moral consideration has continued to expand and has drawn more types of creatures under the umbrella of being worthy of moral consideration.[24]

In a similar way, a commonplace assumption is that unique characteristics possessed by humans make us superior in the order of creation. Reason, for instance, has historically been cited by a number of theologians as the reason why we regard ourselves as superior to animals, and therefore deserving of a different kind of moral consideration. While it might be factually correct to state that certain species have a unique characteristic, it is another thing entirely to claim that such possession automatically entitles them to preferential treatment. So, for instance, let us assume that a number of different animals or species have unique characteristics: humans have reason; bats have echolocation; dogs have an acute sense of smell; whale pods have unique languages; elephants can smell water from miles away; birds can fly under their own power; hummingbirds can hover stationary in the air; rabbits can see behind themselves without turning their head; horses can sleep while standing up; sailfishes can swim as fast as 50–60 miles per hour; goldfish can see in both infrared and ultraviolet light; bald eagles can swim under water; and sheep self-medicate with medicinal plants when ill.

So why should human reason confer preferential moral treatment over all these and many other creatures when they too exhibit many different types of uniqueness? The common answer is because it allows us to create civilization, or to create beneficial technologies, or in some way to do something that is beneficial and critical to securing human well-being. This is another way of saying that reason allows humans to pursue certain ends, which are beneficial to humans. Yet the same thing could be said about the unique characteristics cited above: Each provides its individual possessor as well as the species to which it belongs with some kind of advantage for securing its well-being. So, once again, why does reason confer preferential moral treatment for humans over all other species that also have unique characteristics, when it does the same thing as those with other unique characteristics, namely, help secure its possessor's or species' well-being?

Third, even if a determinate notion of superiority could be established on the basis of the possession of certain characteristics, the moral meaning attached to such superior status is still an open question. While a hierarchically ordered universe is often used as a conceptual tool to give preference to the superior at the expense of the inferior and to make the latter's destiny one of subservience to the former, according to Andrew Linzey this should not be the case. From a Christian perspective, in which God becomes the model for the superior/inferior relationship, this traditional dynamic should be inverted, so that instead of the inferior existing to serve the needs of the superior, the superior's meaning and worth is found in enhancing the well-being of the inferior, even if that entails considerable suffering on the part of the superior. Just as God (the superior) became incarnate, suffered, and died for us (the inferior), so likewise we must regard ourselves as servants to those creatures over whom we have power and control.[25]

These reservations about the characteristics approach underlying anthropocentrism, however, do not lead Berry to conclude that we ought to embrace an egalitarianism that regards all creatures as equal and deserving of similar treatment. Berry is leery about the psychological leveling effect he perceives with the notion of equality, which puts a premium on sameness and tends to minimize differences mentally. Instead of relying on the concept of equality, Berry prefers to universalize the hierarchy of importance, as he calls it:

> We do indeed need equal opportunity to be our different selves, but our roles are different. There has to be an equal opportunity for things to be what they are, but that does not make an egalitarian society in members lose their qualitative differences, the distinctive grandeur that each

possesses in a unique manner and to a unique degree. Egalitarianism is quite ambivalent in its understanding and consequences ....

Regarding egalitarianism and hierarchy, I suggest that, rather than diminish hierarchy, we universalize it. Everything is at the top of the hierarchy in its own way. When it comes to swimming the fish are at the top. When it comes to flying, the birds are at the top. When it comes to bearing peaches, peach trees are at the top. When it comes to being a person's own specific self, that person is at the top. When it comes to reflective thinking, humans are the best. But just because we humans are the best in one area does not mean that we are the best absolutely. The thing that is best absolutely is the community of the planet, the community of species.[26]

Berry clearly has little affinity for traditional hierarchical thinking, and his inclination from beginning to end is not to attempt to order the universe but to celebrate the enormous diversity that God's creative powers have brought about. There is a robust element of joy in Berry's writings for each creature and species, as each represents the culmination of a long stretch of biological evolution, with each one equipped with precisely the kind of bodies, minds, feelings, inclinations, and attributes that have made it fit to survive and flourish in its respective environment. Each has its place on planet Earth, and each one contributes something valuable to the functioning of Earth's vital processes. From earthworms that pulverize and fertilize topsoil, to squirrels that spread acorns and expand the range of oak trees, to wolves who keep deer and elk populations in check and thereby create habitat for songbirds and a host of other species, to humans who have an uncanny mental aptitude for building sophisticated tools—each creature and species has a particular place and function, according to Berry, none better or worse, just different.

Berry and the Stewardship Paradigm: A Comparative Assessment

Thus far my analysis has focused on using Thomas Berry's New Story as a way to critique the anthropocentrism underlying the familiar stewardship paradigm in Catholic environmentalism. In order to make a normative statement that Berry's line of thought is more intellectually cogent and persuasive than the stewardship paradigm, however, a comparative analysis of both according to criteria relevant to the adequacy of a model for contemporary Catholic environmentalism would be most helpful, if not necessary. To this end, I will briefly develop the criteria endorsed for assessing the strength of theological models by the noted ecotheologian Jame Schaefer,[27] which cover a broad range of considerations, from foundational to methodological to highly practical, and then use them as a means to assess the comparative advantages of one over the other.

Schaefer develops five criteria that are necessary "to the task of developing a model of the human that is responsive to our ecologically destructive age."[28] First, a theological model must be rooted in a religious faith tradition, with the presumption that the more deeply rooted the model is in a tradition's primary texts, doctrines, and teachings of notable theologians, the more likely it is to garner widespread acceptance among the faithful. Second, a model must cohere with knowledge gained in other disciplines, especially contemporary "scientific findings about the physical world." Third, a model "should be positively relational to other species and physical systems" and avoid any type of dualistic thinking that places humans "over or apart from other entities," and it should also respect every creature's unique contribution to the ecosystem it inhabits. Fourth, a model must specify the kind of behavior needed today, with preference given to the model that can be more descriptive in the behavior it prescribes or proscribes. Finally, the model should identify the particular religious motivation underlying the transformation in attitude and behavior.[29]

Criterion 1. The stewardship paradigm, being grounded theologically in the first creation account in Genesis, in addition to being the preferred theoretical framework for recent popes constructing their respective versions of Catholic environmentalism, anchors it firmly in a religious faith tradition; indeed, many Catholics would consider this convergence of Scripture and papal teaching to culminate in one of the most authoritative forms of teaching within Catholicism. Thomas Berry, on the other hand, wants to distance himself from biblical creation accounts, and he prefers to turn to contemporary science in order to construct his New Story. In Berry's opinion, biblical creation accounts might possess intellectual credibility in a premodern context, and while they assuredly contain some spiritual or metaphorical insights, there is little doubt in Berry's mind that contemporary science gives us a far more accurate and comprehensive understanding of physical reality and the universe, and to this extent ought to be given preference when constructing a cosmology. Moreover, the robust anthropocentrism of the first creation account in Genesis, which was far more environmentally benign in the context of low population density of the ancient Hebrews and the primitive state of their technology that limited their influence over and degradation to natural systems, becomes highly problematic in our contemporary context in which some have even suggested that our historical epoch be named the Anthropocene to denote the pervasive human influence on Earth's natural systems.[30] So while Berry would certainly agree with Schaefer that a theological model should be rooted in a religious faith tradition, he would also insist that not all elements of a faith tradition are equal, and while some seminal stories in sacred texts served a purpose historically to teach and bind adherents to a particular vision of God and the universe, such a vision can become outdated, and perhaps even counterproductive, as circumstances change and knowledge about the universe accumulates over time. While it appears at first glance that the stewardship paradigm better fulfills the first criterion of being anchored in a particular religious tradition, perhaps Berry's attempt to construct a new cosmology actually does more justice to a contemporary notion of God that has emerged through the fertile discussion between scientists and theologians, and as such might be more faithful to a religious tradition that places a premium on openness, development, and appropriating new insights from various disciplines that could supplement, or perhaps even alter, our understanding of the divine.

Criterion 2. Beginning with the second criterion, the comparative advantages of Berry's New Story over the stewardship paradigm start to become apparent. The stewardship paradigm, having its theological foundation in the first creation story in Genesis, does not offer any fertile bases for incorporating scientific insights at that level. It does, however, allow and perhaps even benefit from, a certain engagement with science at the practical level in order to discern how stewardship gets embodied most effectively in the daily lives of Christians, especially when something akin to best practices standards get codified for a wide range of issues such as greenhouse gas emissions, participating in agriculture, resource use, pollution associated with one's preferred lifestyle, and so on.

Similar to the stewardship paradigm, Berry's New Story relies on scientific data and insights on the practical level in order to figure out the best method for contributing to overarching goods such as the promotion of biodiversity. Yet Berry's New Story goes far beyond the partial practical engagement with science by making contemporary scientific cosmology the foundation of his anthropology and ethics. So, in his *The Universe Story*, Berry begins with the "primordial flaring forth" (which many call the "big bang"), and charts the trajectory of the unfolding universe through the formation of galaxies, supernovas, suns, and then moves into the dynamism of evolution which induces continual change at every level of creation, Earth's history which includes the emergence of one-celled organisms, and the eventual explosion of life forms on our planet during the Cenozoic period, which in turn greeted the newly emerged humans with a rich array of diverse habitats and possibilities for living. Berry's *The Universe Story* is not simply a fertile conversation partner with religion and theology; it is an attempt to refashion the grand metanarratives of religion and science via the latest scientific findings about our universe, and to this extent, it meets Schaefer's second criterion as fully as possible.

Criterion 3. The stewardship paradigm is perhaps most notorious for regarding humans as distinct from and superior to the rest of creation, as the first creation account in Genesis, which is the theological foundation of the stewardship paradigm, claims that humans are the only creatures made in God's image and likeness and are also mandated to subdue the Earth and are given dominion over other creatures by God. This is precisely the kind of dualism that Schaefer thinks should be resoundingly rejected by Christians, and it has also been decried by a number of influential ecofeminists.[31] The relational possibilities based on a non-dualistic cosmology abound in Thomas Berry's New Story, as humans are regarded as one species among many on Earth. To be sure, Berry would readily concede that humans might have unique capabilities, as do many other types of creatures, but the important point for Berry is that each species has a vital role to play in the ongoing maintenance and health of the ecosystems it inhabits, regardless of any unique characteristics it happens to possess. Quite clearly, Berry's New Story meets this criterion far better than the stewardship paradigm.

Criterion 4. This is perhaps the most important criterion, as a theological model that cannot give a determinate trajectory to the specific kind of behavior consistent with that model is unhelpful or, even worse, counterproductive in the context of an ecological crisis. As I argued above, the stewardship paradigm suffers from a foundational theological vacuity that is virtually insurmountable, as the term "dominion" proves to be the critical concept giving practical directionality to the stewardship model, yet when each pope attempts to add more specific content to that term through the use of qualifiers like "love" and "wisdom"[32] (Pope John Paul II), or by recommending that dominion ought to be exercised responsibly[33] (Pope Benedict XVI), or by specifying that dominion does not justify "absolute domination over other creatures"[34] (Pope Francis), even a sympathetic reader will be perplexed at the lack of content provided by the stewardship paradigm, beyond the most general exhortations. Furthermore, even if terms like love, wisdom, and responsibility could be given more determinate content, critical questions still need to be addressed explicitly about the exercise of stewardship: For whom or what? and To what end(s)? These questions are rarely asked by proponents of the stewardship paradigm, but the answers invariably inferred in their writings are, for humans in order to realize some human benefit. In other words, the foundational vacuity of the stewardship paradigm not only leaves room for a consistent and robust anthropocentrism to fill in the blanks where the stewardship paradigm leaves off, but it also leaves open a dizzying array of options on the practical level that might be consistent with the dictates of the stewardship paradigm, with no way to determine whether any are better than the others.

One could argue that such lack of specific directionality is actually a strength of the stewardship paradigm, as it allows for regional and local variation and acknowledges that environmental solutions are often contingent upon particular conditions, which are best known by individual agents in the situation. While there is a kernel of truth to these claims, a student of environmental history will undoubtedly be far more concerned with the all-too-human abilities to rationalize, brutalize, pollute, and destroy. As Clive Ponting writes at the end of his magisterial *A Green History of the World*, citizens of modern industrial societies are quite predictable in their view and treatment of nature: they believe they are disconnected from it, superior to it, and they exploit it with impunity.[35] Given our consistent track record of abusing nature, one overarching objective of any environmental ethic ought to be to provide a sufficiently robust set of moral criteria to give a determinate practical trajectory to its adherents and to minimize the human tendencies to rationalize, obfuscate, and destroy.

Thomas Berry's cosmology and the principle of promoting biodiversity that emerges from it, on the other hand, provide considerably more substantive ethical bite than the stewardship paradigm. To be sure, the amount and type of biodiversity will vary from ecosystem to ecosystem, and while there might be realistic disagreements about the manner of measuring biodiversity accurately, the ethical mandate is abundantly clear for Berry: act in such a way that biodiversity is not undermined, and ideally act in such a way as to promote biodiversity. What this entails practically is an honest assessment of our daily behavioral patterns and the ways in which they affect biodiversity directly or indirectly, in addition to organizing our institutions to ensure that they support and promote biodiversity.

Criterion 5. The last criterion focuses on whether a model identifies a particular motivation that provides "an ultimate theological reason for bringing about a transformation in attitude and behavior."[36] Both models are quite strong in this regard. For its part, the stewardship paradigm provides an anthropology that understands humans as extensions of divine agency on planet Earth, who are commissioned by God to carry out the divine plan for creation by working to realize certain ends during our terrestrial life. As I noted above, these ends, which are practical specifications of the general dictum to be good stewards of creation, tend to be a bit opaque the further one descends into detail, but there can be little dispute that a proponent of the stewardship paradigm understands that one must continually strive to become properly ordered internally not only in order to avoid sinful behavior, but also so that one can successfully pursue behavior consistent with good stewardship over creation.

Thomas Berry's insistence on promoting biodiversity, on the other hand, provides an equally clear motivation by placing human agency within the cosmic unfolding of creation via the dynamics of biological evolution, which has not only resulted in an explosion of myriad life forms on planet Earth but also the emergence of new characteristics that provide enhanced relational possibilities with God, insofar as certain creatures can understand and respond to divine love knowingly and intentionally. By promoting biodiversity, humans are cooperating with the inherent dynamism of biological evolution to generate new types of creatures with a wide variety of capabilities, and especially given our robust human social desires and the intense satisfaction we receive from fulfilling relationships, we can readily grasp the momentous worth of intentionally creating a universe that is replete with opportunities for God to be in relationship with many different kinds of creatures. Just as we humans find a profound sense of satisfaction in a good marriage or a devoted friendship, so too we can cherish the thought of sculpting our little part of creation in such a way that brings God so much relational bliss.

In the final analysis, while the stewardship paradigm and Berry's New Story show comparable strengths on two of Schafer's criteria for assessing the adequacy of theological models, Berry's New Story fares far better on the other three criteria, which are coherence with the findings of contemporary science, non-dualism, and practical ethical guidance. If Catholic environmentalism is going to become more intellectually convincing among the theologically informed, then it is clear that it would benefit enormously by incorporating the essential insights of Berry's New Story when reconstructing the theological foundations of Catholic environmentalism, especially the priority of promoting biodiversity, which is the organizing principle of Berry's cosmology and ethics and the raison d'être for God's creative activity. In the process, Catholic environmentalism might also find that it begins to appeal to many non-religious people with an intellectual allegiance to contemporary science, in addition to being able to provide ethical direction to many who would appreciate some determinate, practical advice on environmental issues—and both would certainly be most welcome to a planet thirsting for a brighter future.

Conclusion: The Gamble of Anthropocentrism

Lynn White's seminal "The Historical Roots of Our Ecological Crisis," which attributes to Christian anthropocentrism and the stewardship paradigm the massive environmental degradation that had occurred in the Western world, might have proved to be a moment of grace, even though most theologians have dismissed White's allegations, claiming that he either misunderstood the biblical texts in question or misdiagnosed the cause-effect relationship between Christian anthropocentrism and environmental degradation. In other words, what could have been a moment of clarity, openness, and self-reflection in the Christian theological community proved to be a long-term entrenchment, the central thrust of which was to bolster and defend the familiar stewardship paradigm.

This leads to a rather odd situation currently. On one hand, Lynn White and Popes Francis, John Paul II, and Benedict XVI unanimously agree that the Western world is experiencing severe environmental degradation, and absent some concerted effort and effective change that start reversing these environmental trends there could be catastrophic results for humans and other denizens of planet Earth. On the other hand, Lynn White and the popes fundamentally disagree on the causes of this widespread degradation, with White claiming its basis in an anthropocentric worldview that regards humans as the pinnacle of creation and material creation as instrumentally valuable only insofar as it satisfies human needs and desires, while the popes claim instead that human weakness, selfishness, and sin are the culprits—not the underlying cosmology and anthropology.

While it is difficult, if not impossible, to determine which constituency has identified more accurately the cause–effect relationship between environmental degradation and underlying theological beliefs, I think it is safe to say that there has never been a notable groundswell of support in the Catholic world for papal environmentalism in terms of changing behavior on a widespread basis. I have argued throughout this book that the stewardship paradigm is theologically inadequate, yet an equally troubling element is that it seems to be incapable of changing hearts and minds or of garnering sufficient political support even to make a dent in the ongoing, and in many cases precipitously increasing levels of, environmental destruction. To be sure, there are Catholic pockets of sustainability and green practices, but these tend to be confined to intentional communities such as religious orders and congregations. As far as most of the 1.4 billion Catholics on planet Earth, levels of consumption and environmental degradation largely mirror that of the dominant culture in which they are located. So, despite nearly thirty-five years of dedicated papal attention to environmental matters and three different popes relying on the stewardship paradigm to attempt to induce behavioral change among Catholics, environmental degradation continues unabated, and today the prospect of potential system-wide difficulties and maybe even collapses seem more and more likely, which Pope Francis points out forcefully in *Laudato Si'*.

If theological beliefs are not rarefied, ahistorical, disembodied truths but expressions grounded in and conditioned by cultural needs and aspirations, then now seems the perfect time to begin the shift away from the stewardship paradigm that has failed to fire the moral imagination or to achieve the behavioral modifications needed in order to start reversing large-scale environmental degradation in favor of something akin to Thomas Berry's New Story that recognizes both the grandeur of natural processes begun and supported by God that have culminated in such an astonishing array of life on planet Earth, as well as our limited, albeit important, role as conscious, rational agents who can intentionally cooperate with God's creative power in bringing about such a cornucopia of lifeforms in our corner of the universe. The universe story being carried out by God is grandiose, large, mind-boggling, and extraordinarily fecund, and it should excite humans almost beyond belief to realize that we are a part of a universe-wide process of unfolding that is delectable to God if it goes well. As it turns out, whether it goes well might depend on us more than any other species, and most especially in our ability to self-limit and not to interrupt and degrade the many creative processes that God has begun on planet Earth. While conscious, widespread self-limitation might seem a bit strange to most contemporary Christians who have been conditioned by the stewardship paradigm to think of everything as ordered to the satisfaction of our needs and desires, being an integral part of a such a stupendously creative divine project ought to excite our imagination and give us the internal resolve to embark upon a gentler and more environmentally benign presence to the universe. Such will be a grand undertaking, but it is one to which I am absolutely convinced we are called—and one to which we ought to respond with joy as our chapter in the universe story.

Notes

1.   Thomas Berry, *The Great Work: Our Way into the Future* (New York: Three Rivers Press, 1999), 26.
2.   Thomas Berry and Brian Swimme, *The Universe Story: From the Primordial Flaring Forth to the Ecozoic Era* (San Francisco: Harper Collins, 1992), 73–5.
3.   Berry and Swimme, *The Universe Story,* 74–5.

4.　Berry, *The Great Work*, 29.

5.　Noel Preston, "The Great Work: Toward an Eco-Centric, Global Culture," *Social Alternatives* 26 (3) (2007) 7–8.

6.　Berry and Swimme, *The Universe Story*, 243.

7.　Berry and Swimme, *The Universe Story*, 259.

8.　Peter Ward, *Under a Green Sky: Global Warming, the Mass Extinctions of the Past, and What They Can Tell Us About Our Future* (New York: Smithsonian Books, 2008).

9.　Pope John Paul II, "The Ecological Crisis," #1.

10.　Pope Benedict XVI, "Message for the Celebration of the World Day of Peace," #5.

11.　There will be a separate chapter on Pope Francis later, which will develop his version of environmentalism extensively.

12.　Pope Francis, *Laudato Si'*, #21.

13.　Pope Francis, *Laudato Si'*, #161.

14.　Thomas Berry, *Befriending the Earth: A Theology of Reconciliation Between Human and the Earth* (Mystic, CT: Twenty Third Publications, 1991), 94.

15.　Thomas Berry, *Selected Writings on the Earth Community* (Maryknoll, NY: Orbis Books, 2014), 70.

16.　Berry and Swimme, *The Universe Story*, 259.

17.　Berry, *The Dream of the Earth*, 35.

18.　Berry, *Befriending the Earth*, 106.

19.　Andrew Linzey, *Animal Theology* (Urbana and Chicago: University of Illinois Press, 1995).

20.　Pope John Paul II, "The Ecological Crisis," #3.

21.　Pope Francis, *Laudato Si'*, 118.

22.　Pope Francis, *Laudato Si'*, 81.

23.　Carl Safina, *Beyond Words: What Animals Think and Feel* (New York: Henry Holt and Company, 2015).

24.　Peter Singer, *Animal Liberation*, reissue edition (New York: Harper Perennial Modern Classics, 2009), chaps. 5 and 6.

25.　Linzey, *Animal Theology*, chaps. 2 and 3.

26.　Berry, *Befriending the Earth*, 102.

27.　Jame Schaefer, *Theological Foundations for Environmental Ethics: Reconstructing Patristic and Medieval Concepts* (Washington, DC: Georgetown University Press, 2009), 268–9.

28.　Schaefer, *Theological Foundations for Environmental Ethics*, 268.

29.　Schaefer, *Theological Foundations for Environmental Ethics*, 268–9.

30. Julia Adney Thomas, Mark Williams, and Jan Zalasiewicz, *The Anthropocene: A Multidisciplinary Approach* (Medford, MA: Polity Press, 2020); Timothy W. Luke, *Anthropocene Alerts: Critical Theory of the Contemporary as Ecocritique* (Candor, NY: Telos Press Publishing, 2019); and Christophe Bonneuil and Jean-Baptiste Fressoz, *The Shock of the Anthropocene: Earth, History, and Us* (Brooklyn: Verso, 2016). On the other hand, some have suggested that renaming a geological epoch after one's species is a signal illustration of the heights of arrogance to which we are capable of ascending.

31. Ivone Gebara, *Longing for Running Water: Ecofeminism and Liberation* (Minneapolis: Augsburg Fortress, 1999); Rosemary Radford Ruether, *Gaia & God: An Ecofeminist Theology of Earth Healing* (New York: Harper Colling, 1992); and Val Plumwood, *Feminism and the Mastery of Nature* (London: Routledge, 1993).

32. Pope John Paul II, "The Ecological Crisis," #3.

33. Pope Benedict XVI, *Caritas et Veritate*, #50.

34. Pope Francis, *Laudato Si'*, #67.

35. Clive Ponting, *A Green History of the World: The Environment and the Collapse of Great Civilizations* (New York: Penguin, 1991), 406.

36. Schaefer, *Theological Foundations for Environmental Ethics*, 269.

3

Laudato Si''s Unfinished Business:

Chastened Anthropocentrism and the Priority of Biodiversity

Pope Francis's *Laudato Si'* (2015) represented a watershed moment in the Catholic Church. In addition to being the first papal encyclical on environmental matters, *Laudato Si'* is notable for breaking new ground in a number of important ways: its analysis of practical environmental issues is unprecedented in its breadth and depth among papal documents on the environment; its exploration of the possibility of love as an ethical framework for Catholic environmentalism signals a fertile avenue for grounding Catholic environmentalism theologically outside of the traditional stewardship paradigm; and its development of practical moral principles, especially of the precautionary principle, interjects a new and robust framework for assessing environmental policies.

Yet amidst all this notable newness in *Laudato Si'* is a development that could potentially have seismic implications for Catholic environmentalism, both theoretically and practically. Ever since the emergence of papal environmentalism as a distinct branch of theological inquiry with Pope John Paul II's "The Ecological Crisis," papal documents on the environment have developed and defended a robust anthropocentrism, in which human interests[1] determine environmental policy and provide the moral justification for behavioral patterns that have widespread implications for the broader well-being of creation. Pope Francis in *Laudato Si'*, however, is exceptionally nervous about his papal predecessors' anthropocentrism, and he is careful to place limits on the degree to which he thinks the satisfaction of human interests functions as a moral justification. This is something almost entirely new, not only in Catholic environmentalism but also in Catholic theology generally, as anthropocentrism has dominated the theological landscape for nearly two millennia.

In what follows, I review the anthropocentrism of Popes John Paul II and Benedict XVI, and then show the ways in which Pope Francis's anthropocentrism breaks from that of his papal predecessors. While it is clear that Francis is charting a new course theoretically, I also argue that his version of anthropocentrism is indeterminate practically. However, several elements of *Laudato Si'* lend themselves to a distinct orientation that does offer a great deal of practical texture for thinking about policies, behavioral patterns, and individual lifestyles. To this extent, Pope Francis provides Catholics with the beginnings of a new non-anthropocentric environmental ethic.

A Brief Review of The Papal Predecessors: John Paul II and Benedict XVI

Christian anthropocentrists, whether Catholic or Protestant, follow a typical pattern in establishing their anthropocentrism theologically. Almost universally they develop what is commonly called the "stewardship paradigm," which grounds Christian environmentalism biblically in the first creation account in Genesis, which in turn leads to several common assertions about humans and our place in creation: (1) that humans are qualitatively different from everything else in creation, having been the only species made in the "image and likeness" of God (Gen. 1:26); (2) that because of our privileged status, God has given humans the task of exercising "dominion" over all creation (Gen. 1:26, 28); (3) that this dominion requires humans to be "stewards" or "caretakers" or "managers" of creation and to cultivate and renovate creation; (4) and that this stewardship is circumscribed by God's wishes for creation. This last point is important for Christian anthropocentrists, as they will quickly point out that human dominion over creation is always exercised in the context of God's purposes for creation. In other words, the goal of human dominion is first and foremost to mold creation into something fitting to God, and not simply to use it to satisfy human interests. So even though humans have a pivotal role to play in managing creation, there are definite limits to what humans are allowed to do to creation—at least in theory.

Pope John Paul II follows this pattern closely in his earlier works. He begins his analysis with the first creation account in Genesis, in which humans are made in the image and likeness of God,[2] which according to Pope John Paul II not only establishes the superiority of humans over other creatures,[3] but also grounds human dignity as the proximate norm for morality.[4] As a result of humans' special place in the order of creation, the first words that God speaks to humans (Gen. 1:28) is the mandate to subdue creation and to have dominion over creation.[5] Pope John Paul II is quick to point out, however, that neither subduing nor exercising dominion over creation entails any absolute right of disposal over it, and he uses both garden metaphors and adjectives qualifying human dominion in order to specify further the type of limitations God has placed on humans. So he writes that Adam and Eve were placed in the Garden of Eden with "the duty of cultivating and watching over it," so there is no indication of any "indiscriminate possession of created things."[6] Likewise, God imposes limits on human dominion over creation:

> The dominion granted to man [*sic*] by the Creator is not an absolute power, nor can one speak of a freedom to 'use and misuse,' or to dispose of things as one pleases. The limitation imposed from the beginning by the Creator himself and expressed symbolically by the prohibition not to 'eat of the fruit of the tree' (cf. Gen 2:16-17) shows clearly enough that, when it comes to the natural world, we are subject not only to biological laws but also to moral ones, which cannot be violated with impunity.[7]

In Pope John Paul II's later works, he follows the same structural pattern established in his earlier writings, with a few notable shifts in his presentation of the stewardship paradigm. He adduces other biblical evidence to bolster the legitimacy of human dominion over creation, citing passages from Wisdom and the Psalms to illustrate the glory and honor bestowed on humans by God.[8] He also becomes more direct and forceful about the privileged place of humans in the order of creation, writing that Genesis "places man at the summit of God's creative activity, as its crown, at the culmination of a process which leads from indistinct chaos to the most perfect of creatures. Everything in creation is ordered to man and everything is made subject to him."[9] Yet in spite of this exalted place of humans in the created order, Pope John Paul II is quick to assert that the dominion granted to humans is qualified and must be exercised by humans with "wisdom and love."[10] Of course, this strategy of qualifying "dominion" with additional terms is only successful if the qualifiers are sufficiently precise to give the reader a clear idea about what constitutes wise or loving behavior, and there is no discussion in his later works that would provide such clarity.

As Pope John Paul II moves from the theological foundations of the stewardship paradigm to more practical matters, no textual evidence suggests that anything other than human interests are relevant for environmental policy or moral justification of behavior. Indeed, everything points in the opposite direction. As the pope writes, the overarching context for moral decision-making is respecting human dignity: *"the dignity of the human person ... is the ultimate guiding norm for any sound economic, industrial or scientific progress."*[11] When the pope turns next to an analysis of the principle of the common good, he makes it clear that God is only interested in an equitable distribution of Earth's goods among humans: "'God destined the earth and everything it contains for the use of every individual and all peoples.'"[12] When the pope articulates a new right to a "safe environment," he recommends that this right be enshrined in the United Nations Charter of Human Rights, which implies that this right extends only to humans.[13] When affirming the sanctity of life and prohibiting unjust aggression against it, his singular concern is the life of humans, not any non-human life.[14] The pope's discussion of a "new solidarity" clearly refers to a solidarity among humans for the sake of humans.[15] When he moves into an analysis of poverty and the environment, he is singularly interested in the way in which environmental degradation affects humans, especially poor humans.[16] His discussion of warfare is clearly focused on the human hardship brought about by protracted large-scale violence.[17] Finally, in discussing the aesthetic value of creation, the pope notes the "deep restorative power" and the "peace and serenity" that are engendered by contemplating nature in all its grandeur, yet it is obvious that the pope is extolling nature's beauty perceived by humans for the sake of human enjoyment.[18] So while Pope John Paul II is keen to point out that anthropocentrism must be limited theoretically by the moral order instituted by God, there is nothing in any of his writings to indicate that any tangible limits exist, nor anything to indicate that anything other than human interests factor into the process of moral deliberation and judgment.

Pope Benedict XVI cleaves closely to Pope John Paul II and identifies the stewardship paradigm as the foundation for Catholic environmentalism, repeating the four essential points highlighted above.[19] Also like Pope John Paul II, he notes the theoretical limits to anthropocentrism, stating that our stewardship of creation precludes any "absolute domination,"[20] and that we must envision our place in creation as "God's co-worker."[21] Yet when Pope Benedict XVI moves from theological foundations to practical issues, his analyses focus exclusively on human interests, despite the limited anthropocentrism he endorses. For instance, when he discusses the issues of potable water, energy use, rural development, and climate change, nothing but human considerations are given any attention.[22] When he considers the principle of the universal destination of creation's goods, he is only concerned with an equitable distribution of these goods among humans. As he writes, "The goods of creation belong to humanity as a whole."[23] When he cites the oft-used future generations principle as a way to promote conservation currently, he is thinking only of future generations of humans, not future generations of animals or rivers or mountains or ecosystems.[24] So in the end, similar to Pope John Paul II, even though Pope Benedict XVI maintains intellectual allegiance to a chastened anthropocentrism, either his ability to provide practical illustrations of those limitations is lacking, or his limited anthropocentrism is more of a rhetorical strategy that has little practical applicability. Based on the textual evidence, I think it is fair to say that Pope John Paul II and Pope Benedict XVI are robust anthropocentrists, with the satisfaction of human interests the sole criterion by which environmental decisions ought to be made.

Pope Francis (2013–2025)

Unlike his papal predecessors, Pope Francis wants to tread gingerly on the topic of anthropocentrism, as he thinks certain versions of anthropocentrism are at the heart of current environmental destruction in addition to being theologically problematic, and he goes to great lengths to specify the version of anthropocentrism that he is willing to endorse. Even though he flirts with love language at the beginning in *Laudato Si'* and elevates St. Francis of Assisi as a model for Catholic environmentalism,[25] he eventually abandons this love language in preference for the familiar stewardship paradigm and its four themes, including the biblical mandate that humans have been given dominion over all creation. Yet Francis is quick to point out that even though the term "dominion" has earned a poor reputation in some circles for promoting the "unbridled exploitation" of nature by "domineering and destructive" humans,[26] this is an aberrant interpretation that needs to be rejected. He writes,

> Although it is true that we Christians have at times incorrectly interpreted the Scriptures, nowadays we must forcefully reject the notion that our being created in God's image and given dominion over the earth justifies absolute domination over other creatures. The biblical texts are to be read in their context, with an appropriate hermeneutic, recognizing that they tell us to 'till and keep' the garden of the world (cf. *Gen.* 2:15). 'Tilling' refers to cultivating, plowing or working, while 'keeping' means caring, protecting, overseeing, and preserving. This implies a relationship of mutual responsibility between human beings and nature. Each community can take from the bounty of the earth whatever it needs for subsistence, but it also has the duty to protect the earth and to ensure its fruitfulness for coming generations.[27]

The upshot of these considerations, according to Pope Francis, is that human dominion over creation needs to be understood as "responsible stewardship"[28] that recognizes that the Earth is God's, first and foremost, and is given to us to manage according to divine dictates.

Shifting his theological strategy, Pope Francis then focuses on the intrinsic value of everything in creation. Citing the Catechism of the Catholic Church, Pope Francis notes that the value given by God to everything in creation undercuts any thoroughgoing anthropocentrism:

> The Catechism clearly and forcefully criticizes a distorted anthropocentrism: Each creature possesses its own particular goodness and perfection …. Each of the various creatures, willed in its own being, reflects in its own way a ray of God's infinite wisdom and goodness. Man [*sic*] must therefore respect the particular goodness of every creature, to avoid any disordered use of things.[29]

In a similar way, Pope Francis explains that "the ultimate purpose of other creatures is not to be found in us" but in God,[30] which means that their raison d'être is not derived from their ability to satisfy human needs and desires, but to give glory to God.

Pope Francis devotes an entire section of *Laudato Si'* to delineating the limits of anthropocentrism. In section "III. The Crisis and Effects of Modern Anthropocentrism," Pope Francis identifies the "technical mind" as the hallmark of modern anthropocentrism, which embodies the Baconian vision of material reality as something to be manipulated, controlled, and used by humans without reference to any value or meaning in that material reality beyond the satisfaction of human desires. Quoting Romano Guardini, Pope Francis writes: "[T]he technological mind sees nature as in insensate order, as a cold body of facts, as a mere 'given,' as an object of utility, as raw material to be hammered into useful shape; it views the cosmos similarly as a mere 'space' into which objects can be thrown with complete indifference. The intrinsic dignity of the world is thus compromised."[31] The psychological effect of this "Promethean vision of mastery over the world"[32] is not only divesting created reality of any intrinsic value or meaning, but also a "practical relativism" in which the satisfaction of immediate human interests is consistently heralded as the most laudable objective of the current technological regime, with all other considerations being blithely dismissed as inconsequential and irrelevant.[33] When this "culture of relativism" becomes pervasive, the "use and throw away mentality" it engenders eventually starts to seep into our relationships with other humans, so that we come to regard them as mere objects to be controlled and manipulated to our advantage. Now, large-scale and organized criminal activities such as human trafficking, sexual exploitation, and the drug trade become not only thinkable, but easily rationalized, according to Pope Francis.[34]

Given the considerable attention Pope Francis gives to critiquing aberrant versions of anthropocentrism and to outlining the version he endorses, one would expect to see clearly how his understanding of legitimate anthropocentrism gets embodied practically. Yet, like his papal predecessors, who endorsed a theoretically chastened anthropocentrism while embracing an unrestricted practical anthropocentrism, Pope Francis's treatment of practical environmental issues follows the same pattern and fails to show how, or to what extent, anything other than human interests factor into practical moral decision-making. So, for instance, Pope Francis claims that the natural environment should be regarded as "a collective good, the patrimony of humanity," which implies that non-humans have no right to the collective good.[35] The principle of the universal destination of Earth's goods entails "a shared inheritance, whose fruits are meant to benefit everyone,"[36] with "everyone" apparently meaning only humans. Medical experimentation on animals is permissible if it contributes to caring for humans or to saving human lives.[37] The foundation of the principle of the common good is "respect for the human person," and its goal is to give "social groups and their individual members" (i.e., humans) access to the goods necessary for their well-being.[38] The pope's analysis of mercy, while moving and challenging, never considers anything other than humans to be an appropriate object of either human or divine mercy.[39] On a wide range of practical issues, ranging from pollution to climate change to freshwater to global inequality to genetically modified organisms to intergenerational justice, all are framed around the human interests at stake, and there is never any indication that anything other than human flourishing factors into the pope's analyses. Thus, despite substantive theoretical reservations about certain strands of anthropocentrism and considerable time devoted to outlining his chastened anthropocentrism, Pope Francis, similar to his papal predecessors, ends up embracing an unrestrained practical anthropocentrism in which only human interests are relevant at the level of policy decisions or individual behavior.

Developing a Chastened Anthropocentrism: The 50/50 Principle and Practical Ethics

Pope Francis clearly wants to break from the robust anthropocentrism of his papal predecessors, but for whatever reason, he does not provide any practical guidance as to how this chastened anthropocentrism either gets incarnated in our daily lives or provides concrete directives in the policy arena. This is not a strike against Pope Francis, in my opinion, as others even more vociferous and thoroughgoing in their rejection of anthropocentrism have failed to articulate the practical contours of a chastened anthropocentric environmental ethic.[40] Moreover, the long and dominant historical track record of anthropocentrism in Catholicism has made it the unquestioned background in which Catholic theology has been constructed, which means that there are historically very few sources, ideas, or concepts from which Pope Francis can draw in order to begin crawling his way out of the anthropocentric paradigm. So even though Francis's discomfort with the anthropocentrism of his papal predecessors is apparent and his commitment to a chastened anthropocentrism is explicit in *Laudato Si'*, in the end its practical texture remains opaque as he provides not even the vaguest blueprint of the contents of this chastened anthropocentrism. Charting a new course is never an easy feat; but doing so after steadily sailing in the opposite direction for many centuries is potentially vexing and unnerving.

Several of Pope Francis's comments on key topics, however, coalesce into a platform that offers a more determinate trajectory to his chastened anthropocentrism, which in turn leads to an endorsement of what I will call the 50/50 principle, which does provide practical direction. Let me develop these points and then explain how they converge on the 50/50 principle.

First, Pope Francis regards all of creation as an object of love, and the appropriate posture toward creation is one of "awe and wonder" and a feeling of intimacy "with all that exists."[41] According to him, we must start thinking about this love for all creation along the lines of the intense passion felt for a lover in a romantic relationship, as such intense feelings are the best basis for understanding the love we ought to feel toward the created order, which is the progenitor of everything good that we experience, and we also ought to regard our fellow non-human creatures as united to us "by bonds of affection."[42]

This link between our emotions and nature is a critical move for Pope Francis, as it resists the contemporary tendency either to background our natural environments by relegating them to the status of being the unimportant and inconsequential backdrops in which valuable human interactions and activities occur,[43] or to regard our environments in typical Baconian fashion as realms that need to be revamped, changed, and manipulated in order to serve the needs of humans, and thereby to become valuable. In either case, nature is not understood as something that evokes warm feelings from us simply by being itself, but only when it manages to transcend our psychological backgrounding by providing something for us in the way of valuable resources or recreation or aesthetic experiences. In other words, nature becomes an occasion of positive feelings only when it benefits humans in some way.

In a similar way, the discipline of Christian ethics has long militated against any robust connection between our affectivity and nature. Typically, the strongest positive emotional movements are associated with "love," and in Christian ethics this love takes its shape from the Great Commandment, which is recorded in the synoptic Gospels during Jesus's encounter with a lawyer: "Teacher, which is the great commandment in the Law?" And he said to him, "You shall love the Lord your God with all your heart and with all your soul and with all your mind. This is the great and first commandment. And a second is like it: You shall love your neighbor as yourself. On these two commandments depend all the Law and the Prophets" (Matt. 22:35-40).[44] Recent influential discussions of love among Christian ethicists[45] have largely assumed that God and humans are the only appropriate objects of love, with most of the discussion centering around the issues of which humans are to be given priority in the order of love and which types of love (agape, eros, and philia) are the most legitimate. The Christian ethical tradition is quite clear that where the "heart" is concerned, God and humans have pride of place, but it is highly ambivalent about anything else in creation also being worthy of entering the domain of emotional connection. Thus, for Pope Francis to get Catholics to recognize that love extends to nature and non-human creatures and rightly includes all the effusive feelings commonly associated with romantic love is a bold move, to be sure.

Second, Pope Francis maintains that every creature possesses intrinsic value given by God, which means that regardless of its practical utility to humans, each creature has a dignity that must be acknowledged and respected.[46] Pope Francis mentions three ways in which this intrinsic value is attributed to creatures.[47] The first is the fact that every creature is "a locus of [God's] presence," which pertains not only to animals, but to plants as well. As Francis writes, "The Spirit of life dwells in every living creature and calls us to enter into relationship with him."[48] Another reason is that creatures have a destiny and purpose that are independent of humans, which rest in God alone.[49] This eschatological promise extends to every creature and involves its ultimate transformation in Christ: "Eternal life will be a shared experience of awe, in which each creature, resplendently transfigured, will take its rightful place."[50] Yet perhaps the most important consideration for the attribution to intrinsic value is that creation is an act of divine freedom done out of love and a desire to share the divine life with everything that exists. Therefore, as Francis writes, we are called to mirror the tenderness with which God loves all creatures:

> Creation is in the order of love. God's love is the fundamental moving force in all created things: 'For you love all things that exist, and detest none of the things that you have made; for you would not have made anything if you had hated it' (Wis 11:24). Every creature is thus the object of the Father's tenderness, who gives it its place in the world. Even the fleeting life of the least of beings is the object of his love, and in its few seconds of existence, God enfolds it with his affection.[51]

In becoming embodiments of this tender divine love for all creatures,[52] we humans must cultivate our affection for creatures, become conscious of and concerned about their plight and hardships, and act for the sake of their well-being.[53] As Francis writes in a prayer at the end of *Laudato Si'*, we are called to stretch ourselves in order to extend love to every creature:[54]

> God of love, show us our place in this world
> as channels of your love
> for all the creatures of this earth,
> for not one of them is forgotten in your sight.[55]

The pope also claims that ecosystems have intrinsic value, in addition to the value they possess to all individual creatures who depend on the health and bounty of the larger systems in which they move and live.[56] So, according to Pope Francis, from the smallest of microbiota to the health and well-being of our planet, every creature and every ecosystem within creation has intrinsic value.

These first two points, namely, that creation is an object of love and that Catholics are called to recognize the dignity and intrinsic value of all creatures, make it difficult to imagine how we are supposed to respect and love bearers of intrinsic dignity without also trying to foster and protect the broader environments that make their lives possible and fulfilling. Pope Francis repeatedly points out that all life on Earth is interconnected and that we need diverse and healthy ecosystems in order for humans, as well as every other species, to flourish. The goods and services provided by diverse ecosystems, which we often take for granted, are simply astonishing: water purification, topsoil fertility and health, shelter and building materials, air purification, carbon sequestration, detoxification and decomposition of wastes, climate stabilization, pollination of crops, pest and disease control, nutrient recycling, ecosystem resilience to threats and stresses, moderation of climate extremes, a broad array of medicines and pharmaceuticals, aesthetic and spiritual value, and the joy for biophilic creatures like us living on a planet teeming with diverse creatures being among the most apparent.[57] The well-being of every living creature is intimately dependent on Earth's biodiversity, so even if ecosystems and the goods and services they produce are regarded purely for their instrumental value, there is still a decided preference to encourage ecosystems that support a rich array of biodiversity which makes them resilient, productive, and fecund.

Third, a key tenet of Pope Francis's environmentalism is that the created order is a conduit through which God becomes manifest. In other words, nature is "a magnificent book in which God speaks to us and grants us a glimpse of his [*sic*] infinite beauty and goodness," and he cites Romans 1:20 to the effect that God's power and divinity have become manifest through creation since the beginning of the universe.[58] Moreover, Francis notes Thomas Aquinas's dictum that God is best represented by a multiplicity of creatures, as no one creature can adequately encapsulate the divine goodness; on the contrary, the more varied and diverse the body of creatures, the better the complexity of God is made manifest.[59] Thus, for Francis, there is a direct link between religiosity and the ability to imagine the fullness of God and our lived environments, especially the degree to which our lives are full of meaningful contact with other creatures. Bland, uniform worlds of sameness are therefore likely to breed a type of mental desiccation that will be a serious liability to anyone striving to know and to love God, insofar as such a sterile environment will necessarily limit one's imagination and impoverish the ability to understand the fullness of the divine. Lived environments that honor our native biophilia, on the other hand, and put us into regular contact with a wide array of different creatures and natural settings will reflect the complexity and grandiosity of the divine and provide a more fertile platform for being able to know and love God.

Fourth, Pope Francis laments the ongoing truncation of biodiversity on Earth, both the declining biodiversity hotspots such as tropical rain forests and coral reefs and the many benefits and resources they could have provided to humans,[60] as well as the extinction of so many species that diminishes creation's ability to mirror the divine reality adequately. This ongoing problem of declining biodiversity, according to Pope Francis, is placed squarely on humankind's shoulders: "Because of us, thousands of species will no longer give glory to God by their very existence, nor convey their message to us. We have no such right."[61] In Pope Francis's opinion, sustainability ought to be the hallmark of every ecosystem managed by humans,[62] and biological hotspots that contain an abundance of biodiversity such as rain forests in the Amazon, Congo, or Borneo must be preserved and protected by law.[63]

Finally, in order to achieve the health and well-being of ecosystems worldwide, Pope Francis is convinced that the withdrawal of human influence is often the best policy, as intervention into ecosystems often results in unforeseen negative side effects,[64] which in turn need additional human intervention to rectify, with potentially new and unanticipated negative side effects emerging from these well intended interventions, and on and on this "vicious cycle" of intervention and negative side effects continues, with no end in sight: "But a sober look at our world shows that the degree of human intervention, often in the service of business interests and consumerism, is actually making our earth less rich and beautiful, ever more limited and grey, even as technological advances and consumer goods continue to abound limitlessly."[65]

These five central considerations for Pope Francis coalesce into an environmentalism that places biodiversity on Earth as an overarching good that sets the context for our actions and policies, as each of the aforementioned points, whether directly or indirectly, readily leads to an endorsement of preserving or increasing biodiversity as the comprehensive planetary common good.[66]

Yet other normative moral principles espoused by Pope Francis presuppose biodiversity. The principle of the common good is intimately connected to biodiversity, as it is hard to imagine any long-term realization of the common good absent a robust underlying biodiversity making those goods possible.[67] Intergenerational justice and solidarity, which focus on the question, "What kind of world do we want to leave to those who come after us, to children who are now growing up?"[68] are also connected to biodiversity as one of the necessary prerequisites for future generations to lead flourishing lives. Finally, appropriate gratitude to God for the wondrous gift of life and divine generosity offered through the stupendous bounty of creation requires us to imitate that generosity and to undergo an ecological conversion that fosters an awareness of our universal communion with other creatures as well as encourages a simple lifestyle that promotes the conditions in which all of creation flourishes, which includes biodiversity.[69]

Biodiversity and the 50/50 Principle

Given the ethical priority of biodiversity and its ongoing maintenance on our planet as the centerpiece of Pope Francis's ecological vision, I propose that Catholics embrace what I call the 50/50 principle[70] and place it front and center on our moral radar screen, which I think best embodies the chastened anthropocentrism that Pope Francis wishes to embrace practically. The 50/50 principle consists of the following two components, the first one psychological and the second one normative: (1) that we ought to function as if only 50 percent of Earth is ours to manage and cultivate for our purposes, with the other 50 percent being regarded as the domain of non-human interests to be satisfied; and (2) that when we choose an action, pattern of behavior, or a policy, protecting and/or promoting biodiversity on Earth must be a consistent benchmark of our decision-making process and actual choices. Let me explain each of these two criteria.

The first component of the 50/50 principle is intended to highlight the fact that we are one species among an almost mind-boggling number of other species who share our bountiful Earth. Scientists have identified and classified 1.2 million animal and plant species thus far, but the best estimates for the total number of species, which includes those yet undiscovered, is 8.7 million! Here are some of the species with which many of us are most familiar: dogs, wolves, jackals, foxes, grizzly bears, polar bears, black bears, sloth bears, red pandas, giant pandas, raccoons, skunks, badgers, polecats, weasels, minks, giant otters, sea otters, smooth-coated otters, walruses, northern fur seals, southern fur seals, northern sea lions, elephant seals, leopard seals, Weddell seals, harp seals, harbor seals, civets, clouded leopards, pumas, jaguarundis, cheetahs, lynxes, servals, hyenas, dwarf mongooses, Liberian mongooses, roe deer, moose, musk deer, caribou, Nearctic deer, fallow deer, bison, cattle, Asian buffalo, African buffalo, elands, impalas, wildebeests, pygmy antelopes, springboks, Saharan gazelles, dik-diks, goats, ibexes, sheep, Rocky

Mountain goats, muskox, oryx, reedbucks, pronghorn antelope, giraffes, okapi, peccaries, camels, hippopotamuses, gray whales, humpback whales, sperm whales, Amazon river dolphins, narwhals, belugas, killer whales, common dolphins, porpoises, bats, armadillos, mice, opossums, kangaroos, wallaby, hedgehogs, shrews, cottontail rabbits, hares, pikas, platypus, rhinoceroses, anteaters, sloths, baboons, macaques, gray langurs, gorillas, chimpanzees, orangutans, gibbons, howler monkeys, spider monkeys, tamarins, squirrel monkeys, lemurs, bushbabies, African elephants, Asian elephants, beavers, pocket gophers, guinea pigs, pacas, porcupines—and this represents an almost infinitesimally small fraction of the known species!

This small snippet of life on Earth is intended to impress on us the grandiosity of God's creative activity, which over millions of years has produced the most fecund planet in the known universe, with life found literally everywhere, from the driest desert to miles below Earth's surface to the scalding water surrounding hydrothermal vents on the ocean floor to microbes locked in icebergs for millions of years. Whether an environment is hot or cold, wet or dry, acid or alkaline, temperate or tropical, welcoming or forbidding, life is resilient and adaptable and constantly changing, and it exists almost everywhere we look. But more importantly, this small snippet ought to convey the fact that we are a very minute part of a bountiful planet—literally one species out of potentially almost 9 million other species!—each treasured by God, each adding to the diversity of our planet, and each contributing something irreplaceably valuable with its presence and functioning. Given that we are simply one species among such a rich tapestry of millions of species on Earth, the first prong of the 50/50 principle is quite generous to us, perhaps even extravagantly so, in specifying that humans ought to function as if 50 percent of the Earth were ours to use exclusively for our purposes. Indeed, the thought of any other one species commandeering one-half of our planet and getting to control its resources and use them solely for the benefit of its own species would be met by us with disbelief, if not outright derision and disdain. So to regard one-half of Earth as ours to cultivate and manage solely for the benefit of our species, *Homo sapiens*, is quite a generous allotment, indeed.

The psychological effect of the first prong of the 50/50 principle should cause Catholics to internalize an attitude that regards creation as a bountiful gift from God to be enjoyed by every creature, that embraces the fact that God is passionately in love with all creatures and desires for every creature to be brought to its proper fulfillment, and that causes us to regard ourselves as belonging to a "sublime communion" of creation, as Pope Francis calls it, which recognizes our dependence on other creatures and natural systems that make our lives possible and worthwhile, in addition to engendering a heartfelt sense of gratitude and appreciation for the many ways in which other creatures benefit us so enormously. Phrased a bit differently, Catholics ought to regard—and according to Pope Francis, to **feel!**—as if other creatures are part of our family, united through dependence, mutuality, reciprocity, and bonds of affection. Much like St. Francis of Assisi in his famous "Canticle of Brother Sun and Sister Moon," in which he uses familial metaphors to describe aspects of creation (brother sun, sister moon, brothers wind and air, sister water, brother fire, mother earth), Pope Francis states that we are linked by unseen bonds with other creatures that form a "universal family" which ought to fill us with a "sacred, affectionate, and humble respect."[71]

Unfortunately, the vast bulk of residents of Western industrialized countries do not even come close to honoring the dictum that we ought to function as if 50 percent of Earth belongs to other species. To the contrary, we typically function as if we have the right of disposal over the entire planet, and that nothing should stand in our way of appropriating whatever we want in order to satisfy our needs and desires. This psychology of entitlement has also recently been coupled with the historically unprecedented ability to satisfy our desires, and we have arrived at a very odd place on Earth in which evolutionary processes have birthed a species so dominant and powerful that the future of life on Earth literally depends on our choices and policies.[72] Gifted with a large cranium and opposable thumbs for grasping, we humans have proven to be highly adept developers of technologies, and we have done so with a vengeance, systematically fashioning tools to augment and transcend our natural powers, allowing us to revamp the contours of ecosystems worldwide and to remake our entire planet into a system for satisfying human needs and desires. While we complain about invasive species, we humans are easily the most invasive species ever to make an appearance on Earth, occupying virtually every ecological niche on the planet. We also as a species use resources that would require 1.75 Earths to sustain indefinitely at current levels of consumption,[73] with projections as high as 2.6 Earths needed by 2050 if current trends continue.[74] Unfortunately for ourselves as well as for the rest of the planet, as our appetite for consumer goods becomes ever more rapacious, our consumption levels continue to increase, as well as the human population on Earth, which by the end of this century is projected to climb as high as 9.5–12.7 billion from the current world population of 8.1 billion,[75] with an increasing percentage of that population aspiring to embrace the consumptive lifestyles of the world's economic elite.

In terms of biocapacity, which represents the amount of available sustainable resources on our planet, our acquisitiveness becomes even more ostentatious. Over the past fifty years, human demand for overall renewable resources and ecological services increased by nearly 140 percent, with our demand for cropland rising over 125 percent and our carbon footprint increasing over 260 percent![76] Humans and our domesticated livestock now comprise an astonishing 96 percent of all mammal biomass on Earth,[77] while human fishing has depleted 85 percent of fish stocks significantly with 90 percent of "big fish" species (tuna, sharks, marlin) having suffered significant losses.[78]

This trend of humans continually appropriating more of the Earth's productivity bodes very ominously for biodiversity on Earth, as the remaking of our planet according to the marching orders of one species has inaugurated a new biological holocaust, dubbed by scientists as the "sixth extinction."[79] Today, every biological taxon is experiencing significant decline, with extinction rates many orders of magnitude higher than the background extinction rate. Amphibians are probably faring the worst, with scientists estimating that over one-third of all amphibian species are facing likely extinction, which represents an extinction rate between 25,000–45,000 times the natural background rate![80] Thirty-one percent of bird species in the United States are of "conservation concern," with 192 species being at extremely high risk of going extinct. Of the 1.3 million known invertebrate species evaluated, 30 percent have been deemed to be at risk of extinction. One-fifth of the world's mammal species are listed as endangered, threatened, or vulnerable, with 50 percent of primate species headed toward oblivion. Of all plant species evaluated by the International Union for the Conservation of Nature, 68 percent are deemed to be threatened with extinction. Overall, extinction rates are over 1000 times higher after humans emerged on Earth compared to before.[81]

Fortunately, biodiversity on Earth can be increased through human actions and policies. Biodiversity hotspots such as tropical rain forests and coral reefs,[82] which contain a disproportionately high number of species, cover only around 2.3 percent of Earth's surface, which means that focused conservation efforts on these areas could be quite successful at protecting biodiversity. Important as biodiversity hotspots are, however, focusing on them is equivalent to conservation triage, and at some point we need to turn our attention to our lived environments, to our neighborhoods, cities, and local ecosystems and try to discern new types of habits and relationships that can engender more biodiversity.

On the broadest level, Catholics ought to embrace two initiatives that hold the most promise for preserving biodiversity on Earth. The first is to encourage our federal legislators to ratify the Convention on Biological Diversity (1992), to which nearly every country on our planet is a party, with the glaring exception of the United States. The Convention on Biological Diversity is the first and most comprehensive plan to ensure the "conservation of biological diversity, the sustainable use of its components and the fair and equitable sharing of the benefits arising out of the utilization of genetic resources,"[83] which mandates that each country formulate a national plan for promoting biodiversity, including establishing a series of protected areas that contain valuable types of biodiversity, protect ecosystems and natural habitats outside these protected areas that contribute to biodiversity, and rehabilitate and restore degraded ecosystems.[84] The Convention on Biological Diversity sought to institutionalize the preservation of biodiversity as an obligatory feature of the national decision-making process of every country's legislative process, and it has succeeded in doubling protected areas worldwide, among other practical accomplishments.

The second notable initiative was the recent "Kunming-Montreal Global Biodiversity Framework," which was the final document issued by the 15th meeting of the Conference of the Parties (2022). The Kunming-Montreal framework attempts to increase biodiversity across our planet by agreeing to realize the following goals by 2050: (1) to increase the area of natural ecosystems substantially; (2) to halt anthropogenic species extinctions, and to reduce the overall extinction rate by tenfold; (3) to use and manage biodiversity resources sustainably; (4) and to provide adequate financial resources for countries to implement their national strategies.[85] In turn, the Kunming-Montreal framework identifies twenty-three specific targets that are consistent with these overarching goals, four of which are germane to our purposes:

- To bring the loss of high areas of biodiversity to near zero by 2030.
- To bring at least 30 percent of degraded ecosystems under restoration efforts by 2030.
- To ensure that at least 30 percent of ecosystems designated as sensitive areas for biodiversity are conserved and managed by 2030.
- To conserve and help threatened species recover in order to regain their ecological meaningfulness.
- To reduce pollution risks, especially those posed by agricultural chemicals and hazardous industrial chemicals.[86]

Hailed as the Paris Agreement for biodiversity, the Kunming-Montreal framework is easily the boldest initiative ever to protect biodiversity worldwide, especially what has become known as the 30×30 target that seeks to protect 30 percent of our planet's land and oceans by 2030—a gargantuan area that represents almost innumerable ecosystems. If the goals of the Kunming-Montreal framework are realized and the levels of biodiversity are maintained, this could be one of the defining moments in which humans offer an enormous gift to life on planet Earth and reverse a consistent track record of truncating biodiversity with our destructive appetites and life-destroying systems.

Unfortunately, in addition to never ratifying the Convention on Biological Diversity, the United States is also not a party to the Kunming-Montreal framework. This does not necessarily imply that the United States federal government is uninterested in promoting biodiversity, as we are free to pass federal legislation that parallels or goes beyond the Kunming-Montreal framework whenever we want. Nor should it be assumed that being a party to the Kunming-Montreal framework automatically results in the realization of the goals and targets of this agreement. History is littered with idealistic international agreements that in the end turn out to be little more than wishful thinking. Being a party to the Kunming-Montreal framework, however, would certainly raise awareness of this momentous biodiversity initiative and could potentially result in a new national commitment to biodiversity programs that would reap enormous benefits for Americans and beyond. To this extent, American Catholics ought to be vocal about the value of the Kunming-Montreal framework and tell our legislators either to become a party to the framework or to introduce federal legislation that strikes a similar note for preserving biodiversity.

While initiatives like the Kunming-Montreal framework are irreplaceable for protecting biodiversity on a large-scale, an equally vital element in preserving biodiversity occurs on a much smaller scale, which places a premium on local initiatives and individual efforts. Biodiversity varies widely according to geography and the kinds of flora and fauna possible in one ecosystem might be very different in another ecosystem, so it should be expected that promoting biodiversity in densely wooded southeastern Pennsylvania will be very different than in the arid areas of Nevada or Utah. Likewise, working to protect biodiversity in the Badlands of South Dakota will look nothing like doing so in the Florida Everglades. Each particular ecosystem has different species and densities of animals and plants, along with unique sets of symbiotic and predatory relationships, so a great deal depends on the particularities of ecosystems and the different kinds of policies and activities that actually promote biodiversity.

When our gaze is focused more locally, several considerations crystallize. There is a small cluster of direct causes that are widely implicated in the staggering extinction rate today: global climate change, habitat loss, pollution, invasive species, and overexploitation of species,[87] with overpopulation and rapacious consumption levels being the two principal engines behind these direct causes. The good news here is that these causes are potentially reversible, if we can muster both the political will power and individual resolve to make a change for the better.

To this end, Catholics ought to focus on two issues, global climate change and our industrialized agriculture system, in order to make the biggest impact on reversing the trend in declining biodiversity. This century, global climate will become the most pernicious threat to biodiversity, affecting every ecosystem and interjecting planetary wide unpredictability and stress that will make life difficult for everyone and everything, and there is a good chance that unless significant reductions of greenhouse gas emissions in the neighborhood of 7 percent annually worldwide yearly are attained in the next ten to fifteen years that the worst case scenario is almost virtually assured, which would be an unmitigated disaster the likes of which human history has never witnessed. Nothing comes close to representing such an ominous, malevolent threat to life on Earth, which ought to put global climate change front and center on the moral radar screen of Catholics.

Perhaps more surprising to most people is the way in which our food production system is implicated in biodiversity loss. Of the direct causes mentioned above (global climate change, habitat loss, pollution, invasive species, and overexploitation of species), industrialized agriculture is implicated in three of them, which makes it the current leading cause of biodiversity loss worldwide, and it is estimated that food production accounts for anywhere from nearly one-fourth[88] to over one-half[89] of all greenhouse gas emission per year, which makes food production one of the leading causes of global climate change.

So how does a Catholic committed to the 50/50 principle approach agriculture and food production? Recall that the first prong of the 50/50 principle is the psychological reminder that we need to share Earth with the myriad other creatures that inhabit our fecund planet, and we continually need to reinforce the mental habit of nurturing a psychology of sharing the bounty of creation with non-humans, so that it becomes second nature to regard Earth as the home to all creatures, large and small. The second prong of the 50/50 principle, on the other hand, functions normatively and refers to our actions, and it specifies that when we choose an action, pattern of behavior, or a policy, protecting and/or promoting biodiversity on Earth must be a consistent criterion of our decision-making process and actual choices. The purpose of this second prong is to move beyond psychological habituation to the realm of action and to push Catholics to begin to make actual changes to our everyday patterns of behavior that promote biodiversity. Motivation and good intentions count for a lot in the moral sphere, but actual results are necessary if the paramount good of biodiversity on planet Earth is going to be preserved, which means that there has to be a consistent transition from motivation to action in the practical sphere.

Two overarching concepts should be kept front and center on our radar screen as we start to imagine ways to implement the 50/50 principle in our lives: self-limitation and symbiosis. Given today's cultural climate of highly consumptive lifestyles, in which the typical ecological footprint for a citizen of a highly industrialized Western democracy is highly injurious to biodiversity, self-limitation is probably one of the best and most direct ways to protect biodiversity, as it is possible to take a precise inventory of one's consumer habits, to identify the principal malefactors among those habits, and then either to stop or modify them. On a large scale, self-limitation can be a highly beneficial strategy to promote biodiversity, as it allows us to remove or lessen the negative impacts of our presence from certain ecologically sensitive areas and to allow natural systems in those areas to reestablish themselves. Our national park system is a good illustration of the power of self-limitation, as curbing the human footprint in our national parks has allowed us to preserve a great deal of the biodiversity that existed in those areas before they became national parks.

The second concept, symbiosis, which is often called mutualism, refers to the fact that humans are always enmeshed in a web of relationships that affects other species and ecosystems, and we not only need to be conscious of this interdependence but we also need to reorganize our lifestyles and patterns of behavior to become a more beneficial presence to those affected by our actions. More specifically, symbiosis means that we should consistently strive not only to be a blessing to other creatures affected by our lives, but also to conduct our lives in such a way that biodiversity is enhanced by our presence.

Self-limitation and symbiosis lend themselves to a very discernible trajectory in terms of supporting agriculture. As I have written elsewhere,[90] the vast majority of food in the United States is produced by an industrial system of farming that has the following characteristics: increasing mechanization and the replacement of human labor with machines; regional specialization; capital intensiveness; uniformity and monocultures; synthetic chemicals (fertilizers, herbicides, and pesticides); hybrid seeds; and the consumption of an exorbitant amount of fossil fuels. This agricultural system has resulted in an explosion of calories available to the average American and an abundance of cheap processed food, but by almost every other standard of assessment it fails miserably. It floats on a sea of fossil fuels, which makes it unsustainable. It separates producer and consumer by large distances, so that every food product in the United States travels an average of 1500 miles between producer and consumer, which is an extravagant waste of energy! It has resulted in historically high rates of topsoil erosion—and healthy, fertile topsoil is the lifeblood of agriculture. The use of synthetic inputs has resulted in pesticide resistance and long-term nutrient deficits in the topsoil. Worst of all, it is one of the most injurious systems known today to biodiversity, as its monocultures intentionally eliminate any competition for food or nutrients, which effectively makes the fields of industrial agriculture to be dead zones for everything but a few opportunistic animal species and the crops cultivated for human consumption.

A first order of business for Catholics wishing to make their lifestyles more beneficial to biodiversity on our planet, then, is to create and support alternatives to industrial agriculture that reduce fossil fuel consumption, pollution, and the use of injurious synthetic chemicals while also being beneficial to other creatures. This last clause is important, as the point of the 50/50 principle is not simply to create systems that are more beneficial to humans, but consistently to consider the needs and interests of other creatures as we imagine alternative ways to order our lifestyles and patterns of behavior.

In my opinion, the best way to do this in the agricultural sector is to embrace E. F. Schumacher's dictum "Small is Beautiful,"[91] as small-scale, local agriculture has a number of advantages over its industrial counterpart. Indeed, a decade ago the United Nations shifted the bulk of its funding efforts to small-scale agriculture, due to the fact that it is more efficient and productive (when inputs versus outputs are measured) than its industrial counterpart, thereby being the easiest and surest route to food security and sustainability, especially for the world's poor.[92] The meteoric rise of urban gardening has been a potent force in combating malnutrition in impoverished urban centers, in addition to overcoming the debilitating effects of food deserts in many of these areas.[93] As it turns out, small is not only beautiful, but sometimes the most viable option for securing nutrient-dense food, a healthy diet, and for fighting poverty.

Gardening, which represents the smallest and most local method of food production, is often regarded today as a relic of a bygone era, but there is little doubt that growing one's own food is vastly superior to supporting our industrial system of food production. Let me take my garden as an illustration of the different ways in which the 50/50 principle can be embodied in a small-scale agricultural system. My garden is structured to allow me to contribute to biodiversity in two principal ways: (1) by designating one-half of my garden space to feed and shelter other creatures; and (2) by allowing me to withdraw my support of industrial agriculture by growing my own food, which indirectly reduces conditions that adversely affect biodiversity. I provide shelter and food for other creatures in two ways. I consider toads to be centerpiece of my integrated pest management system, which allows me to garden organically, as they are voracious predators and do an admirable job of controlling the populations of slugs, snails, and Japanese beetles. So the first order of business in the spring is to tip over a couple clay pots and bury them halfway in the dirt in order to attract toads. The second order of business is to plant flowers, most of which are indigenous to southeastern Pennsylvania, which are adapted to my particular soils and provide food, shelter, and breeding grounds for many types of insects, birds, and small mammals in my area. I also have to admit to having a certain soft spot for sunflowers, as each of the hundreds of seeds on a large sunflower head also contains a single flower filled with succulent nectar, with the result that at any point during the day there might be dozens of bees and butterflies and bugs on the sunflowers in my garden. Moreover, after the sunflower seeds develop and dry a bit, goldfinches will start making regular visits, hanging upside down on the large flowers, pulling off individual seeds and shelling them with their beaks, and chirping at each other as they enjoy munching on the tasty seeds. During the afternoon when the sun is high in the sky and accentuating the brilliant yellow and black goldfinch feathers, the beauty of the goldfinches is borderline sublime.

Food production is maximized in my garden by a combination of traditional gardening and vertical gardening. Bamboo poles harvested from a neighbor's property provide sturdy columns for vining plants to climb, and lashing the poles together and adding some netting adds even more area for the vining plants to grow. Cold weather crops such as spinach, lettuce, snap peas, and kale are planted in the late winter or early spring and then removed after the weather warms in favor of the summer crops, which this year were tomatoes, eggplants, carrots, onions, green beans, potatoes, cucumbers, watermelons, zucchinis, summer squashes, cilantro, and basil. After the summer season is finished, either another crop of spinach is planted or a cover crop such as winter rye or clover is sown.

One of the benefits of gardening is that a great deal of kitchen waste can be composted and then returned to the garden as nutrient-dense topsoil. Especially in southeastern Pennsylvania, the topsoil of which has a high clay content, gardening can be challenging as water absorption is difficult. Composting over many seasons has markedly improved the porosity and texture of my garden's topsoil, which has resulted in more vibrant and healthier plants.

The benefits of my garden for promoting biodiversity are legion. The direct benefits are that for a large portion of every year, my garden provides food and shelter for dozens of species of insects, flies, moths, butterflies, bees, birds, and small mammals. In turn, all these creatures provide food for predators and their young. While my garden is certainly not a game changer for the biodiversity of the larger ecosystem, it is nonetheless a small oasis of biodiversity in a suburban ecosystem dominated by Kentucky bluegrass and parking lots, and the food and shelter it provides make a tangible difference to numerous creatures in my area.

There are indirect benefits to biodiversity for my garden as well. Every vegetable bought from the grocery store travels an average of 1,500 miles from producer to consumer, and the energy for almost all these miles comes from burning fossil fuels; every vegetable from my garden travels an average of twenty feet from producer to consumer (unless shared with my neighbors, which might require walking a block or two), and it is fueled by me walking those twenty feet with vegetables in my hands. Plus, every vegetable consumed from my garden results in less demand for industrial agriculture and the many ways in which it is hostile to biodiversity. In an age in which global climate change and industrial agriculture represent two of the most formidable threats to biodiversity worldwide, my garden represents a friendliness to biodiversity that is obvious.

My point here is neither to engage in self-congratulatory backslapping nor to sell gardening as a sine qua non for the promotion of biodiversity. Gardening is simply one way in which I, using the resources and tools at my disposal, can create a small system that supports biodiversity in my area. The more important point is that the 50/50 principle ought to become a mainstay of a properly functioning conscience and something that arises consistently as Catholics attempt to find new and creative ways to sculpt lives that are pleasing to God. To this end, the drivers of biodiversity loss worldwide (global climate change, habitat loss, pollution, invasive species, and overexploitation of species) ought to be a source of regular individual consideration for Catholics as we assess how we unwittingly cause or participate in these drivers of biodiversity loss and the many ways in which our lives and habits can be improved to make our presence more benign to all creatures on Earth.

Only 43 Percent Human, or More Microbe Than Human: From Anthropology to Zoology

Before a baby is baptized and welcomed into the Catholic community, he or she has already undergone a momentous—and highly beneficial!—baptism of microbial biodiversity as his or her gracious welcome to life outside the womb. As an expectant mother's body begins to prepare for the birthing process, her birth canal starts undergoing a dramatic renovation as a veritable explosion of bacteria growth occurs to help her baby get its best start in life, both by exposing the baby to bacteria that create enzymes to help break down breast milk,[94] as well as to myriad other bacteria that protect it against common ailments,[95] which is why babies delivered vaginally compared to those delivered via c-section have lower rates of allergies, asthma, coeliac disease and obesity later in life.[96]

This microbial baptism marking a baby's entrance to life outside the womb is only the beginning of an intimate, symbiotic relationship between the human body and the literally thousands of species of microbes that exist on and in it. As the recently launched Human Microbiome Project (HMP), which involves research at nearly eighty universities and scientific institutions, has shown, the human body has over 10,000 distinct microbial species living in and on our bodies, and in some cases, even inside our cells. These microbes consist of bacteria, viruses, fungi, and archaea and their numbers in and on the human body are simply mind-boggling. While the average human body is comprised of approximately 30 trillion cells, it is also home to microbes that have 39 trillion cells, leading one scientist to note that in terms of cellular composition, we are only 43 percent human![97] In terms of genes, the human body has roughly 20,000 protein-coding genes, while our microbiome has 8 million genes, or 360 times more![98] Indeed, microbes exist in such almost unfathomable numbers in and on our bodies that it might be more accurate to describe ourselves as more microbe than human,[99] with one scientist quipping that each one of us is more aptly described as a zoo than as one distinct human: "Even when we are alone, we are never alone .... When we travel, they come along. When we die, they consume us. Every one of us is a zoo in our own right—a colony enclosed within a single body. A multi-species collective. An entire world."[100]

Yet numbers are not the whole story. Our microbiome is responsible for myriad processes and functions throughout our bodies that are absolutely essential to human health. Our gut microbiome, which has to be resilient enough to survive in one of the harshest environments for life characterized by high acidity and low oxygen, regulates fat storage, activates genes in cells that allow for nutrient absorption, breaks down toxins, and helps create new blood vessels.[101] It also regulates the production of "good" cholesterol, which is linked to heart health, affects the levels of blood sugar in the blood and thereby can help prevent the onset of diabetes, and fosters the production of neurotransmitters that are vital for mental health, especially the alleviation of depression.[102] In addition, our gut microbiome helps break down many of the carbohydrates, lipids, and proteins in the foods we eat and makes available a wide variety of nutrients to our bodies to absorb, as well as producing beneficial compounds like vitamins and anti-inflammatories that our bodies cannot produce on their own.[103]

While scientists are continuing to discover the manifold health effects of our gut microbiome, other areas of our microbiome have been shown to be just as vital to our health and welfare, as they have been linked to a host of different conditions and effects including Parkinson's disease, the effectiveness of cancer drugs, depression and autism,[104] the immune system's response to foreign invaders,[105] improved stress responses, anxiety and depression reduction,[106] breast and prostate cancers, cardiovascular diseases, respiratory and allergic diseases,[107] kidney stones, Alzheimer's disease, strokes, circadian rhythms and sleep cycles,[108] metabolic syndrome, type 2 diabetes, liver disease, high blood pressure, and micro-nutrient deficiency, among others.[109]

While we have known for quite some time that biodiversity within ecosystems is not only an indispensable element of their resilience, adaptability, and fecundity, the extensive catalog of benefits to humans stemming from this biodiversity is breathtaking: water purification, topsoil fertility and health, shelter and building materials, air purification, carbon sequestration, detoxification and decomposition of wastes, climate stabilization, pollination of crops, pest and disease control, nutrient recycling, ecosystem resilience to threats and stresses, moderation of climate extremes, a broad array of medicines and pharmaceuticals, aesthetic and spiritual value, and the joy for biophilic creatures like us living on a planet teeming with interesting and diverse creatures that pique our curiosity and provide abundant opportunities for the exchange of care, affection, and awe.

Yet hundreds of thousands of years after the emergence of modern humans, we are just now discovering that the biodiversity within ecosystems is a reflection of the biodiversity that exists inside our bodies, which is every bit as critical to our health and well-being. As Pope Francis reiterates over and over again in *Laudato Si'*, we are connected to everything in the universe and we are intimately dependent upon the staggering array of symbiotic relationships that nurture our minds and bodies, without which our lives would either be severely impoverished or impossible. Yet the more we look within ourselves, the more we recognize that biodiversity is not simply a feature of ourselves, but it is literally what we are. We are zoos, comprised of thousands of mutually supportive creatures, all with a particular purpose that serves the whole. At the very least, the fact that the daily functioning and maintenance of our bodies are so dependent on thousands of invisible tiny creatures should engender awe and wonder about the mysteriousness, grandiosity, and complexity of creation. Yet it should also create an enormous amount of gratitude in us, not only to God as the author of all life and goodness, but to the innumerable creatures on, in, and around us who make our lives possible. They quietly bless us every day with their presence, make our lives possible, and allow us to realize all the goods that give our lives meaning and purpose—and for these myriad blessings, we ought to be enormously grateful.

Yet this only begins to broach the value of biodiversity on Earth. While biodiversity is obviously highly beneficial to humans, it is also highly valuable to God. Part of Pope Francis's agenda in *Laudato Si'* is to circumscribe the anthropocentrism that has dominated Catholic theology for millennia and to chart a new theological course that is more theocentric in structure and content. This long-standing anthropocentrism has resulted in theological speculation reaching ever greater heights of self-absorbed navel gazing. Elizabeth Johnson summarizes this trajectory well: "[O]ver the centuries … theology narrowed its interests to focus on human beings almost exclusively. Our special identities, capacities, roles, sinfulness, and need for salvation became the all-consuming interest. The result was a powerful anthropocentric paradigm in theology that shaped every aspect of endeavor."[110] According to Johnson, Christology was cast as good news for humans, while the biblical theme of cosmic redemption was conveniently overlooked, and a theology of creation relegated nature to the status of an unimportant backdrop for the grand divine–human interaction. As a result, "Theology lost touch with the universe."[111]

Fortunately, this self-obsession and accompanying constriction of the Catholic theological imagination has begun to wane recently, as many have begun to question the validity of this trajectory. The United States Conference of Catholic Bishops has called for a *"God-centered and sacramental view of the universe"*[112] that rejects the assertion that nature is merely a repository of resources for humans to use and affirms that the enormous biodiversity found on Earth not only "manifests God's glory" but is also "part of the divine plan."[113] Similarly, the Catholic bishops of Alberta, Canada, also promote a sacramental view of the universe that recognizes that God is revealed through "the dynamic life forces of our universe" and decry the current loss of biodiversity as "an affront to the Creator."[114] The Canadian Conference of Catholic Bishops claim that nature is "a continuing revelation of the divine" and that theological speculation must acknowledge that humans are a part of a "vast community of life on Earth" that gives glory to God.[115] The Catholic Bishops of the Columbia River Watershed claim that "mountains and valleys, forests and meadows, [and] rivers and plains reflect the presence of their Creator,"[116] that God is lovingly concerned about all creation,[117] and that God sent Christ "to reconcile all things … whether those on earth or those in heaven."[118] The comfortable anthropocentrism that has functioned as the unquestioned and implicit background of theological speculation for millennia has begun to unravel, which in turn has allowed theologians to begin articulating and defending larger goods such as biodiversity, which is the sine qua non for the health of ecosystems, oceans, and our entire planet.

This ongoing expansion of the theological frontier beyond an anthropocentrism that locates value and meaning in creation only to the extent that it satisfies human interests opens a door to a foundational theological question. Prescinding entirely from the benefits that biodiversity provides to humans, Would God prefer an Earth with abundant biodiversity compared to one with very little to no biodiversity? To this question, I offer an emphatic "Yes!" Perhaps the most widely shared sentiment in Scripture is the fact that God is a relational being, meaning that God delights in forging relationships, becoming intertwined in the history of individuals and peoples, showering God's creation with love and grace, communicating the divine life in a way that is understandable to the recipient, drawing close in times of trauma and need, and feeling a wide array of emotions, both positive and negative, as God's creatures suffer, experience happiness and contentment, and strive to attain the ends for which they have been created. To be sure, most Catholics are familiar with the ways in which God's relationality has been directed toward humans, but each of these statements is equally applicable to God's relationships with non-human creatures as well.

Take, for instance, God's relationship with animals in the Old Testament. In the book of Job, which is probably the oldest book in the Old Testament, God appears a bit smitten by two mythical figures, Behemoth and Leviathan (Job 39-41). God waxes eloquently about Behemoth's strong loins, powerful muscles, a tail as stiff as a cedar tree's trunk, bulging sinews in his thighs, and bones as hard as iron. God concludes the effusive praise of Behemoth by declaring him the "masterpiece of all God's work" (Job. 40:19)—high praise, indeed! God's accolades for Leviathan are just as forthcoming as his praise of Behemoth, but mostly because of Leviathan's wildness and his inability to be tamed or controlled by humans. God notes that the common ways to capture and domesticate large wild animals are laughable to Leviathan, as his ferocity, strength, and tenacity make it impossible: "Any hopes you might have [to tame Leviathan] would prove vain, for the mere sight of him would stagger you" (Job. 41:1). Leviathan's fearsomeness has "no equal on earth"—he represents wildness and savagery, a force so completely beyond human control that avoidance is the only reasonable strategy for dealing with him. God is not simply proud of Behemoth and Leviathan—God is rapturous about their superlative strength, independence, and fierceness.

Yet God's admiration and care for animals in the Old Testament is not confined to grandiose and fearsome specimens. God feeds all the animals (Ps. 147:9), mandates rest for beasts of burden (Ex. 20:10 and 23:12, Deut. 5:14), knows all animals and they all belong to God (Ps. 50:10-11), accepts praise from sea creatures (Ps. 148:7), requires care for a sick or injured animal (Deut. 22:4), holds the lives of animals in God's hand (Job 12:10), satisfies the desires of every living thing (Ps. 145:15-16), establishes a covenant with beasts, birds, and creeping things (Hosea 2:18), saves both humans and beasts (Ps. 36:6), uses animals as a way to teach humans (Prov.

6:6–8 and Job 12:7), directs mercy to animals (Ps. 145:9), and is preparing a peaceable kingdom in which all animals will flourish (Is. 11:6).

This affection and care extend into the New Testament as well, where God feeds the birds of the air (Matt. 6:26 and Luke 12:24), knows the plight of all lowly creatures (Matt. 10:29), saves all creatures and brings them into God's inner life (Luke 3:6), forgets not even the lowliest of creatures (Luke 12:6), mandates mercy for suffering animals (Luke 14:5), and sets all of creation free, including animals, from bondage and corruption (Romans 8:19–21).

Given the deep relationality of God and God's love for all creatures, it is quite easy to imagine why God chose to create a planet that over time has come to produce a staggering array of creatures. As a being whose nature is to love and to be in relationship, God prefers to create a universe in which a prodigious number of lifeforms emerge, which can be showered by divine love and experience the goodness of life, and for those creatures capable of responding consciously to these divine promptings, to return that love in gratitude and reciprocal love. Divine love is an endless, overflowing cup, and a planet that is teeming with creatures capable of receiving and basking in this divine love is far preferable to one that is devoid of life and has no possibility of receiving and enjoying the divine love.

Strictly from God's perspective, a universe bursting with biodiversity has to be more enjoyable to God, as it presents more extensive and fertile relational possibilities to God. We humans know this deep-seated relational impulse quite well, as we are naturally geared to bond with a wide range of humans and animals, to appreciate their companionship and friendliness, and to enter into relationships of mutual care and concern. Moreover, as relational beings, too, our natural inclinations prompt us to pursue many different kinds of relationships with many kinds of creatures, from pair bonding, to intimate and lifelong friendships, to more casual friendships, to a wide variety of inter-species relationships with both wild and domesticated animals. Indeed, some of the most satisfying and life-giving relationships occur between humans and our beloved pets, in which we experience something akin to unconditional love and devotion from them. We humans are not only related to and dependent upon a number of symbiotic relationships with other creatures, as Pope Francis reiterates in *Laudato Si'*, but our purpose and meaning in life, in addition to our quality of life, is often directly contingent upon a wide array of relationships with humans and animals.

Just as our relational inclinations cause us to prefer environments in which biodiversity is abundant, so too God vastly prefers a universe in which relational possibilities abound and opportunities for giving and receiving love exist everywhere, from microorganisms that occupy our microbiome or caverns deep underground, to the largest megafauna roaming our planet's vast plains, to denizens of our marvelously biodiverse rain forests, to fishes and whales and dolphins who glide effortlessly through our vast oceans, to the wide variety of humans that exist in virtually every ecosystem on Earth. For God, a planet teeming with life and relational possibilities has to be one of the most satisfying things that can be experienced as it offers almost unlimited possibilities for God to shower creatures with love, care, and mercy and to bask in contentment as creatures enjoy their lives, fulfill their purpose in the universe, and sometimes return God's love with heartfelt gratitude.

This is why putting the 50/50 principle front and center on our moral radar screen is paramount to the Catholic moral identity, as it is one of the surest ways to guarantee that biodiversity continues to flourish on our planet. As the only planet in the universe known to contain life, Earth is the crown jewel of creation, presenting unnumerable possibilities for God's love to be given and received gratefully by creatures great and small. For our part, it behooves us who control the fate of life and biodiversity on Earth to align ourselves with God's wishes that our bountiful planet continue to produce prodigious amounts of biodiversity and to offer new heights of relational possibilities to God. Doing so would not only be one of the grandest things that we humans could achieve, but it would also be a significant move toward the Kingdom of God becoming more palpable in our world—and this would be reason for hearty celebration!

Notes

1.   Some Christian anthropocentrists would object to this statement and point out that they are explicitly theocentrists and thus committed to serving God and to ordering creation according to God's wishes, but it just so happens that God has given creation over to humans to protect, nurture, and cultivate according to our needs and desires, so

theocentrism, when properly understood, entails that only human interests be given consideration in moral decision-making (or whenever there are unavoidable conflicts between human and non-human interests, the former are always given priority). Theologians such as James Gustafson, Rosemary Radford Ruether, and Ivone Gebara, on the contrary, eschew this tight link between theocentrism and anthropocentrism and spend considerable energy explaining the marked discontinuity between the two.

2. Pope John Paul II, *Laborem Exercens*, #4; Pope John Paul II, *Sollicitudo Rei Socialis*, #29.

3. Pope John Paul II, *Sollicitudo Rei Socialis*, #29.

4. Pope John Paul II, *Redemptor Hominis*, #14.

5. Pope John Paul II, *Redemptor Hominis*, #16.

6. Pope John Paul II, *Sollicitudo Rei Socialis*, #29.

7. Pope John Paul II, *Sollicitudo Rei Socialis*, #34.

8. Wisdom 9:1, 2–3 and Psalms 8:6–8.

9. Pope John Paul II, *Evangelium Vitae*, #34.

10. Pope John Paul II, "The Ecological Crisis: A Common Responsibility," (January 1, 1990), #3, http://w2.vatican.va/content/john-paul-ii/en/messages/peace/documents/hf_jp-ii_mes_19891208_xxiii-world-day-for-peace.html (accessed November 27, 2025).

11. Pope John Paul II, "The Ecological Crisis," #7.

12. Pope John Paul II, "The Ecological Crisis," #8, quoting the Second Vatican Council's *Gaudium et Spes*, #69.

13. Pope John Paul II, "The Ecological Crisis," #9.

14. Pope John Paul, *Evangelium Vitae*, #52–67.

15. Pope John Paul II, *Evangelium Vitae*, #10.

16. Pope John Paul II, *Evangelium Vitae*, #11.

17. Pope John Paul II, *Evangelium Vitae*, #12.

18. Pope John Paul II, *Evangelium Vitae*, #14.

19. Pope Benedict XVI, "Message for the Celebration of the World Day of Peace," #6.

20. One wonders, then, whether simple "domination" is acceptable to Pope Benedict XVI, and what kind of policies or behaviors would be consistent with this domination?

21. Pope Benedict, "Message for the Celebration of World Day of Peace," #6.

22. Pope Benedict, "Message for the Celebration of World Day of Peace," #10–13.

23. Pope Benedict, "Message for the Celebration of World Day of Peace," #7.

24. Pope Benedict, "Message for the Celebration of World Day of Peace," #8.

25. Pope Francis, *Laudato Si'*, #10-11.

26. Pope Francis, *Laudato Si'*, #67.

27. Pope Francis, *Laudato Si'*, #67.

28. Pope Francis, *Laudato Si'*, #116.

29. Pope Francis, *Laudato Si'*, #69, citing the *Catechism of the Catholic Church*, 2416.

30. Pope Francis, *Laudato Si'*, #84

31. Pope Francis, *Laudato Si'*, #115.

32. Pope Francis, *Laudato Si'*, #116.

33. Pope Francis, *Laudato Si'*, #122.

34. Pope Francis, *Laudato Si'*, #123.

35. Pope Francis, *Laudato Si'*, #130.

36. Pope Francis, *Laudato Si'*, #95.

37. Pope Francis, *Laudato Si'*, #130.

38. Pope Francis, *Laudato Si'*, #156-7.

39. Pope Francis, *Misericordia et Misera* (November 20, 2016), http://w2.vatican.va/content/francesco/en/apost_letters/documents/papa-francesco-lettera-ap_20161120_misericordia-et-misera.pdf (accessed November 27, 2025).

40. See, for instance, chapter two of James Gustafson's, *Ethics from a Theocentric Perspective*, vol. 1, *Theology and Ethics*.

41. Pope Francis, *Laudato Si'*, #11.

42. Pope Francis, *Laudato Si'*, #11.

43. Val Plumwood, *Feminism and the Mastery of Nature* (New York: Routledge, 1993).

44. See also Mark 12:28-31 and Luke 10:25-28

45. Major figures in this discussion are the following: Anders Nygren, *Agape and Eros*, trans. Philip S. Watson (Philadelphia: Westminster, 1953); and Gene H. Outka, *Agape: An Ethical Analysis* (New Haven, CT: Yale University Press, 1972). Edward Collins Vacek, *Love, Human and Divine: The Heart of Christian Ethics* (Washington, DC: Georgetown University Press, 1994) is the notable exception to this, claiming that non-human creation is a legitimate object of love.

46. Pope Francis, *Laudato Si'*, #69.

47. Denis Edwards, "Earth as God's Creation: The Theology of the Natural World in Pope Francis's *Laudato Si*," *Phronema* 31 (2) (2016): 6.

48. Pope Francis, *Laudato Si'*, #88.

49. Pope Francis, *Laudato Si'*, #83.

50. Pope Francis, *Laudato Si'*, #243.

51. Pope Francis, *Laudato Si'*, #77.

52. For a depiction of the tenderness of Jesus toward creatures, see Pope Francis, *Laudate Deum* (October 4, 2023), #1, https://www.vatican.va/content/francesco/en/apost_exhortations/documents/20231004-laudate-deum.html (accessed November 27, 2025).

53. Denis Edwards, "'Sublime Communion': The Theology of the Natural World in *Laudato Si'*," *Theological Studies* 77 (2) (2016): 382-3.

54. Mary A. Ashley, "In Communion with God's Sparrow: Incorporating Animal Agency into the Environmental Vision of Laudato Sí," *Sophia* 57 (2018): 105.

55. Pope Francis, *Laudato Si'*, #246.

56. Pope Francis, *Laudato Si'*, #140.

57. Secretariat of the Convention of Biological Diversity, *Sustaining Life on Earth: How the Convention on Biological Diversity promotes nature and human well-being* (Switzerland: United Nations Environment Programme, 2000), 3-6, https://www.cbd.int/doc/publications/cbd-sustain-en.pdf (accessed November 27, 2025).

58. Pope Francis, *Laudato Si'*, #12.

59. Pope Francis, *Laudato Si'*, #86.

60. Pope Francis, *Querida Amazonia* (February 2, 2020), #48, https://press.vatican.va/content/salastampa/en/bollettino/pubblico/2020/02/12/200212c.html (accessed November 27, 2025).

61. Pope Francis, *Laudato Si'*, #33.

62. Pope Francis, *Querida Amazonia*, #51.

63. Ibid., #48, 52.

64. Pope Francis, *Laudato Si'*, #41.

65. Pope Francis, *Laudato Si'*, #34.

66. For an insightful analysis of a Catholic notion of the planetary common good, which closely parallels what Pope Francis does with biodiversity in *Laudato Si'*, see Daniel P. Scheid, *The Cosmic Common Good: Religious Grounds for Ecological Ethics* (New York: Oxford University Press, 2016), chap. 2.

67. Pope Francis, *Laudato Si'*, #156-8.

68. Pope Francis, *Laudato Si'*, #160.

69. Pope Francis, *Laudato Si'*, #220-32.

70. The 50/50 principle is borrowed in part from Edward O. Wilson, *Half-Earth: Our Planet's Fight for Life* (New York: Liveright, 2016).

71. Pope Francis, *Laudato Si'*, #89.

72. Elizabeth Kolbert, *The Sixth Extinction* (New York: Picador, 2014), 8.

73. The ecological footprint measures the pace at which we consume resources and generate wastes, compared to the ability of nature to

regenerate new resources and absorb our wastes. To measure your personal ecological footprint, visit one of the following sites: https://www.footprintcalculator.org; https://www.footprintnetwork.org/resources/footprint-calculator; https://ecological-footprint-calculator.climatehero.org; or https://www.epa.gov/ghgemissions/carbon-footprint-calculator (all accessed December 24, 2025).

74. Alessandro Galli, David Lin, Mathis Wackernagel, Michel Gressot, and Sebastian Winkler, "Humanity's Growing Ecological Footprint: Sustainable Development Implications," 2, https://sustainabledevelopment.un.org/content/documents/5686humanitysgrowingecologicalfootprint.pdf (accessed November 27, 2025).

75. United Nations, Department of Economic and Social Affairs, Population Division, *World Population Prospects 2019: Highlights* (New York: United Nations, 2019), 5.

76. Galli, et al., "Humanity's Growing Ecological Footprint," 1.

77. Yinon M. Bar-On, Rob Philips, and Ron Milo, "The biomass distribution on Earth," *Proceedings of the National Academy of Sciences of the United States of America* 115 (25) (2018): 6508.

78. Oceana, "Too Few Fish: A Regional Assessment of the World's Fisheries," https://oceana.org/wp-content/uploads/sites/18/toofewfish41.pdf (accessed December 24, 2025).

79. Richard A. Leakey and Roger Lewin, *The Sixth Extinction: Patterns of Life and the Future of Humankind* (New York: Anchor Books, 1996).

80. International Union for the Conservation of Nature, "*State of the World's Amphibians: The Second Global Amphibian Assessment*" (2023), https://nc.iucnredlist.org/redlist/resources/files/1696400756-SOTWA_GAA2_04Oct2023.pdf (accessed November 27, 2025).

81. Jurriaan M. De Vos, Lucas N. Joppa, John L. Gittleman, Patrick R. Stephens, and Stuart L. Pimm, "Estimating the Normal Rate of Background Extinction," *Conservation Biology* 29 (2) (2014): 452–62.

82. Tim Swanson and Ben Groom, "Regulating global biodiversity: what is the problem?" *Oxford Review of Economic Policy* 28 (1) (2012): 115–16.

83. Secretariat of the Convention on Biological Diversity, *Convention on Biological Diversity* (Montreal: United Nations Environmental Programme, 2011), 4, https://www.cbd.int/doc/legal/cbd-en.pdf (accessed Novermber 27, 2025).

84. Secretariat of the Convention on Biological Diversity, *Convention on Biological Diversity*, 7–8.

85. Conference of the Parties to the Convention on Biological Diversity, 15th Meeting, "Kunming-Montreal Global Biodiversity Framework," (Dec. 2022), 8, https://www.cbd.int/doc/c/e6d3/cd1d/

daf663719a03902a9b116c34/cop-15-l-25-en.pdf (accessed November 27, 2025).

86. Conference of the Parties to the Convention on Biological Diversity, "Kunming-Montreal Global Biodiversity Framework," 9-11.

87. *Global Biodiversity Outlook 2*, 14.

88. United States Environmental Protection Agency, "Global Greenhouse Gas Emissions Data," https://www.epa.gov/ghgemissions/global-greenhouse-gas-emissions-data#Sector (accessed November 27, 2025).

89. Robert Goodland and Jeff Anhang, *World Watch Magazine* 22 (6) (Nov./Dec. 2009) 10-19.

90. Mark Graham, *Sustainable Agriculture: A Christian Ethic of Gratitude* (Cleveland: Pilgrim Press, 2005), and Mark Graham, "The Unsavory Gamble of Industrial Agriculture," in *Just Sustainability: Technology, Ecology, and Resource Extraction*, eds. Christiana Z. Peppard and Andrea Vicini (Maryknoll: Orbis Books, 2015), 105-16.

91. E. F. Schumacher, *Small is Beautiful: Economics as if People Mattered* (New York: Harper Perennial, 2010).

92. Food and Agriculture Organization of the United Nations, *The State of Food and Agriculture, 2012*, https://www.fao.org/3/i3028e/i3028e00.htm (accessed November 27, 2025).

93. Annu Ratta and Jac Smith, "Urban Agriculture: It's About Much More Than Food," *WHY Magazine* 13 (1993): 26-9; Catherine Murphy, *Cultivating Havana: Urban Agriculture and Food Security in the Years of Crisis* (Oakland, CA: Food First, 1999), 1-4; and Lauren Baker and Jin Huh, "Rich Harvest," *Alternatives Journal* 29 (2003): 21-5.

94. Steven A. Edwards, "Our bodies as ecosystems," *American Association for the Advancement of Science*, (November 29, 2012), https://www.aaas.org/taxonomy/term/10/our-bodies-ecosystems (accessed November 27, 2025).

95. National Institutes of Health, "NIH Human Microbiome Project defines normal bacterial makeup of the body," (June 13, 2012), https://www.genome.gov/27549144/2012-release-nih-human-microbiome-project-defines-normal-bacterial-makeup-of-the-body (accessed December 24, 2025).

96. Mun-Keat Looi, "The human microbiome: Everything you need to know about the 39 trillion microbes that call our bodies home," *BBC Science Focus Magazine* (July 14, 2020), https://www.sciencefocus.com/the-human-body/human-microbiome (accessed November 27, 2025).

97. Elizabeth Lee, "We're Only About 43% Human, Study Shows," *VOA News* (May 26, 2019), https://www.voanews.com/a/research-estimates-

we-are-only-about-43-percent-human/4932876.html (accessed November 27, 2025).

98. NIH, "NIH Human Microbiome Project defines normal bacterial makeup of the body."

99. James Gallagher, "More than half your body is not human," *BBC* (April 9, 2018), https://www.bbc.com/news/health-43674270 (accessed November 27, 2025).

100. Ed Yong, "I Contain Multitudes," *BBC Science Focus Magazine* (August 3, 2017), https://www.sciencefocus.com/nature/i-contain-multitudes-by-ed-yong (accessed November 27, 2025).

101. Looi, "The human microbiome."

102. Ruairi Robertson, "How Does Your Gut Microbiome Impact Your Overall Health?" *Healthline* (January 19, 2022), https://www.healthline.com/nutrition/gut-microbiome-and-health (accessed November 27, 2025).

103. NiH, "NIH Human Microbiome Project defines normal bacterial makeup of the body."

104. Gallagher, "More than half your body is not human."

105. Rob Stein, "Finally, A Map of All the Microbes on Your Body," *National Public Radio Online* (June 13, 2012), https://www.npr.org/sections/health-shots/2012/06/13/154913334/finally-a-map-of-all-the-microbes-on-your-body (accessed November 27, 2025).

106. Simon Crompton, "Psychobiotics: Your microbiome has the potential to improve your mental health, not just your gut health," *BBC Science Focus Magazine* (November 21, 2019), https://www.sciencefocus.com/the-human-body/psychobiotics-your-microbiome-has-the-potential-to-improve-your-mental-health-not-just-your-gut-heath (accessed November 27, 2025).

107. Grace A. Ogunrinola, John O. Oyewale, Oyewumi O. Oshamika, and Grace I. Olasehinde, "The Human Microbiome and Its Impacts on Health," *International Journal of Microbiology* (June 12, 2020), https://www.ncbi.nlm.nih.gov/pmc/articles/PMC7306068 (accessed November 27, 2025).

108. Matt Wood, "How the microbiome affects human health, explained," *University of Chicago News* (n.d.), https://news.uchicago.edu/explainer/how-microbiome-affects-human-health-explained#health (accessed November 27, 2025).

109. Igor Spivak, Leviel Fluhr, and Eran Elinav, "Local and systemic effects of microbiome-derived metabolites," (August 29, 2022), https://www.embopress.org/doi/full/10.15252/embr.202255664 (accessed November 27, 2025).

110. Elizabeth A. Johnson, *Ask the Beasts: Darwin and the God of Love* (New York: Bloomsbury, 2015), 2.
111. Johnson, *Ask the Beasts*, 3.
112. USCCB, *Renewing the Earth*, III. Catholic Social Teaching and Environmental Ethics, italics in original.
113. USCCB, *Renewing the Earth*, B. Respect for Life.
114. Bishops of Alberta, Canada, "Celebrate Life: Care for Creation," (October 4, 1998), 3, http://faculty.theo.mu.edu/schaefer/ChurchonEcologicalDegradation/documents/CelebrateLifeCareforCreation-Alberta_000.pdf (accessed November 27, 2025).
115. Canadian Conference of Catholic Bishops, "You Love All That Exists … All Things Are Yours, God, Lover of Life," 1.
116. Catholic Bishops of the Northwest, *Columbia River Watershed*, 1.
117. Catholic Bishops of the Northwest, *Columbia River Watershed*, 7.
118. Catholic Bishops of the Northwest, *Columbia River Watershed*, 9, quoting Colossians 1:20.

4

Go Ahead, Love Beaver Creek! Emotions and Catholic Environmentalism

Nobody outside of southeastern Pennsylvania has probably heard of the nondescript Beaver Creek, but it assumed mythological status in my kids' minds when they were young. Beaver Creek originates from an underground water source several miles northwest of Downingtown, Pennsylvania and meanders through several farm ponds and around a number of suburban subdivisions before depositing its waters into the wider and deeper Brandywine Creek, a local favorite of canoers and kayakers and weekend warriors, particularly of the drinking variety.

Beaver Creek wraps around the outskirts of our subdivision, never more than a two-minute walk away from our house, constantly reminding us of its presence with a towering canopy of sycamore and oak trees shading its waters and establishing a definite boundary between the creek and the well-manicured lawns that adorn our subdivision. Beaver Creek's formidable canopy can be seen from anywhere over the tops of the houses and moving physically from the ordered and controlled world of suburban lawns of Kentucky bluegrass and ornamental shrubbery into the brushy, dense, prickly, shaded, and semi-wild confines of Beaver Creek is like stepping into an alternative dimension. Much like approaching and stepping into a cathedral, entering the confines of Beaver Creek gives one the impression of entering sacred space, in which the usual rules of relating are suspended and give way to something mysterious and magical.

From the time my kids, Peter and Hannah (now 23 and 22, respectively), could walk, Beaver Creek was one of their favorite destinations. Quick one-on-one trips with dad were mainstays on weekdays after work when leisure time or sunlight was limited, but weekends presented the opportunity for lengthier forays to Beaver Creek and almost infinite possibilities for exploration. I can still remember vividly their typical response when asked on a lazy weekend morning whether they would like to "wade the creek" that afternoon, and the instantaneous explosion of glee as they would reply in unison, "Yes! Yes!! Yes!!!" while jumping up and down excitedly. So we would locate some old tee shirts and shorts, don our favorite wading shoes (usually raggedy, worn-out tennis shoes), and proceed to round up a few of their neighborhood friends. I always told their parents that their kids would assuredly come home quite dirty and perhaps a little bit bloody, but I guaranteed that they would come home alive. Even aware of such risks, their parents were always eager to escort them out the door for a Beaver Creek adventure (sometimes with relieved smiles on their faces!). So with the excitable menagerie in tow, off we would head to the creek.

Their enthusiasm always overflowed on the walk there, and soon one of them would break ranks in an effort to get to the creek first, and the others would immediately burst into a sprint in order not to be left behind. Before long, each one would have jumped into the creek and begun splashing and laughing wildly, in a burst of energy unique to young kids—always with unmitigated expressions of joy on their faces. As a parent, seeing such delight on the faces of babes was perhaps the closest thing to the beatific vision for me on this side of the divide, and I still marvel at my fortune of being able to witness first-hand such pure joy.

No trip to Beaver Creek was ever the same, and there was never a plan or objective once we arrived. We simply explored at our own pace, lost track of time, and followed whatever prompted us in the moment. Sometimes this meant finding shiny rocks as we meandered down the middle of the stream and enjoyed the sight of tiny minnows scattering into the shallows to avoid the rambunctious energy headed their way. Other times it consisted in throwing rocks into the soft claylike mud of the creek's banks or trying to sink sticks thrown into the water for target practice, which sometimes mysteriously transformed into battleships and submarines that could do significant damage to the US naval fleet unless sunk by a well-placed rock thrown by one of the kids. Sometimes it shifted into an investigative mode, and the kids slowed down and started paying attention to the flora and fauna surrounding the creek and learned to identify objects of interest. Often it resulted in oohs and aahs as we encountered many of the gloriously colored dragonflies and damselflies that populated the vegetation hanging over the creek's edge. Sometimes it involved scouring the shoreline for animal tracks, and the kids quickly became adept at identifying a number of different tracks. Occasionally, we found some rare gem: a snakeskin that had been shed; a stunning rainbow trout that shared its beauty momentarily before heading into deeper water; a patch of flowers that took one's breath away. Almost always it resulted in a lengthy stop at the "swimming hole," which was deep enough to allow the kids to be completely submerged under water, and wide enough to accommodate all the kids simultaneously, so the swimming hole was perfect venue for slowing down, cooling off, and gliding under water and checking out the schools of fish that called the swimming hole home. Always there was splashing, laughing, curiosity, coolness, exploration, wonder, awe, excitement, relaxation, contentment, and that almost indescribable joy that can only be had in nature.

Beaver Creek also found its way into Pete's preschool lore. While wading the creek one sunny weekend, Pete had wandered ahead of the group and was the first to round a sharp bend. Out of the blue he started screaming, "Dad, a baby cardinal is drowning!" The rest of the kids and I broke into a mad dash, rounded the corner, saw Pete standing near the edge of the creek looking into his cupped hands, with an irritated female cardinal chirping excitedly at him a few feet away. As we approached Pete, he opened his hands and, sure enough, there was a nearly bald cardinal chick in his hands, shivering and looking bewildered. Pete explained that as he rounded the bend he came upon the cardinal, which had apparently fallen out of its nest into the water and was being pushed by the current up against a log jam and was flailing wildly as it kept getting pulled under the water. So Pete scrambled over, scooped it out of the water, and proceeded to incur the wrath of its mother. We began searching upstream and within minutes found what appeared to be a cardinal's nest in a dense shrub overhanging the water and Pete returned the cardinal to its home. "Nice job, buddy," I said to Pete as I ruffled his hair and the other kids sighed in relief. "You saved that baby cardinal!"

The next day at preschool Pete drew a picture about his rescue mission and relayed the story to his classmates during show-and-tell. According to Pete, his fellow preschoolers were awed (but not surprised!) by his bravery and smitten by his kindness to animals, and he quickly assumed the status of a young Steve Irwin, the famed "Crocodile Hunter" and animal rescuer, among them. A note later that week from one of his teachers confirmed that Pete's classmates were duly impressed by his animal-saving skills and now considered him the local authority on all fauna needing assistance.

As my kids grew older and became teenagers, their relationship to Beaver Creek changed, and while wading the creek no longer possesses the allure it once did, Beaver Creek still beckons them back regularly. Pete enjoys going there on the weekends, meeting a friend in the early morning mist to stalk wily rainbow trout, and his eyes always seem to dance when he returns from a fishing trip. Sometimes he even humors his dad by showing me his advanced fishing techniques and the secret lairs he has discovered where big trout hide! Hannah also heads back to the creek on occasion, almost always with me, sometimes to plant wildflowers or milkweeds, sometimes just to bond with me, sometimes to wander aimlessly and to discover something new, and sometimes to capture our photogenic local red fox, whose predictable habits make him a fantastic subject for a budding nature photographer.

Beaver Creek is like a treasured friend to me, and I owe an enormous debt of gratitude to its welcoming waters for all the joy it has brought into my kids' lives. I appreciate Beaver Creek being almost a perfect venue for children to explore the grandiosity of nature, as it presents a cornucopia of delights to the senses and abundant opportunities for play and recreation that are not part and parcel of more human contrived environments, while not presenting genuine dangers that might require extreme parental vigilance in order to keep the little ones safe. This is part of Beaver Creek's allure. While my kids certainly enjoyed many excursions to city parks in our area and the opportunity to run around and burn off their abundant energy, city parks are highly contrived environments that bear a human imprint all the way down. Beaver Creek, although certainly affected by human activities, is not designed as a recreation area, and thus bears the mark of wildness to a greater degree—and this extra bit of wildness is very good for kids. From the poison ivy that seems to lurk everywhere, to the nettles that threaten to prick sensitive skin out of nowhere, to sharp and slippery rocks and wasps and hornets and unstable banks, Beaver Creek presents challenges and potential frustrations that are anathema in settings designed for high-volume human activity. Nonetheless, this added bit of wildness forms part of Beaver Creek's allure, and while my kids would often feel tired after a trip to a city park, after a trip to Beaver Creek they were just as equally tired and yet also more deeply satisfied. Not like the satisfaction of a hearty meal or a job well done, but the satisfaction of being fully alive and basking in the joy that only nature can provide.

I would be remiss, however, if I did not admit my own affection for Beaver Creek, outside of the joy it has brought to my kids. I was born during a time when the cult of child safety had not scared parents into thinking that monsters, human or otherwise, lurked behind every tree, and the phrase "helicopter parents" had not yet emerged in popular nomenclature. Indeed, I, like most kids of my generation, enjoyed an abundant amount of freedom and unstructured time, and was expected to entertain myself when not in school. As a result, I spent an inordinate amount of time exploring the natural wonders in and around my small Midwestern hometown, from farm ponds containing fat bluegills and leeches galore, to the local river containing prized walleyes and smallmouth bass, to meandering hiking trails along creeks and through woodlots, to nature preserves that had been turned back to native tallgrass prairie, to wetlands and sloughs that contained an astonishing array of bird life, to oak savannas and the refreshing coolness they always provided during the hot summer months. Amidst a sea of corn and soybeans that dominated the Iowa landscape, pockets of nature abounded that begged an outdoor aficionado to explore and savor, and whenever I was not in school or playing organized sports, I heeded that call and from a very young age developed an abiding affection for those areas that quenched my thirst for nature.

Beaver Creek, then, evoked all those pleasant emotions of childhood and quickly became one of my favorite local nature haunts after moving into our subdivision. My solitary activities at Beaver Creek ranged from chasing skittish trout, to nature photography, to prayer and meditation, to simply meandering through the trees lining its banks and soaking up the sights and sounds. It was also where I first introduced an elderly rescue dog to a creek, and I will never forget either his initial look of trepidation as I led him to the creek's edge or his eventual look of exquisite satisfaction and he gingerly walked to the middle of the creek and laid down, letting the water flow over his entire body. Beaver Creek was also the site of my attempt to assess whether Roxy, our orange tabby cat, had the makings of an Appalachian Trail hiking companion. Needless to say, the attempt was abject failure, and since then Roxy is quite content to spend her time basking in the sun and keeping an eye out for small rodents rather than hiking with me! For me, Beaver Creek is a friend and a lover, an escape, a reliable source of stimulation and comfort, a glorious display of beauty, and a manifestation of the divine, all rolled into one.

In my opinion, the greatest benefit of my kids' many forays to Beaver Creek was that such contact created a bond of affection and gratitude that will remain with them forever. To be sure, my kids were outdoor aficionados from the very beginning and enjoyed a steady diet of nature adventures while growing up, and there are a number of local places that they remember with fondness. But Beaver Creek was always "the one" for them, as it was a place that not only provided innumerable joyful hours recreating, exploring, and relaxing along its banks, but also because there is an intense bond of intimacy and love that my kids feel for Beaver Creek. They are passionately attached to Beaver Creek and they are fervently committed to preserving it and making sure that its receptive waters are able to caress the bare feet of many generations of kids to come. Like enthusiastic lovers, their affectivity has been fully engaged and directed toward the flourishing of their beloved Beaver Creek, and they would be devastated if it were ever rerouted or replaced by a suburban subdivision or a strip mall or a Wal Mart parking lot.

I recently asked my kids to use single words to describe their experiences at Beaver Creek when they were younger, and to rank the intensity on a scale of 1-10, with 1 being the lowest and 10 being the highest. Here are the results for each, in decreasing order of intensity:

Table 4.1 Beaver Creek Experience Table

Pete	Hannah
Freedom—10	Joy—10
Inspiration—9	Interest—10
Love—8	Love—9
Bravery—7	Refreshing—9
Joy—6	Thankful—9
Pride—4	Awe—8
	Liberated—8
	Gratitude—7
	Peaceful—7

Please keep in mind that data such as these often belie important observations, such as a dad witnessing the smiles, glimmering eyes, and excitement of his kids when discussing and mentally reliving adventures at Beaver Creek years after the fact, even though these observations are highly subjective and do not lead to any objectively supportable judgments. A few notable considerations emerge from these data. First, everything listed was positive, if not highly positive, despite an occasional negative experience at Beaver Creek: a brush with poison ivy or nettles; stubbed toes; cuts and scratches; mud in the eye; and tripping and falling on slippery rocks. Despite the predictable bumps and bruises and adversity, the important memories that characterize my kids' experience of Beaver Creek when they were younger are uniformly positive. Second, these experiences are emotionally laden. Indeed, each word describing their experience is either an emotion or something that is easily connected to an emotion. For my kids, meaningful experiences at Beaver Creek that get stored and later recalled are felt, and often deeply. Third, love and joy are common elements on Pete's and Hannah's list, but the remainder of their lists are different (although if they clarified exactly what is meant by each term, more overlap might emerge). Pete's list contains an action component, insofar as he mentions bravery and pride, which indicate some obstacle or subjective fear that is overcome and followed by a sense of accomplishment. Hannah's list, on the other hand, has a marked element of being captivated (awe and interest) by her experiences at Beaver Creek and then a certain kind of basking in and feeling grateful for those experiences (peaceful, refreshing and liberated; and thankful and grateful, respectively). Thus while certain emotions such as love and joy might appear as common reactions to their forays to Beaver Creek, Pete and Hannah valued different aspects of their experiences there, yet each still treasured their time spent at Beaver Creek. Fourth, and finally, I think their reactions to their Beaver Creek excursions are about as emotionally evocative and multifaceted as it is possible to imagine for my kids, outside of something akin to a near-death experience. I can think of many seminal events in their young lives that many teenagers and young adults would consider to be suffuse with positive emotions—athletic championships, academic accomplishments, getting a driver's license, family vacations, friendships, proms, dating, getting into college—and yet, given what I know about Pete and Hannah, I can say without hesitation that their experiences at Beaver Creek still stand unparalleled for them in terms of providing a richness and a sense of meaningfulness to their lives. The kind of persons my kids have become as young adults has been fostered by the positive and robust emotional repertoire developed through their early experiences at Beaver Creek, which will follow them for the rest of their lives and provide a constant reminder that love and joy are only as far away as the nearest nondescript creek.

Hunter-Gatherers in Contemporary Garb: Biophilia and the Current State of Emotionality

My thesis for the remainder of this chapter is that three moral criteria that are foundational to the Catholic moral identity, namely love, compassion, and promoting biodiversity on Earth, can come to fruition only if we start feeling more connected to the natural realm and becoming passionately attached to the well-being of our local environments and their denizens. Our current environmental crisis, as all the recent popes agree, is real and pressing and will ravage our planet if conditions are not reversed quickly. Indeed, I am convinced that we are sowing the ignominious seeds of our own demise as a species, as well as catapulting our planet toward a near total biocide, unless we make a communal about face, become different kinds of persons, and embrace a more environmentally benign lifestyle, and the only way to do this outside of the eventual scarcity, deprivation, and extreme pain that will assuredly come if business as usual continues unabated is to embrace the innate biophilia that constitutes humans (even though it is currently being suppressed) and, once again, to being to feel passionately and lovingly toward non-human creation.

Although we are living in an unprecedented time in which the scale of environmental destruction encompasses our entire planet, the pattern of humans soiling their nest and rendering local environments uninhabitable is as long as civilization itself.[1] Indeed, human history is littered with illustrations of formerly technologically and intellectually sophisticated societies becoming dependent on unsustainable practices that over time caused insurmountable environmental problems and eventually resulted in abandoning settlements and cities that were once the crown jewels of entire peoples and empires. Until very recently, when this occurred the common strategy for dealing with local environmental degradation was simply to pick up and move somewhere else. Unfortunately, such a strategy is unavailable today, as the scale of environmental degradation is worldwide and the particular types of environmental problems we have created means that their effects are inescapable. There is literally nowhere else to go.

In particular, three large-scale, long-term environmental problems constitute an unholy trinity that will wreak havoc on our planet if they continue unchecked. The first and most ominous is global climate change, which threatens to interject a level of unpredictability so rapidly into our climate that it becomes very difficult, if not impossible, to adjust to such quick system-wide changes. Slow and incremental changes allow lifeforms and civilizations sufficient time to adapt to new conditions, but the pace at which global climate change is occurring currently is simply staggering: the ten warmest years on record have all occurred since 2005, and seven of these ten warmest years have occurred since 2014.[2] This type of change across the entire planet will have dire repercussions for every system that supports life on Earth (freshwater supplies, agriculture, biodiversity, coral reefs, oceans, and forests), with some of the worst case scenarios involving widespread suffering before a mass extinction event.

The second is human population growth, which influential Catholic figures today deny is a problem. Pope Francis, for instance, refuses even to discuss population growth as a potential problem or a moral issue, as he believes that it is used as a cudgel by powerful members of the economic elite worldwide to manipulate less developed countries into embracing internationalist policies that are disadvantageous to the world's poor. In Pope Francis's mind, "demographic growth is fully compatible with an integral and shared development."[3] In other words, population growth is not a genuine problem—conspicuous consumption is—and we need to prevent the economic elite from scapegoating the world's poor and face the real issue directly, which is an unequal distribution of resources. While Pope Francis is an astute student of international politics and the self-interested agendas often promoted by leading international organizations, not acknowledging human population growth as a key driver of environmental degradation today is wishful thinking, at best. Every new person born on our planet requires resources and energy and produces waste and pollution, and even at minimal consumption levels, adding more people to our planet increases the pressure on already stressed ecosystems to produce more while dealing with increasingly adverse conditions—and make no mistake about it, we are adding people to our planet at an astonishing rate!

From the emergence of modern humans around 100,000 years ago until the invention of agriculture approximately 90,000 years later, a mere one **million** humans existed on our planet. After settled agriculture became firmly entrenched, the human population started to skyrocket and it took only another 10,000 years for the human population to reach one **billion** in 1800. In other words, after the widespread adoption of settled agriculture, it took roughly one-tenth of the time for the human population to increase 100-fold! The two billion mark was broached a mere 130 years later in 1930, followed by another one billion humans being added to our planet in 1959, 1974, 1987, 1998, 2011, with the current world population of humans standing at 8.3 billion. The United Nations estimates that there will be nine billion humans in 2043 and ten billion in 2083, which by many accounts probably represents the absolute carrying capacity of humans on planet Earth. Suffice it to say that Earth has never witnessed in its 4.5 billion years of existence such a meteoric rise of one species, which has led to a wholesale renovation of our planet and its systems to meet the needs of this burgeoning human population. Moreover, the unsustainability of adding another one billion humans to our planet every fifteen years is obvious.

This leads to the third major environmental problem, industrialized agriculture.[4] I will be the first to admit that farmers are some of the most adaptive, resourceful, and resilient people I have ever met, and they have done precisely what market forces have encouraged them to do, which is to create an ever more bountiful supply of calories for humans to consume. Yet there are two fatal flaws of industrialized agriculture. One is that the whole system floats on a sea of fossil fuels and its preferred technologies—heavy machinery, herbicides, pesticides, fertilizers, implements—are dependent on a steady supply of oil to manufacture and use and we have already passed peak oil production, which means that oil will become scarcer and more expensive in its terminal phase. The bottom line is that fossil fuels are not a viable option in the long-term and we will have to wean ourselves off the fossil fuel teat sooner rather than later, and to have our entire planet's food production system dependent on them with no viable alternatives on the horizon is risky almost beyond belief. But more importantly, as currently practiced, industrialized agriculture is undermining the natural resource base upon which its life and vitality depend. From topsoil erosion rates that are unsustainable, to salinization and desertification of once fertile farmland, to pesticide resistance that produces "superbugs" resistant to all known pesticides, to the enormous amounts of pollution stemming from agricultural chemical use, industrialized agriculture is perhaps the perfect system to produce copious amounts of cheap food, but it is also a radically unsustainable system that is slowly but surely inching its way toward an ignominious demise. Yet as industrialized agriculture continues on its death march, it will also be expected to produce more and more food, not only for the burgeoning world population but also for the millions of upwardly mobile people who have the desire and are finding the means to transition from a plant-based to a meat-based diet, a choice that requires far higher production rates and puts even more stress on an already seriously burdened system. To meet the dual demands of the burgeoning world population and changing dietary preferences, the United Nations estimates that agricultural production will have to increase by 70 percent this century—a truly mind-boggling number! So, at precisely the time when we need to be transitioning to a more sustainable agricultural system, forces are converging to put pressure on our wasteful, inefficient, and environmentally harmful industrialized agricultural system to produce even more, which means intensifying the practices that have sown the seeds of its own demise. If ever there was a moment in human history when there is a collective realization of a Faustian bargain with the devil that has been made with a worldwide system absolutely necessary for human survival, now would be an opportune time for that moment, as we have cast our lot with an industrialized agricultural system that is not only structurally very fragile and vulnerable, but will assuredly have to come to an end at some point in its current form.

It is hard to imagine a more perfect storm that incrementally yet inexorably increases the odds that a planetary-wide failure will occur at some point, resulting in unimaginable suffering and death, absent a considerable about face in our systems, practices, and lifestyles. Moreover, nearly everyone is well aware of the threats posed by these problems, especially overpopulation and global climate change. The overpopulation issue has received considerable media coverage since the early 1970s when Paul Ehrlich's *The Population Bomb* put it front and center on our national radar screen. Likewise, global climate change is one of the most covered stories today, gaining daily international and national media attention at all levels, being the subject of regular international conferences and accords, with greenhouse gas mitigation efforts forming the centerpiece of many national political administrations. Anyone with even tangential contact with mainstream media will be familiar with the enormous stakes involved in combating global climate change effectively.

Yet what continually astonishes me is the lack of an affective response to global climate change. Despite respected religious leaders sounding the sirens about an impending disaster if global climate change is not brought under control, despite a robust consensus on the threat posed by global climate change by our military, economic, and political leaders, despite near unanimity in the scientific sector that global climate change is real and poses perhaps the gravest threat to life on Earth in human history, despite international agreements to combat climate change, and despite the reordering of economies in North America, Europe, and elsewhere to mitigate greenhouse gasses, there is surprisingly, maybe even astonishingly, such a paltry emotional reaction on the part of so many people to the reality of global climate change.[5]

As I have experienced many times when discussing global climate change with interested Catholic laypersons in a parish setting or with my students in the classroom, attention spans are short on this topic and at some point minds will invariably start to wander and eyes will drift to available visual stimuli, which are key indicators that attention has moved elsewhere to a more mentally enriching environment. Take the same people in the same setting and present to them a snake or a spider, and there might be screaming, adrenaline dumps, fight or flight responses, and general mayhem as they try to put critical distance between themselves and the perceived threat. Likewise, take the same people and present to them a cute puppy or a newborn baby, and they are likely to smile, to feel warm and fuzzy inside, and to emit a steady stream of oohs and aahs as they interact adoringly with the puppy or baby (and probably secretly wish to snuggle for hours with such cuteness). Either scenario involves a rather pitched and intense emotional response, while discussions of or thoughts about global climate change are met by a blasé, apathetic, emotionally nonchalant response. Moreover, while snakes and spiders might represent a legitimate threat to those individuals unfortunate enough to be bitten by the more venomous specimens in either group, the threat posed by global climate change is almost unimaginably more widespread and dire, as it will affect every living creature on our planet for perhaps thousands of years, and it could potentially induce an extinction event like asteroid impacts and volcanic eruptions have in the past. If anything deserves the most intense emotional reaction to rouse our attention and to move us to action, it is global climate change.

So while the unholy trinity of global climate change, a burgeoning and unsustainable human population growth, and a worldwide agricultural system in its terminal phase bear down upon the entire planet and promise long-term system-wide disruption unless radical changes are made—and quickly!—we remain emotionally indifferent and unmoved, even though intellectually we grasp the urgency of our predicament. The reasons for this are twofold. One is the fact that for roughly 98 percent of human history we have been hunter-gatherers, and our inherited predispositions and emotional repertoire were forged during this period when environmental conditions and common obstacles and threats were very different from those faced today. Phrased a little bit differently, there is a mismatch between the emotions that served a valuable purpose during our hunter-gatherer period and appropriate and helpful emotional responses today, as the emotions forged over tens of thousands of years of biological evolution during our prehistory are causing us to misperceive actual threats today and to have no emotional reaction to things that constitute serious threats to our existence. Unless we can find a way to rectify this mismatch and to feel differently, we could be our own worst enemies as we confront major environmental issues this century. Second, our emotional lives are partly pliable and can be sculpted by cultural, social, and religious approval or stricture, and the thrust of our conditioning—and especially our Catholic religious conditioning—is to restrict considerably the scope of our emotional repertoire, especially when it comes to love, which many claim is the heart of Catholic ethics.[6] As I will argue below, our native biophilia, which is also inherited from our hunter-gatherer prehistory, has largely been stifled and subdued by the Catholic theological tradition, and it behooves us to cultivate this biophilia once again.

The Function of Emotions[7]

The driving forces of biological evolution are random genetic mutations, natural selection, genetic drift, and gene flow, and these forces will cause changes in human populations that over time will make humans either more or less fit to survive in their respective environments. Those changes that promote survivability by introducing a new beneficial characteristic into a human population eventually become widespread among that population, and maladaptive changes that decrease survivability become less prevalent and sometimes nonexistent in that population. Biological or genetic evolution moves at a glacial pace compared to cultural evolution and it is limited in terms of the changes it can make, as it only has the existing genetic platform from which to build and to bring out new characteristics and any single alteration that it can induce typically leads only to small changes in survivability. In addition, many of the changes are evolutionary dead ends and lead nowhere. So evolution is both a slow and imperfect system, but given very long periods of time the inexorable force of evolution can produce some spectacular results, both in terms of changes within a species, or overall biodiversity, or the creation of organs or systems or abilities that never existed before. Especially when the entire panoramic sweep of life on Earth is considered, the evolution of life from primitive one-celled organisms to the cornucopia of species that have emerged and flourished on our planet, along with the mind-boggling array of different characteristics that are finely tuned to help their possessors survive in their respective environments, is stupefying. We certainly live in a magical corner of the universe that amply testifies to the enormous creative power of God and if evolution is allowed to continue its momentum on our planet, it portends to attain even greater heights of complexity and diversity and newness in the universe.

It is no surprise that biological evolution, which has created a spectacular array of creatures and characteristics that are uniquely adapted to survive in their respective environments, would also create what we describe as emotions or feelings, which can range from intense reactions to deadly threats that cause a sudden fight or flight response, to feelings of warmth and softness and connection, to preferences of one thing over another not based on any rational reason but simply on a "hunch" or "feeling." As some have noted, these hunches are often our preconscious mind detecting something awry in our immediate environment and causing an emotional alert to trigger conscious advertence to a potential threat. In this way, there is intimate teamwork between reason and the emotions of which we are not even consciously aware, which functions as an early alert system. There is a gamut of emotions, depending on the situation in which one finds oneself, but the common denominator underlying all human emotional responses is that they emerged during our hunter-gatherer prehistory as either inducements to or rewards for action that promoted human survivability in that respective context.

The benefit of emotional responses is not only that they can produce a nearly instantaneous transition to decisive action, which is highly beneficial when sudden threats emerge in one's environment, but that they can steer human behavior in specific directions that have consistently promoted survivability. So, for instance, a person suddenly spotting a snake out of her peripheral vision while hiking along a mountain trail is much better served by immediate overwhelming fear that causes her to jump out of the way, compared to a more deliberate and time-consuming approach that tries to assess the species of the snake to see if it is actually venomous. Fear is a highly adaptive emotion, insofar as it can be a lifesaver when fractions of a second count. In a similar way, the intense protective and nurturing feelings a mother or father gets when coddling his or her baby are far more effective tools for creating a bond of affection that will make mom and dad unreservedly devoted to the baby's well-being, even when significant personal sacrifices have to be made, compared to simply knowing intellectually that one needs to care for one's baby. Knowing the good and feeling the good are very different phenomena, and the two in tandem are perhaps the most effective inducements to actions that humans experience.

Emotions, then, are rational responses to reality that steer humans to act in particular ways and effectively provide helpful shortcuts through more tangled and involved rational processes as well as rewards for preferences for certain behavior over others, and they have proven to be remarkably successful at promoting the survivability of humans during our hunter-gatherer prehistory. From this perspective, not only is it accurate to say that a well-adjusted human should be able to experience a broad array of emotions, but that emotions ought to be affirmed as a fundamental good for humans that have promoted our survivability for millennia. Indeed, it is a good thing that humans are not passionless Vulcans, as we would have had a much more difficult time surviving for tens of thousands of years without a rich repertoire of emotions to help guide our way through the many challenges in our hunter-gatherer prehistory.

Given that humans spent the vast bulk of our history on the African savannas before migrating to Eurasia and then eventually settling all across the globe, one would expect to find that a great deal of our inclinations, preferences, and emotional circuitry correspond to life on the savanna and the kind of traits that would enhance human survivability in that context, and that is precisely what the empirical data suggest. Perhaps one of the most critical emotions for survival is fear that produces an instantaneous response to immediate threats, and humans today have a cluster of fear responses that are culturally and socially invariant, the most documented of which is fear of snakes and spiders.[8] But our fear response extends to other stimuli as well, including heights, enclosed places, sharks, dogs, and large carnivores such as lions and tigers.[9] Interestingly enough, as more of the world's human populations becomes concentrated in urban areas and direct contact with snakes, spiders, and sharks becomes increasingly unlikely for residents of large cities, there does not seem to be any waning of the fear response to these stimuli, while it is much easier to extinguish a fear response to things that actually pose a much greater danger in urban areas, such as cars and guns and knives. What this shows is that long-standing prepared associations to stimuli are very difficult to overcome, while cultivating learned associations to actual dangers that have little connection to our prehistory can be difficult to establish.

While risk avoidance was a daily undertaking for our prehistoric ancestors on the African savanna, a far more expansive set of biophilic inclinations, preferences, and positive emotional rewards was solidified to aid in their survivability. For instance, one key advantage of bipedalism coupled with eyesight being the dominant method of gathering environmental information for ancient hunter-gatherers on the African savanna is the ability to see over the top of the savanna's grasses and to detect threats from long distances, which would either allow for a furtive escape from danger or time to formulate a defensive plan. Whether a lion pride on the hunt, or a roving pack of hyenas, or a grass fire, or a storm, being able to detect threats from a distance was highly advantageous. As a result, humans have developed a marked preference for savanna-like or park-like environments dominated by short grasses that allow for considerable visual openness and surveillance, scattered trees or small groupings of trees in which it is difficult for predators to hide, and various escape routes.[10] So when people possess the economic wherewithal to be able to choose to live in an upper-class area, they typically choose either an immediate environment (such as a yard) that resembles a savanna or an area that has a number of open green spaces and parks.[11]

In addition to a preference for savanna-like environments, prehistoric hunter-gatherers would take a keen interest in their local topography, as no savanna is the same. Likely places for predators to launch an attack; the location of water holes and plants that could provide water; the location of fruit bearing trees and bushes and the particular times during which they are actively flowering and producing fruit; plants that could be eaten or used domestically or to create tools; specific areas that offered an abundance of game animals, and conversely areas in which predators are rarely found; places that attracted migratory animals—intimate, detailed knowledge of all these would have aided enormously in securing the basic necessities for prehistoric hunter-gatherers, which means that an abiding curiosity and interest in concrete particulars about one's local environment, an enthusiasm for exploring new areas and new facets of one's immediate environment, and a fascination for discovering new things in natural settings would have served our prehistoric ancestors quite well—and those same traits are found in abundance among humans today.[12]

Another inclination that emerged during our hunter-gatherer period was a strong attraction to ecosystems that showed evidence of abundant water sources, as consistent and regular access to water is not only one of the most basic needs of humans,[13] but water also is an attractant to animals that can be hunted, and in a coastal context, can provide an abundance of shellfish, crustaceans, and fish.[14] So ecosystems that show signs of water availability (widespread presence of green shrubbery or plants, diverse animal species) are going to be strongly preferred by humans over ecosystems that indicate water scarcity (deserts, little or brown and dry vegetation, few animal species), and some of the most positive reactions will be to ecosystems that have running water (streams or rivers) or bodies of water (ponds or lakes). It is also one of the reasons why artwork containing waterfalls and other water scenes are found to be highly aesthetically pleasing to humans.[15]

I said earlier that humans today are hunter-gatherers in contemporary garb, and I think the evidence robustly supports widespread commonalities among the inclinations, preferences, and emotional repertoire between contemporary humans and our prehistoric ancestors. A handy catchphrase to encapsulate this shared cluster of propensities is biophilia, an idea popularized by Edward Wilson and Stephen Kellert, which indicates an affinity for and a tendency to focus on life and lifelike processes. We revel in life and in all its forms and the conditions that have supported human survivability from human prehistory, and our emotional circuitry, including our likes and dislikes, our preferences, and myriad feelings of awe and wonder and happiness and love and joy have been solidified through evolutionary pressures that rewarded humans for seeking conditions that promoted their survivability. These biophilic inclinations are the reason why humans today have such well-defined preferences: open spaces versus spatially restricted views;[16] biodiversity versus a paucity of animal life; easily traversable topography versus one filled with tripping and falling hazards; green versus brown vegetation; separated or single trees versus thick forests; natural versus urban or built environments; and curvilinear or irregular versus rectilinear or regular forms and edges. The Yahwist author of the second creation account in Genesis might have come close when he described humans as earthy beings made from dirt, but evolutionary biologists have gone a step further and shown convincingly that we are not simply generic earth creatures, but creatures whose inclinations, emotional repertoire, and robust preference for life and lifelike processes were forged and solidified on the African savanna.

While our inherited emotional circuitry and system of preferences served humankind very well for millennia, one of the fundamental problems today is that the environmental problems posing the greatest risk do not automatically trigger our risk detection system, which tell us to be alert for the presence of spiders and snakes and tigers and tight spaces and visually restrictive areas and other threats in our immediate environment. Ongoing, incremental change to habitats, or the accumulation of greenhouse gasses in the atmosphere, or the slow loss of biodiversity, or increasing desertification of once fertile agricultural land—while these large-scale problems might lead to system wide collapse if left unchecked, none of these induce the kind of heightened emotional response in humans that would cause mental warning flags to be raised, so even though the best scientific data available let us know the likely dire outcome of ignoring these problems, many people are simply emotionally unmoved by knowing about these issues, even when the knowledge is extensive, bolstered by solid scientific data, and foreboding in its consequences for all life on Earth.

The only way we are going to emerge from this century with major planetary systems intact and thriving is to act decisively to reverse major environmental problems, and the only way to do this effectively is to reignite the connection and affection toward creation that is part and parcel of our biophilic heritage, but which has also been suppressed and largely forgotten today. This is easier said than done, however, as we are at the end stages of a multifaceted process that has incrementally stripped nature of anything that would evoke our affection and cause us to feel—viscerally and primordially—intimacy with anything in nature, outside of other human beings.

Sources of Emotional Disaffection From Nature

The sources of this disaffection with nature are many and varied, but the first worthy of mention is the general animosity between reason and the emotions in Catholic moral theology, which sows more than a bit of distrust toward the emotions as mostly distractions and obstacles in the pursuit of the good. The dominant framework for understanding emotions in Catholic moral theology is an oppositional model[17] that, first, regards emotions as separate and distinct from rationality, and second, frequently portrays the emotions as undermining the dictates of reason by their urgency. Particularly in the Thomistic tradition, which dominated Catholic moral theology from the late 1800s to the Second Vatican Council and is still highly influential today through the work of renowned theologians as well as being incorporated into the Catechism of the Catholic Church, emotions are rarely presented as anything but obstacles and distractions to the machinations of good moral reasoning. Henry Davis, for instance, who was one of the most influential neo-Thomists in the English-speaking world during the twentieth century, considers emotions in the context of human freedom being the necessary prerequisite for a human act, or an act that if fully attributable or transferable to the agent's character, and his singular concern is that emotions become so passionate that they effectively diminish or obliterate the ability to choose freely. Davis is aware that emotions can often rouse us to action, which can eventually lead to the pursuit of good, but the ultimate arbiter of human action is "right reason," and regardless of whether emotions support or detract from considered judgments, the ideal is to have an unencumbered and detached human reason that can assess a situation in all its concrete particulars and present accurate information for the person to choose the right course of action.[18]

Davis neither understands emotions as rational responses to reality nor does he regard emotions as anything but potential obstacles to reason in making sound judgments.

Thomas Slater, another influential twentieth-century English-speaking Catholic moral theologian, is similarly concerned about the possibility of emotions diminishing the degree to which an action can be chosen freely, as well as the subjective responsibility that can be assumed under the duress of extreme emotions.[19] The Catechism of the Catholic Church corroborates this oppositional model, claiming that the pursuit of the human good is governed by reason, and that the emotions must be trained by reason to desire the good.[20] Emotions are simply givens of nature, and through the process of reinforcing those beneficial to an individual's pursuit of beatitude and restraining or ignoring those impeding a life of holiness, the ideal situation over time is to have one's emotions habituated to desire the good consistently. So once again, emotions are not rational responses to reality or aids to the smooth and effective functioning of reason, but potential obstacles that need continual monitoring and reinforcement in order not to interfere with a person's pursuit of the good. Even though Thomas Aquinas, whose thought Davis and Slater are attempting to condense and to present to a seminary audience, recognizes the value of having emotions allied with reason, so that they are trained to respond positively to the good as determined by reason,[21] the overarching posture toward emotions in recent Catholic moral theology has been to regard them either as potential irksome distractions that lead moral reasoning astray, or as serious threats that so swamp rationality and create such intense desire that they threaten to extinguish even the ability to make free choices.

Another source of disaffection with nature, according to the environmental philosopher Val Plumwood, is the European colonial mentality that has come to dominate politically and culturally in the Western world in the past few centuries. The logic of colonization, according to Plumwood, employs several subtle psychological strategies to legitimize a series of dualisms that bifurcate the moral universe, create a rigid hierarchy, and ultimately establish a master/slave mentality in which the slave's purpose is simply to serve the master. The process of disaffection begins with "backgrounding," which attempts to establish that the other (in this case, nature) is inessential, unimportant, maybe not even worth noticing, and relatively inconsequential. Once the backgrounding process has been undertaken and established psychologically, the next step is to move toward a radical exclusion that not only solidifies nature as an inferior through the construction of a hierarchical system in which the other occupies a low rung on the ladder of importance but also denies any identification or empathy or sympathy or likeness with the other. This "radical exclusion," as Plumwood calls it, is intended to establish the other as totally different, and therefore not worthy of any affection or care. The next phase is instrumentalization or objectification, whereby the other is deemed to be valuable only insofar as it provides something valuable to beings higher on the hierarchy; outside of the service provided to the genuinely valuable beings, however, the inferior has no inherent value or internal raison de être. Finally, the last stage involves attaching derogatory nicknames to the other, which not only reinforces and perpetuates the other's inferior status but also causes the other to internalize that sense of inferiority. According to Plumwood, this master/slave mentality has been employed during the colonization period and afterward by humans toward nature, which has culminated in a utilitarian attitude toward nature that regards it merely as a repository of natural resources or natural capital that gets value and significance only in relation to the satisfaction of human needs and desires.[22] Furthermore, and perhaps more importantly, as something that possesses instrumental value alone, nature is not the object of affection or intimacy. Nature has become just like the many other tools or objects that get their meaning from the way in which they benefit human life, such as hammers, toilets, pencils, laptops, couches, chairs, and end tables. The tools might provide a valuable service and be recognized for their usefulness, but never does the thought cross anyone's mind that we ought to feel emotional intimacy with a hammer or a toilet and to work actively for its well-being. Instead, these feelings of affection ought to be directed to the humans who give meaning and value to the tools, not to the tools themselves.

For Sallie McFague, prior to the rise of modern science, nature was alive, rich in meaning, full of subjects with whom humans could relate personally, and a conduit for the divine that gave glimpses into the inner life of God. After the Renaissance, and especially after the emergence of Isaac Newton's mechanical universe, the idea of nature as significant for us, multivalent in meaning, a fitting topic for literature and poetry and intense personal experiences, "becomes nothing more than an object to be analyzed, dissected, and commodified."[23] The spectacular success of modern science has given it pride of place among the disciplines, and today its tools of quantification and measurement, its allegiance to the scientific method, its posture of objectivity and detachment, and its ultimate result of objectifying everything under the sun is regarded as the most legitimate language by which to understand and to relate to nature. Under the regime of modern science, nature not only loses is subjecthood, but it also becomes little more than an object to be manipulated and controlled.[24]

For Richard Bulliet, settled agriculture and the gradual intensification of food production into what is known today as industrial agriculture are responsible for the current alienation that many experience from nature. According to Bulliet, the hunter-gatherer stage of human existence was characterized by nature assuming mythical, religious, cultural, and symbolic dimensions, and there was no sense of the bifurcated universe in which humans were separate from, or superior to, nature.[25] With the emergence of agricultural pastoralism, however, there is a marked diminishment of the spiritual and mythical qualities of nature, and the emergence of a utilitarian mentality that starts to truncate the value of nature to its practical benefit to humans. As agricultural pastoralism gave way over time to industrial agriculture and a massive food production system emerged that allowed a small fraction of the population to feed the masses, which in turn allowed for the emergence of civilization, specialization, and rapidly increasing human populations that are more and more concentrated into dense urban areas, even fewer people have any meaningful contact with nature. For most denizens of urban areas today, their biophilic impulses have few opportunities to be satisfied and they become trapped in an almost completely human-contrived world, lonely and estranged from the types of nature experiences that have soothed and stimulated humans since time immemorial.[26]

While these cultural, scientific, and developmental forces have had tangible effects on the ways in which contemporary Catholics experience nature, there are several salient elements of the Catholic theological tradition that wittingly or unwittingly contribute to the ongoing disaffection with nature as well. As I discussed earlier at length in Chapter 1, the long-standing anthropocentrism in Catholic theology, which is still alive and well today despite Pope Francis's recent attempt to circumscribe it in his encyclical *Laudato Si'*, cannot be underestimated in terms of its ability to habituate Catholics to the idea that humans are the pinnacle of creation and that value is bestowed upon creation to the extent that it can be transformed and manipulated in order to satisfy human needs and desires. In this context, creation is, at best, an object of concern only insofar as it needs to be cultivated, transformed, and maintained properly in order to produce goods for humans, and nature is rarely understood as anything more than a storehouse of resources that exists to satisfy human needs and desires.

Rivaling the stewardship paradigm in its ability to foster a robust disaffection with nature is the contemporary concept of love, which has been preached from the time of the early Church through contemporary times as being the bedrock of the Christian moral life. Described as "the basic moral standard,"[27] the "pattern and prototype,"[28] and "the basic norm and distinctive pattern of the Christian life,"[29] the love commandments and the influence of the concept of love remain unparalleled for the Catholic moral life. No other concept has so fired the Christian moral imagination, has been a beacon of light for those desiring to follow in the footsteps of Jesus, and been the subject of theological debate and discussion since the inception of Christianity. Even someone as esteemed for his theological acumen as St. Augustine can recommend one pithy command to his flock that encapsulates the Christian moral life: love, and do what you will; for according to St. Augustine, nothing can spring from love except goodness.[30]

There are three Greek words in the New Testament that are commonly translated as "love": agape, philia, and eros. Agape is associated with an altruistic, giving, and self-sacrificing form of love; philia is understood as love of a friend or of a friendship; and eros is a fiery and passionate love that is often equated with romantic affection. Theological speculation from St. Augustine to Thomas Aquinas to contemporary popes has consistently shown a marked preference for agape over the others as the purest form of love, and when a theologian today talks about love, he or she almost invariably means agape, and not one of the other two types of love.

The important point to note about the ascendance of agape as the standard bearer for Christian love is that it need not imply any emotional movement or connection at all. Unlike eros, which is saturated with some of the most deeply held emotions, agape entails two things: an action intended to be beneficial to the other and some kind of sacrifice on the part of the agent. Nothing about an agapeic act entails any kind of emotion; indeed, agape is often lauded precisely because the actions it inspires are so often perceived to be overcoming significant emotional resistance. Agape is purely a rationalist and voluntarist form of love, as it entails knowing the good for the other and willing that good through an action intended to secure the well-being of the other. Both philia and eros, on the other hand, have a robust emotional component to them, as friendships and intimate or sexual relationships are typically accompanied by a whole range of feelings of affection and intimacy toward the beloved. In my opinion, this decided preference of agape over philia and eros need not imply any overt animosity toward the emotions, but it does reinforce to the long-standing suspicion in Christianity about the value of emotions, either because the moral life is perceived to have little to do with emotions or because the emotions frequently lead us astray from performing right actions, especially when such actions are personally costly.

The typical exhortation on love from Catholic leaders today, then, is going to portray agape as the highest form of love, with an emphasis on the costliness and sacrifice frequently involved with such love. So Pope John Paul II claims that "Real love is demanding. I would fail in my mission if I did not clearly tell you so. For it was Jesus—our Jesus himself—who said: 'You are my friends if you do what I command you' (*Jn* 15:14). Love demands effort and a personal commitment to the will of God. It means discipline and sacrifice."[31] Similarly, Pope Benedict XVI reiterates the self-sacrificial nature of Christian love and holds up Jesus's willingness to accept death on a cross in order to achieve the salvation of humankind "as love in its most radical form."[32]

The triumph of agape in the Catholic theological tradition as the most authentic form of love has cemented a marked indifference toward the moral relevance of the emotions for the moral life, in addition to steering the academic theological conversation toward questions that have nothing to do with the emotions and everything to do with the scope of Christian love, which in turn surreptitiously assumes the higher the level of difficulty, the purer the form of love—and what could be more difficult than loving some anonymous, abstract person whom one will never know or meet who lives halfway across the world? Yet these are precisely the kinds of issues that dominate the contemporary discussion of Christian love. So questions about the validity of "special relations," which is a euphemism for family and those near and dear, and whether they should be loved more than strangers; or the legitimacy of universal love and impartiality toward everyone; or whether agape and self-love are compatible in some way; or whether it is proper to exclude anyone or any groups of people from the category of the "neighbor"[33] are the foci of theological discussion today.

Another equally important effect of agape's dominance in Christian theology is the tightly constricted scope of Christian love, which has two objects, God and humans. Commentators who espouse love as the apogee of the Christian moral life invariably tout the "Great Commandment" as the linchpin to understanding love, a version of which is contained in each of the synoptic Gospels (Matt. 22:34-40; Mark 12:28-31; and Luke 10:25-37) and affirmed in the Pauline epistles (Romans 13:9-10; Galatians 5:14). When asked about the greatest commandment by an interlocutor, Jesus replies that one must love God with all of one's heart and soul, and one's neighbor as oneself. In the Gospels of Mark and Matthew, the dialogue ends there, but in Luke's gospel, the young lawyer questioning Jesus asks a follow up question, Who is my neighbor? to which Jesus tells the Parable of the Good Samaritan, which is perhaps one of the most famous stories in the Western world. The upshot of all three renditions of the Great Commandment is that there are three objects of love: God, oneself, and one's neighbor. There are other passages that extend love to one's enemies, but regardless of which particular tribe or class of people is designated as an appropriate object of love, the important point is that love in the New Testament is directed at either God or humans, not nature.

Even for those few who attempt to extend the concept of love beyond God and humans to nature, they typically end up following a pattern of regarding agape as the only legitimate form of love to be directed toward nature, and thus the real ethical debate for them is the scope of that love, or what parts of nature are legitimate objects of love, and which types of acts are consistent with that love. Take, for instance, one of the most thoughtful and comprehensive statements on the topic, James Nash's *Loving Nature*. Nash, too, is convinced that love is the indispensable bedrock of the Christian moral life, stating that "love is the integrating center of the whole of Christian faith and ethics. If so, a Christian ecological ethic is seriously deficient—if even conceivable—unless it is grounded in Christian love."[34] Since Christian love is based on fidelity to God, cooperating with God, and respecting what God is trying to do in the universe, "humans are called to love what God loves, to value what is valued by the Source of Value."[35] This leads Nash to affirm that love ought to be directed at all of creation:

> An ecological ethic that is rooted in the Christian faith is a reasonable extension of love to the whole creation, in order to re-present the all-encompassing affection and care of God. Since God's love is unbounded, loyal Christian love is similarly inclusive or universal. This love resists confinement of any sort. It punctures all forms of ethical parochialism, as a number of interpreters have testified.[36]

Based on this universalism, Nash then reinterprets the Parable of the Good Samaritan, claiming that love of nature is simply the love of neighbor "universalized in recognition of our common origins, mutual dependencies, and shared destiny with the whole creation of the God who is all-embracing love." In this sense, the task of Christian environmentalism is to "define the character and conduct of the good neighbor, the ecological equivalent of the good Samaritan."[37] While Nash's *Loving Nature* ought to be commended for attempting to extend love beyond the sphere of humans, he still adheres to the dominant paradigm of understanding love as an action and spending the bulk of his time trying to figure out the appropriate characteristics of that love, which leads to extensive discussions of beneficence, justice, rights, responsibilities, and the political implications of love. In the end, love ends up for Nash being cut out of an intellectualist cloth just as much as the Christian ethicists he is attempting to correct.

The practical upshot of these considerations is that significant cultural, political, and religious forces converge to produce a profound disaffection and alienation from a substantive emotional relationship with creation for contemporary Catholics. Love is exclusive and reserved for God and other human beings, and the emotional component of love is bracketed in favor of love as sacrificial actions for the sake of others. With each passing year, more people find themselves in situations in which regular and meaningful contact with nature becomes more elusive, which prevents more people from being able to feel the deep satisfaction and stimulation of direct contact with nature. Dominant contemporary Western political and cultural trends habituate us into a bifurcated psychological universe in which humans are separate from and superior to nature, which places value on nature only insofar as it can meet human desires and needs.

In consequence, emotional attachment to particular natural areas is becoming more of an oddity for contemporary American Catholics. Nature is simply the backdrop for the more important activities of working, making a living, and raising a family, and the closest contact many have with nature is occasionally noticing it while driving to and from work. Nature has been thoroughly backgrounded and now simply serves as a silent sentinel, its raison d'être being to remain as unobtrusive as possible, yet ever ready to provide a steady supply of natural resources in order to satisfy our ever increasing consumer demands.[38] No longer a conduit of the divine or worthy of reverence or even worth noticing for its own sake, nature has become something of a Heideggerian standing reserve,[39] a storehouse of resources that can be called into action whenever human desires beckon, garnering our attention only when it misbehaves or thwarts our desires or is needed for something. Far from being a mother, or a friend, or an object of love, nature has become nothing more than an obsequious servant whose purpose is dutifully to serve those invited to the banquet table day after day and year after year, without complaining or resisting, and without expecting anything more than an occasional cold utilitarian glance from the banqueters.

For hunter-gatherers in contemporary garb who are biophilic to the core, this disaffection from what has historically been one of the most potent sources of emotional vitality and connection and satisfaction is perhaps the profoundest transition to occur in recent memory. As Glenn Albrecht states, "My emotional compass, my inherited biophilia, instinctively directs me to beautiful and biologically rich environments where I want to be 'in place' with as much place attachment as possible,"[40] but today we are "emotionally lost" and entering an age of solastalgia[41] in which loneliness, depression, and chronic distress will become widespread, which stems directly from lack of contact with nature and the emotional stagnation that corresponds to it.[42] For Albrecht, this is tantamount to an emotional death:

> The emotional death I am thinking about occurs when some humans no longer even have a reaction to the end, death, or loss of nature. There is no emotional presence to bear witness, as all remaining biota are ignored as irrelevant to the life projects of individual humans. With technological isolation from raw nature in the digital age, this form of emotional death becomes commonplace. Distracted by, for example, the small screen, people no longer notice nature. It is no longer physically or conceptually out there: it effectively no longer exists …. They hear … nothing. They see … nothing. Their senses and their emotions for connecting to life outside the Anthropos have died.[43]

If Albrecht is correct and our emotional disaffection with nature is almost complete, very little stands in the way of the predatory systems and destructive patterns of behavior from continuing unabated. Our best, and perhaps only, hope to reverse these nefarious trends is to rekindle our love for nature, to allow our biophilic cravings to be satisfied, and to begin once again to feel passionately and viscerally connected to our small parcel of creation.

These main points noted by scholars, namely, that we are biophilic beings who crave contact with nature and are happiest and healthiest when we have regular direct contact with nature, are strongly corroborated in the empirical data emerging from studies on our relationship with nature. Some of these findings show the benefits of even minimal contact: indirect, subliminal exposure to natural environments consistently evokes positive feelings;[44] the sight of trees from one's own home affects relaxation and comfort levels;[45] the presence of trees in inner city and suburban environments are correlated with feelings of safety;[46] a view of trees versus a view of a brick wall during a hospital convalescence reduced the amount of narcotics needed for patients as well as reduced postoperative complications and shortened the overall hospital stay;[47] and even a virtual experience of nature is associated with stress reduction.[48]

Direct and more sustained contact with nature, on the other hand, provides myriad benefits on a number of levels. Psychologically, nature contact is responsible for so-called transcendent experiences of awe, wonder, and humility, and it also occasions reflective thinking about important existential realities such as the quality of one's life and the worth of personal goals.[49] It is also correlated with feelings of elation,[50] lower rates of depression and stress,[51] relief from mental fatigue,[52] a broad array of prosocial tendencies,[53] increased positive emotional states,[54] lower rates of psychiatric disorders,[55] increased birth weight of babies, increased levels of physical activity for children, and lower rates of obesity and neurodevelopmental issues,[56] among many others.

While the empirical data on contact with nature corroborates what proponents of biophilia have been asserting for decades, namely, that we crave and are happiest and healthiest when we have regular and direct contact with nature, for nearly fifty years there has been a steady decline in the amount of time Americans spend in nature, with one commentator stating that "a massive retreat of *Homo sapiens* from the natural world is underway"[57] and another claiming we are suffering from a "nature deficit disorder" pandemic, a phrase coined to describe the cluster of psychiatric disorders associated with too little time spent in nature.[58]

The most recent comprehensive national study on Americans' relationship to nature, *The Nature of Americans* (2017),[59] notes not only the decreasing amount of time Americans spend in nature, but perhaps more importantly, the increasing disconnect between the kind of experiences Americans desire to have in nature and their ability to have those experiences. The majority of adults surveyed regarded their interests in nature to be either their most enjoyable interest, or among their most enjoyable interests, with a majority also reporting that their interests in nature had remained unchanged over time or had grown.[60] Compared to their parents, 79 percent of the adults claimed that their interests in nature were similar or greater. The data "suggest an American public that remains highly interested in nature in general."[61] On an emotional level, a majority of respondents claimed that their love of nature is one of their strongest feelings, with 79 percent claiming that smells and sounds associated with past positive experiences in nature help them recall some of their fondest personal memories, and a majority testifying to the importance of pets in their lives and the emotional bond they forged with family pets.[62]

This widespread desire for meaningful nature experiences, however, does not automatically translate either into more time spent in nature or quality experiences in nature, as indoors-oriented hobbies and recreational activities currently predominate over outdoors-oriented activities, with two-thirds of the national sample claiming that there are more important issues in their lives than their interests in and concerns for nature. Competing priorities for time, attention, and finances are often cited as prime factors that impede quality time in nature, along with built environments that are often bereft of any inkling of possibilities to enjoy nature as well as new technologies and media being major distractions for Americans.[63] American adults have the added burden of showing a decided preference for experiencing pristine and remote nature areas, which brings along added burdens of greater travel, cost, and time to partake in these contacts with nature.[64]

The overriding impression gleaned from *The Nature of Americans* study along with other relevant data is that Americans attribute an enormous amount of value to nature experiences and the desire to partake in meaningful nature activities is as great as it has ever been. Yet there currently exists "a profound *interest-action gap* in Americans' relationships with nature,"[65] insofar as the actual time spent in nature has been steadily decreasing for decades, with children experiencing the steepest decline. Today an American child spends less time outdoors than at any other time in American history, averaging between four and seven **minutes** per day of unstructured time outside, while spending an average of seven and a half **hours** per day using electronic media.[66] The practical upshot is that while desire for contact with nature is high, so is the level of discontent and frustration with the inability actually to engage in meaningful nature experiences for many Americans, coupled with the inevitable affective disconnection from nature that has ensued as a result of dwindling nature experiences.

This bodes ill for a few important reasons. As biophilic beings who crave a wide array of contact with nature and desire to feel connected emotionally with elements of nature, our decreasing direct contact with nature will inevitably become manifest in some way, whether in increasing rates of depression, unhappiness, or some other key indicators of human well-being. Second, as Sallie McFague argues, we can only love those things we know, which implies that if we are going to fall in love with some aspects of nature, we will have to become familiar with them—and there is no good way outside of direct experience to get to know nature well. Knowledge might be generated by books, magazine articles, and websites on our laptops, but love will emerge only when all our senses— sight, smell, touch, hearing, taste—begin to uncover and savor the beloved in all its different textures and qualities. Third, if we are going to cooperate with God's activity in making our planet even more a cornucopia of biodiversity unparalleled anywhere in the known universe, then falling in love with nature emerges as an urgent directive for Catholics, as it encourages a wider and more benevolent connection to creation, or at least to parts of creation. When we love, we pay attention to, nurture, protect, spend time with, and become fiercely attached to, our beloved. Even in our beloved's absence, the feelings of connection and joy are still present, as are well wishes directed toward the beloved. If Catholics loved parts of nature like my kids love Beaver Creek, they would be passionately engaged in making sure that their favorite nature areas are treated with the respect they deserve and that their health and vitality were guaranteed for generations to come, and if push came to shove, their sense of dedication and commitment would prompt them to stand up and fight the good fight against those intent on undermining their cherished nature areas.

Such an attitude is aptly illustrated by Thomas Berry, who relays an experience when he was eleven years old and his family moved from a settled part of his hometown to an area on the edge of town that was a bit wilder, having a creek and meadow behind his family's new house. Here is his account of his first trip across the creek and encountering the meadow:

> The field was covered with white lilies rising above the thick grass. A magic moment, this experience gave to my life something that seems to explain my thinking at a more profound level than almost any other experience I can remember. It was not only the lilies. It was the singing of the crickets and the woodlands in the distance and the clouds in a clear sky …. [A]s the years pass this moment returns to me, and whenever I think about my basic life attitude and the whole trend of my mind and the causes to which I have given my efforts, I seem to come back to this moment and the impact it has had on my feeling for what is real and worthwhile in life.

> This early experience, it seems, has become normative for me throughout the entire range of my thinking. Whatever preserves and enhances this meadow in the natural cycles of its transformation is good; whatever opposes this meadow or negates it is not good. My life orientation is that simple. It is also that pervasive. It applies in economics and political orientation as well as in education and religion …. [This meadow] has none of the majesty of the Appalachian or the western mountains, none of the immensity or power of the oceans, nor even the harsh magnificence of desert country. Yet in this little meadow the magnificence of life as celebration is manifested in a manner as profound and as impressive as any other place I have known in these past many years.[67]

Berry clearly fell in love with the meadow behind his house at an early age, and this experience of falling in love ended up giving his entire life a directionality, an ethical bearing, and a fierce emotional attachment to the meadow that never dimmed, even many years after Berry moved away from his boyhood house. Many of us with similar childhood loves of creeks or meadows or woodlots or wetlands can, decades later, recall vividly the many pleasurable moments in our favorite nature spots, playing, exploring, relaxing, swimming, digging, collecting, and savoring the joy that seemed to be in inexhaustible supply when present in these spots.

Humans loving nature is both good for us and good for God. Not only is time spent in nature deeply satisfying to us, but it also creates bonds of affection to different parcels of creation that get expressed in caring, nurturing, and protecting those favored parcels, and this protective attitude is perhaps the most effective bulwark against biodiversity loss.[68] Our planet could certainly use a widespread ecological conversation among the world's 1.4 billion Catholics that leads to biodiversity protection across the globe, and there could be no better way to foster this goal than to have Catholics fall passionately in love with our little parcels of creation.

Rekindling the Flame: Learning to Love Nature Again

While agape has emerged triumphant as the most legitimate form of love in Catholic moral theology, what is sorely needed right now is something akin to eros for nature, a fiery, passionate, and visceral attachment to creation that not only satisfies our biophilic cravings but also prompts us to protect and nurture all those objects of love experienced in nature. Agape might be ideal for pushing the boundaries of human generosity and for encouraging altruistic behavior beyond the confines of friends or family or community, but eros and the deep feelings it engenders are far more effective at motivating behavior, as it forms a constitutive aspect of our native biophilic constitution.

Pope Francis is one of the few in the Catholic moral tradition who openly promotes the importance of this passionate, fiery love. Commenting on his namesake, Saint Francis of Assisi, in his encyclical *Laudato Si'*, Pope Francis lauds Saint Francis's use of romantic love as the basis for our relationship to creation:

> Just as happens when we fall in love with someone, whenever [St. Francis] would gaze at the sun, the moon or the smallest of animals, he burst into song, drawing all other creatures into his praise. He communed with all creation, even preaching to the flowers, inviting them 'to praise the Lord, just as if they were endowed with reason.' His response to the world around him was so much more than intellectual appreciation or economic calculus, for to him each and every creature was a sister united to him by bonds of affection. That is why he felt called to care for all that exists .... If we approach nature and the environment without this openness to awe and wonder, if we no longer speak the language of fraternity and beauty

in our relationship with the world, our attitude will be that of masters, consumers, ruthless exploiters, unable to set limits on their immediate needs. By contrast, if we feel intimately united with all that exists, then sobriety and care will well up spontaneously.[69]

Lest the point be lost on the reader, this is about as far from the dominant stewardship paradigm and its view of nature as a storehouse of resources to be managed as can be imagined. St. Francis of Assisi was a lover, and by modeling a love for creation based on romantic love, Pope Francis has invoked perhaps the most potent form of love known to humans, outside of perhaps a parent's love for his or her child. This is the kind of love that moves mountains and prompts outrageous acts of bravery, irresistible daydreams, sleepless nights, eloquent poetry, intense longings, wedding vows, and heartbreaking Shakespearean tragedies.

In promoting a rekindled love of nature, I want to avoid one major potential pitfall. Love is often represented as the apogee of the moral life in Catholic moral theology, and while I have no desire to dethrone love's pride of place in the moral life, I also do not want to denigrate the importance of other emotions that are necessary precursors to love and, in this sense, the building blocks out of which love emerges. Whether we take Thomas Berry's experience of the meadow across the creek, or my kids' love for Beaver Creek, or some of my favorite childhood or current nature destinations, love always emerges after extended experience and familiarity and an affirmation of the desirability of the place in question. So, for instance, Pete and Hannah did not fall in love with Beaver Creek before they experienced it; it was only after feeling its cool waters, sinking their toes into its muddy banks, admiring its many smooth rocks and glistening fish, watching the translucent dragonflies that adorned the shrubbery on its banks, and spending many hours playing, investigating, and relaxing in its soothing waters did they come to love it. Prior to love is the experience of the beloved and the many characteristics that make it loveable, and as the beloved is experienced a panoply of emotions emerge that signal an affirmation of the goodness of the beloved[70]—joy, gratitude, awe, wonder, reverence, peace—which can become abiding dispositions or pieties, as James Gustafson calls them, that provide directionality to one's life. But more importantly, these emotions that emerge from experience with the beloved form the basis for love, which means that without these emotions love would never emerge. So while love might be the end stage of a process of experience, discovery, the emergence of feelings, and eventually the realization of being in love, it depends upon a range of prior emotions emerging and signaling the beloved's goodness, and in this sense they ought to be recognized for their vital importance, even indispensability, within the full sweep of love.[71]

Cultivating Love

In what follows I want to focus on the best scenarios for the types of experiences that will cause children to fall in love with nature. American adults, as *The Nature of Americans* study conveys, tend to set impossibly high standards for their nature experiences, preferring those that are more "pristine," expensive, time consuming, and more remote than children, and as we start to describe the contours of positive nature experiences for children, my hope is that adults will see ideas for implementing similar strategies for themselves in their lives. In other words, we adults need to take a page from the children's play book. But my focus on children is also because they are perhaps being hit hardest by the lack of time in nature, and by laying out a constructive agenda for getting kids into nature, perhaps adults will see the value and ease with which nature experiences await.

The data on positive nature experiences for children suggest a pattern that is emotionally engaging and satisfying. First, positive nature experiences tend to be highly social events for children, and years after the fact many recount their favorite childhood activities as being those involving special nature activities done with friends and family. Many adults prefer isolated nature experiences, in which they spend many hours in solitude engaged in various activities. Children, on the other hand, strongly prefer to be in the company of others, whether parents or relatives or friends, and a quality nature experience almost invariably involves a child being able to share that experience with a close friend or family member. Indeed, an almost universal trait of renowned environmentalists is that as children they had a particular family member whose love for nature was impressed upon them at an early age and who consistently took the child into nature and shared all the joy, delight, and fascination that they experienced in nature with the child. Emotional contagion has long been recognized among humans, and children absorb the positive feelings of adults and friends who accompany them on their jaunts into natural areas.

Second, the best nature experiences for children are local.[72] Backyards, nearby parks and open spaces, woods and lakes and creeks close by—nature for children does not need to be grandiose, pristine, or involve considerable travel; nature is part and parcel of their daily lives and typically within a short walk outside the front door. Indeed, the vast majority of unforgettable nature memories reported by children happened locally.[73] I vividly remember when my kids were young and how easily they could become fascinated with myriad things in our backyard: bugs underneath the leaves of garden vegetables, grubs found in freshly tilled dirt, the numerous birds that flitted overhead, the different textures of bark and grass and weeds, the butterflies that targeted sources of nectar, the edges of the fence where the taller grass often held insect or small rodent surprises. Their senses of wonder and awe were consistently activated by pedestrian and mundane things in our backyard, and when their attention waned they simply moved onto another parcel of the backyard to have the wonder and awe emerge all over again. This bodes quite well for parents and adults who are mentoring children, as it minimizes the resources necessary to provide children with meaningful and emotionally satisfying nature experiences.

Third, a great majority of children—nine out of ten—report that nature experiences made them happy (nine out of ten parents concurred with this self-reporting), in addition to lifting them out of episodes of sadness and decreasing feelings of stress and anxiety. Eight out of ten children reported an increase in problem-solving skills, clear thinking, and a willingness to experiment with new ideas. Parents corroborated the psychological gains of their children's contact with nature, noting increases in creativity, resourcefulness, and the ability to overcome obstacles, in addition to a number of social gains in terms of their children making and deepening friendships. From both the children's and parents' perspectives, nature experiences offered a legion of benefits, and there is a tight connection between both personal happiness and a wide range of personal skill sets associated with time spent in nature.

Fourth, and perhaps most importantly, not all nature experiences are equal in their ability to evoke positive emotions or a perceived connection to nature. The positive effects of virtual nature contacts pale in comparison to direct nature contacts, and the quality of nature experiences is more important than the amount of time spent in nature.[74] One study found that absorption in nature is the linchpin to experiencing awe and wonder, which in turn fosters positive emotional states such as happiness, joyfulness, and contentedness. The capacity for absorption in nature is determined by the characteristics of the setting, with those offering more diversity, more textures and sounds and sights, and more possibilities for exploration being the preferred ones.[75]

Perhaps the most informative body of work, which corroborates the study cited immediately above on absorption, but which provides a more detailed template for nature experiences directly applicable to children, is that of Marketta Kyttä, who popularized what is known as the "Bullerby model"[76] for assessing environmental child friendliness and the ability of nature experiences to evoke positive emotions. According to Kyttä, there are four general types of environments, each of which has varying degrees of child friendliness: Wasteland, Cell, Glasshouse, and Bullerby. A Wasteland environment is one in which there is little incentive for children to explore and investigate, since the features of this environment are uniform and bland and uninteresting. Urban environments replete with concrete and steel and human-shaped artifacts, with few objects considered to be "natural," typify this kind of environment. A Cell environment, on the other hand, limits the freedom and knowledge of children to discover possibilities for interacting with the environment. Much like a dog confined exclusively to a backyard and oblivious to what lies beyond the high fence, children living in a cell lack direct experiential data from which to conceptualize the possibilities for interacting with nature. In contrast, a Glasshouse environment may present manifold interesting and inviting possibilities for a child, but the child is prohibited from engaging his or her full range of senses to experience the environment, either due to design, rules, or parental restrictions on freedom, and most of the meaningful information they get in this environment comes via second-hand sources, such as tour guides, signs, books, or online sites. Zoos that exclude any interaction other than seeing animals behind glass or steel bars is one example, as are hikes through nature areas in which getting off the path is prohibited or butterfly houses that prohibit touching the butterflies. The Bullerby environment, according to Kyttä, is the most deeply satisfying for children and the best for evoking a wide range of positive emotions, and it possesses the following characteristics: (1) children are free—and encouraged—to explore independently; (2) the possibilities for interaction are not only perceived by the children, but can also be shaped and utilized by them; (3) the environment is polymorphic, which means that it allows for a wide range of uses; and (4) the more diverse and varied the environment in terms of its lifeforms, textures, shapes, features, and possibilities for exploration, the better.

The Bullerby model provides a helpful template for parents, relatives, friends, and mentors envisioning satisfying nature experiences for children, and it is critical to understand two important points. First, not all environments are equal in providing the kind of stimulating and fulfilling nature experiences that kids crave. In my estimation, the most common mistake is for caretakers to assume that time spent outdoors on playgrounds, jungle gyms, and athletic fields constitute a "nature experience." While these activities are fantastic for energy management and provide a number of psychological and physical benefits, they are governed by a series of rules or by the design of the equipment, which conveys a web of socially accepted meaning about how they are to be used. This limits the freedom of children to generate their own meaning and to explore an array of options as to how they would like to give shape to their experience. For children, the best nature experiences are ones in which they can take charge, go where they want to go, explore on their own terms, and investigate whatever they find interesting. For parents who have internalized rigid social expectations about hovering over their children, granting the amount of freedom conducive to a deeply satisfying nature experience for them can be quite difficult, but the desire to control and micro-manage will only thwart a child from enjoying his or her time in nature. Indeed, perhaps the best thing for a child to experience all the grandiosity of nature available to her is to be encouraged by the adults in her life to explore anything in nature that piques her interest, and not to be afraid to investigate, touch, feel, examine, learn about, and use all her senses to take in as much of nature as she wishes.

This leads to a related point. Do not underestimate the power of unstructured time in nature, or to meandering or apparently aimless wandering. Adults tend to be task oriented and consider non-goal-oriented behavior to be wasting time. For children, however, this allows them to gravitate to things they find interesting and to experience whatever they want on their own terms. This is not only good for children, though, as parents, if they grant their children freedom in nature, will quickly learn their child's interests and likes and dislikes, which in turn might provide critical information about other potential nature experiences that might be enjoyable to a child. As I quickly learned as a parent, the more unstructured time I offered to my kids to explore the wonders of our little part of creation, the happier and more fascinated with nature they became, and the more I learned about their unique idiosyncrasies and different ways of interacting with whatever interested them in nature. Plus, it is always heartening as a parent to see all the smiles of delight on the faces of children as they freely explore and satisfy some of their deepest cravings to feel connected to nature.

Based on the Bullerby model, a handy rule of thumb to keep in mind is that children are explorers with an insatiable appetite for discovering the world around them, which should prompt parents to begin to pay attention to different facets of their local environment as potential nature areas to be explored by their children. To be sure, there is nothing wrong with nature areas designed to be used by children: parks, beaches, hiking trails, boardwalks through wetlands, flower gardens, petting zoos, working farms, etc. These assuredly provide many hours of stimulation for children. But try to notice all the nature areas that are relatively nondescript and rarely noticed by people moving about to conduct the business of everyday life. The small creek buried underneath a canopy of tall trees; the wetland sporting impressive cattails and red-winged blackbirds that can be seen from inside one's car; the retention pond adjacent to a shopping mall that supports healthy populations of frogs, dragonflies, and sunfish; the unruly edges behind a strip mall that sport a surprising array of flora and fauna; the overgrown areas around highway entrances and exits; the abandoned railroad tracks; the wooded areas at the back of dead end roads; the semi-wild borders around industrial parks; and unkempt fence lines and hedgerows, among many others. We adults are conditioned not even to notice these areas, and if we do notice them, we are conditioned socially to disregard them as potential areas to be explored, since they were neither intended nor designed with that purpose in mind. But these are precisely the areas that can be magical to children, as they provide hours of unstructured time with a cornucopia of unknown wonders to be explored and savored! No agenda, no destination, no purpose other than to investigate whatever piques a child's interest.

For parents, the principal obstacle to making these unobtrusive, nondescript, local nature areas a mainstay in your child's life are the quizzical and disapproving looks that you will assuredly get from passersby whose facial expressions will convey unambiguously that you really should not be there—especially with delicate children in tow! Trust me, for many years I was the object of myriad scornful looks when our nature adventures took me and my kids to more public destinations, but after a while I took it as a badge of honor that I could convey, however imprecisely, to all the well-heeled denizens of suburbia that these largely ignored parcels of nature are worthy objects of investigation for biophilic children whose favorite activity was to explore our grandiose natural world.

The fate of our planet, and of God's desire to create a world replete with relational possibilities by generating ever greater levels of biodiversity on Earth, might very well hinge on our efforts to allow our children's native biophilia to blossom into the savory flower of love—a love that relishes its beloved, enjoys spending time together, expresses gratitude to God who made it all possible, and seeks passionately to protect its beloved like it would a spouse or a child. So take your kids and chase butterflies, wade a creek, explore a woodlot, plant wildflowers, catch frogs, swim in a pond, watch birds, go fishing, learn tree identification, pick wild berries, track animals. Immerse your kids in nature, discover your own version of Beaver Creek, and then watch that joy, fascination, and delight emerge as they fall in love with their little parcel of God's creation. Not only will you thank your lucky stars that your kids feel vibrant and fully alive when exploring the wonders of the natural world, but you might also feel a sense of hope about a more benign and sustainable future for life on Earth—and our world needs hearty doses of both right now!

Notes

1. Norman Yoffee and George L. Cowgill, *The Collapse of Ancient States and Civilizations* (Tucson: University of Arizona Press, 1991); Guy D. Middleton, *Understanding Collapse: Ancient History and Modern Myths* (New York: Cambridge University Press, 2017); Jared Diamond, *Collapse: How Societies Choose to Fail or Succeed*, rev. ed. (New York: Penguin, 2011); and Joseph A. Tainter, *The Collapse of Complex Societies* (New York: Cambridge University Press, 1990).

2. Rebecca Linsey and LuAnn Dahlman, "Climate Change, Global Temperature," https://www.climate.gov/news-features/understanding-climate/climate-change-global-temperature (accessed November 27, 2025).

3. Pope Francis, *Laudato Si'*, #50.
4. For a synopsis of the significant risks associated with industrialized agriculture, see Mark Graham, "The Unsavory Gamble of Industrial Agriculture," in *Just Sustainability: Technology, Ecology, and Resource Extraction*, eds. Christiana Z. Peppard and Andrea Vicini (Maryknoll: Orbis Books, 2015), 105-16.
5. Debra J. Davidson, "Rethinking Adaptation: Emotions, Evolution, and Climate Change," *Nature and Culture* 13 (3) (Winter 2018): 378-9 notes the contemporary phenomenon of widespread recognition of an urgent problem and the insufficient responses to it.
6. James F. Keenan, S.J., *A History of Catholic Theological Ethics* (New York/Mahwah: Paulist Press, 2022), 18-21.
7. In what follows, I am going to use the terms emotion and feeling interchangeably, even though they are technically different phenomena. Robert Solomon argues convincingly, in my opinion, that feelings are simply physical sensations that have no underlying cognitive basis. Things such as a raindrop striking one's skin, or a cool breeze wafting across one's face, or a kidney stone passing are all illustrations of a "feeling," or a simple physical sensation. Emotions, on the other hand, include physical sensations but they go beyond that by including some "sophisticated and subtly structured perceptions of the world." In other words, emotions are feelings in response to intellectual evaluations or perceptions of reality. For an extended analysis of this distinction, see Robert C. Solomon, *True to Our Feelings: What Our Emotions are Really Telling Us* (New York: Oxford University Press, 2007), 137-41.
8. Robert S. Ulrich, "Biophilia, Biophobia, and Natural Landscapes," in *The Biophilia Hypothesis*, eds. Stephen R. Kellert and Edward O. Wilson (Washington, DC: Island Press, 1993), 77.
9. Eleanora Gullone, "The Biophilia Hypothesis and Life in the 21st Century: Increasing Mental Health or Increasing Pathology," *Journal of Happiness Studies* 1 (2000): 298.
10. Ulrich, "Biophilia, Biophobia, and Natural Landscapes," 89.
11. Joe Hinds and Paul Sparks, "The Affective Quality of Human-Natural Environment Relationships," *Evolutionary Psychology* 9 (3) (2011): 452.
12. John P. Simaika and Michael J. Samways, "Biophilia as a Universal Ethic for Conserving Biodiversity," *Conservation Biology* 24 (3) (2010): 904.
13. Gullone, "The Biophilia Hypothesis," 294.
14. Ulrich, "Biophilia, Biophobia, and Natural Landscapes," 90.
15. Ulrich, "Biophilia, Biophobia, and Natural Landscapes," 91-2.
16. Gullone, "The Biophilia Hypothesis," 299.

17. Michael L. Spezio, "The Neuroscience of Reasoning and Emotion in Social Contexts: Implications for Moral Theology," *Modern Theology* 27 (2) (April 2011): 348.

18. Henry Davis, *Moral and Pastoral Theology*, vol. 1, *Human Acts, Law, Sin, Virtue* (New York: Sheed and Ward, 1935), 20-2.

19. Thomas Slater, *A Manual of Moral Theology*, vol. 1 (New York: Benzinger Brothers, 1908), 17-40.

20. Catechism of the Catholic Church, #1767.

21. For an insightful synopsis of Thomas Aquinas's thought on emotions, see Diana Fritz Cates, *Choosing to Feel: Virtue, Friendship, and Compassion for Friends* (Notre Dame: University of Notre Dame Press, 1997), 16-30.

22. Val Plumwood, *Feminism and the Mastery of Nature* (New York: Routledge, 1993), 48-55.

23. Sallie McFague, *Super, Natural Christians: How We Should Love Nature* (Minneapolis, MN: Augsburg Fortress, 1997), 59-61.

24. McFague, *Super, Natural Christians*, 88-90.

25. Richard Bulliet, *Hunters, Herders, and Hamburgers: The Past and Future of Human-Animal Relationships* (New York: Columbia University Press, 2005), 41.

26. Bulliet, *Hunters, Herders, and Hamburgers*, 42.

27. Joseph A. Allen, *Love and Conflict: A Covenant Model of Christian Ethics* (Nashville: Abingdon Press, 1984), 49.

28. Gene Outka, *Agape: An Ethical Analysis* (New Haven: Yale University Press, 1972), 149.

29. Paul Ramsey, *Deeds and Rules in Christian Ethics* (New York: Charles Scribner's Sons, 1967), 2

30. St. Augustine, *Sermon on 1 John 4:4-12*, #8.

31. Pope John Paul II, "Homily of His Holiness John Paul II," Boston, Monday, October 1, 1979, https://www.vatican.va/content/john-paul-ii/en/homilies/1979/documents/hf_jp-ii_hom_19791001_usa-boston.html (accessed November 27, 2025).

32. Pope Benedict XVI, *Deus Caritas Est*, #12.

33. For a signal illustration of these concerns, see *The Love Commandments: Essays in Christian Ethics and Moral Philosophy*, eds. Edmund N. Santurri and William Werpehowski (Washington, DC: Georgetown University Press, 1992).

34. James A. Nash, *Loving Nature: Ecological Integrity and Christian Responsibility* (Nashville: Abingdon Press, 1991), 139.

35. Nash, *Loving Nature*, 141.

36. Nash, *Loving Nature*, 142.

37. Nash, *Loving Nature*, 143.

38. Val Plumwood, *Feminism and the Mastery of Nature* (New York: Routledge, 1993).

39. Martin Heidegger, *The Question Concerning Technology and Other Essays* (New York: Harper Perennial Modern Thought, 2013).

40. Glenn A. Albrecht, *Earth Emotions: New Words for a New World* (Ithaca: Cornell University Press, 2019), 25.

41. For Albrecht, solastalgia means distress caused by environmental change.

42. Albrecht, *Earth Emotions*, 10-11.

43. Albrecht, *Earth Emotions*, 67-68.

44. A.E. van den Berg, S. L. Koole, and N. Y. van der Wulp, "Environmental preference and restoration: (How) are they related?," *Journal of Environmental Psychology* 23 (2003): 135-46.

45. R. Kaplan, "The nature of the view from home: Psychological benefits," *Environment and Behavior* 33 (2001): 507-42.

46. F. E. Kuo, M. Bacaicoa, and W. Sullivan, "Transforming inner-city landscapes: Trees, sense of safety, and preference," *Environment and Behavior* 30 (1998): 28-59.

47. Roger S. Ulrich, "View through a window may influence recovery from surgery," *Science* 224 (Apr. 27, 1984): 420.

48. Jessica Stanhope, Martin F. Breed, and Philip Weinstein, "Exposure to greenspaces could reduce the high global burden of pain," *Environmental Research* 187 (2020): 1-10.

49. Melissa R. Marselle, et al., "Pathways linking biodiversity to human health: A conceptual framework," *Environment International* 150 (2021): 1-22.

50. H. A. Passmore and A. J. Howell, "Nature involvement increases hedonic and eudaimonic well-being: A two-week experimental study," *Ecopsychology* 6 (2014): 148-54.

51. Eugenia C. South, Bernadette C. Hohl, Michelle C. Kondo, John P. MacDonald, and Charles C. Branas, "Effect of Greening Vacant Land of Mental Health of Community-Dwelling Adults," *Journal of the American Medical Association* 1 (3) (2018): 1-14.

52. S. Kaplan, "The restorative benefits of nature: Toward an integrative framework," *Journal of Environmental Psychology* 15 (1995): 169-82.

53. J. W. Zhang, P. K. Piff, R. Iyer, S. Koleva, and D. Keltner, "An occasion for unselfing: Beautiful nature leads to prosociality," *Journal of Environmental Psychology* 37 (2014): 61–72.

54. M. G. Berman, E. Kross, K. M. Krpan, M. K. Askren, A. Burson, P. J. Deldin, and J. Jonides, "Interacting with nature improves cognition and

affect for individuals with depression," *Journal of Affective Disorders* 140 (2012): 300–5.

55. Kristine Engemann, Carsten Bocker Pedersen, Lars Arge, Constantinos Tsirogiannis, Preben Bo Mortensen, and Jes-Christian Svenning, "Residential green space in childhood is associated with lower risk of psychiatric disorders from adolescence into adulthood," *Proceedings of the National Academy of Sciences* 116 (11) (March 12, 2019): 5188-93.

56. Mohammad Zahirul Islam, Jessika Johnston, and Peter D. Sly, "Green space and early childhood development: A systematic review," *Review of Environmental Health* 35 (2) (2020): 189-200.

57. Laurence E. Smith, "More Time Out in Nature is an Unexpected Benefit of the COVID-19 Sheltering Rules," *Scientific American* (April 26, 2020), https://blogs.scientificamerican.com/observations/more-time-out-in-nature-is-an-unexpected-benefit-of-the-covid-19-sheltering-rules (accessed November 27, 2025).

58. Richard Louv, *Last Child in the Woods: Saving our Children from Nature-Deficit Disorder* (Chapel Hill: Algonquin Books, 2008); Richard Louv, *The Nature Principle: Reconnecting With Life in a Virtual Age* (Chapel Hill: Algonquin Books, 2012).

59. Stephen R. Kellert, David J. Case, Daniel Escher, Deniel J. Witter, Jessica Mikels-Carrasco, and Phil T. Seng, *The Nature of Americans: Disconnection and Recommendations for Reconnection* (2017), accessed at natureofamericans.org.

60. Kellert, et al., *Nature of Americans*, 50-1.

61. Kellert, et al., *Nature of Americans*, 52.

62. Kellert, et al., *Nature of Americans*, 69-70.

63. Kellert, et al., *Nature of Americans*, 267-84.

64. Kellert, et al., *Nature of Americans*, 64-5.

65. Kellert, et al., *Nature of Americans*, *National Executive Summary Excerpt* (2017), 3, italics in original.

66. National Recreation and Park Association, *Children in Nature: Improving Health By Reconnecting Youth With the Outdoors*, 1, https://www.nrpa.org/uploadedFiles/nrpa.org/Advocacy/Children-in-Nature.pdf (accessed November 27, 2025).

67. Thomas Berry, *The Great Work: Our Way Into the Future* (New York: Random House, 1999), 12-14.

68. Louise Chawla, "Childhood Experiences Associated with Care for the Natural World: A Theoretical Framework for Empirical Results," *Children, Youth, and Environments* 17 (4) (2007): 147.

69. Pope Francis, *Laudato Si'*, #11.

70. Jules Toner, *The Experience of Love* (Washington, DC: Corpus Books, 1968), 40-1.
71. James M. Gustafson, *A Sense of the Divine: The Natural Environment from the Theological Perspective* (Cleveland: Pilgrim Press, 1994).
72. Kellert, et al., *Nature of Americans*, 152-4.
73. Kellert, et al., *Nature of Americans,* 156.
74. Matthew E. Ballew and Allen M. Omoto, "Absorption: How Nature Experiences Promote Awe and Other Positive Emotions," *Ecopsychology* 10 (1) (Mar. 2018): 26-7.
75. Ballew and Omoto, "Absorption," 31-4.
76. Marketta Kyttä, "Environmental child-friendliness in the light of the Bullerby Model," in *Children and Their Environments: Learning, Using and Designing Spaces*, eds. C. Spencer and M. Blades, (New York: Cambridge University Press, 2006), 141-58.

5

The Least Among Us: Environmental Toxicants and Children

When my children were babies, my wife would pump her breast milk, store it in the refrigerator, and I would be responsible for the late-night bottle feedings. Whenever Peter, our firstborn, would start to stir, the race was on to get the milk warmed as soon as possible, as he would explode in anger if more than a few minutes lapsed before some milk started warming his stomach! Hannah, on the other hand, had the patience of a saint, and did not mind a reasonable delay, especially if I held her and talked to her while getting her bottle ready. Pete and Hannah are now recent college graduates, and whenever I reminisce about pleasurable bonding moments with them when they were babies, I always return to their late-night bottle feedings as a source of exquisite joy. The nights were quiet and calm and dark, just my baby sleeping quietly in a bassinette as I read or wrote nearby. At the first sign of stirring, I would go to the bassinette, greet Pete or Hannah in hushed tones, and start talking quietly and lovingly, not rushing the process but allowing him or her time to wake up slowly. When eyes were opened, arms and legs were stretched, and smiles were being directed my way, I would lift Pete or Hannah out of the bassinette and head to the kitchen to get the bottle ready. Once the milk was sufficiently warm, I would sit on the couch, lean back, pull Pete or Hannah onto my chest, insert the nipple, and feel the satisfaction and relaxation creep over my baby's body as the milk started flowing freely. Pete liked to watch my face as he fed, assiduously scanning every nook and cranny, sometimes finding a part of my face that warranted an occasional quizzical look, but never getting too distracted to interrupt his steady sucking. Hannah liked to interact as she fed, playing with my face, cooing at me, sometimes even temporarily suspending her sucking to smile at me. At some point, the warm milk acted like a narcotic and the sucking would cease, eyes would start getting heavy, little bodies would relax, and sleep would eventually return after yawns and stretches. This moment was absolutely blissful—baby cradled on my chest, shared body warmth, dark and quiet all around, rhythmic baby breaths soothing me, the love of my life sleeping quietly in my arms.

Yet amidst this cherished intimacy between parent and child was an unwelcome cognitive rupture, occasioned by the knowledge that the milk I was giving my babies was likely contaminated by a number of environmental toxicants that had accumulated in my wife's body since the time when she was an infant, especially the lipophilic ones that are stored in body fat, which were then liquefied when her breast fat was transformed into milk and passed along to our babies. Today the range of toxicants commonly found in human breast milk is expansive: polybrominated diphenyl ethers (PBDEs), Bisphenol A (BPA), phthalates, polyvinyl chloride, polychlorinated biphenyls (PCBs), heavy metals (lead, mercury, cadmium), perchlorate, perfluorinated chemicals (PFCs), hexachlorobenzene, cyclodiene pesticides, volatile organic compounds (VOCs), polyfluoroalkyl substances (PFAS), DDT, arsenic, and dioxin, among the most worrisome. As Florence Williams puts it, "When we nurse our babies, we feed them not only the fats, sugars and proteins that fire their immune systems, metabolisms and cerebral synapses. We also feed them, albeit in minuscule amounts, paint thinners, dry-cleaning fluids, wood preservatives, toilet deodorizers, cosmetic additives, gasoline byproducts, rocket fuel, termite poisons, fungicides and flame retardants."[1]

Pete, our firstborn, received the bulk of the environmental toxicants in my wife's body, as he ingested roughly thirty years of the load that had built up in her body, while Hannah, our second child, ingested disproportionately less, having arrived less than two years after Pete was born. Nor is this situation unique to my wife. Every woman living in an industrialized country ingests a number of environmental toxicants, and every one of these women who breast feeds her child will pass along many of these toxicants to her baby. It is simply a fact of life today—a deeply unsettling and disturbing fact—that our physical environment is a locus of contamination from which nobody is spared, especially the youngest and most vulnerable. Thus, while biological evolution has over millennia created an ideal form of nutrition for babies that will nurture them through the critical developmental window of infancy, environmental toxicants will pollute that form of nutrition so pervasively that major health organizations now feel compelled to issue statements on whether breast milk is actually preferable to formula for babies![2] The mantra "breast is best," long a mainstay of pediatricians' advice, is no longer self-evident in our contaminated world.

Such is the bizarre universe of environmental toxicants, which upends common sense and traditional health advice, creates classes of threats invisible to the normal channels of human perception, undermines the health of the most vulnerable, and infiltrates our bodies from all quarters—air, soil, water, food, our lived environments. It is a universe in which lives are shortened, capacities for flourishing diminished, hopes for a brighter future are dashed, moral responsibility is like sand slipping through a sieve, and cause–effect relationships are elusive at best. It is a bedeviling, frightening, and maddening universe, in which even the most sacred and intimate rituals and bonds can be fraught with opacity and potential moral guilt, despite our best intentions. And, truth be told, it can be a downright brutal and savage place for our children, who almost always bear the brunt of our increasingly toxic world.

This chapter explores two stories as a port of entry into the morally problematic world of environmental toxicants, PCBs (polychlorinated biphenyls) and the so-called "Body Burden Report" (2005). PCBs are some of the most extensively studied environmental toxicants, which provide something of a prototype for understanding the uniqueness of environmental toxicants and the moral conundrums they pose. The "Body Burden Report" is a startling exposé of the extent of environmental contamination and its ability insidiously to shape even the very beginnings of human life in the womb. From both stories a number of moral considerations emerge, which will clarify the kinds of policies and behavioral patterns that are necessary to create a loving and compassionate universe for the weakest and most vulnerable among us.

Polychlorinated Biphenyls (PCBs)

The first polychlorinated biphenyl (PCB)-like chemical, a byproduct of coal tar, was first discovered in 1865 and a mere sixteen years later the industrial and domestic potential of this chemical was recognized and the first PCBs were being synthesized. By 1914, enough PCBs had entered the environment to leave measurable amounts in the feathers of birds in museums today, and by 1927 the Anniston Ordnance Company moved to full-scale industrial production of PCBs.[3] PCBs are a family of 209 different chemicals that are renowned for their extreme stability and flame retardant properties, even when subjected to very high temperatures, which makes them extremely useful as insulators to prevent fires.[4] PCBs were one of the most commercially popular synthetic chemicals during their time with a wide variety of uses. A favorite in the electrical industry, PCBs were commonly used as liquid insulation in transformers where the potential for sparks, and therefore fire, was high. They were also used in paints, varnishes, adhesives, lacquers, moisture proof paper, plasticizers, and inks, and they were commonly used as a protective or decorative coating on wood, metal, brick, stone, concrete, and fabric surfaces. From yachts and barges, to steel bridges and buildings, to masonry floors and the walls of houses, to concrete swimming pools, to traffic paints—the uses of PCBs continued to grow. Indeed, in time they even found their way into chewing gum and dentures![5]

Despite the early resounding commercial success of PCBs, by the early 1930s—only a few years after commercial production commenced—health problems emerged among plant workers manufacturing PCBs, with acne-like pustules on their faces and bodies, and loss of appetite, energy, and libido as well as other skin ailments being reported by twenty-three of the twenty-four plant workers.[6] Other early warning signs emerged among plant workers in the 1930s: symptoms of systemic poisoning due to PCB fume inhalation; evidence of increased incidence of liver disease among PCB plant workers, and subsequent studies on rats showing severe liver damage even at low concentrations, with a follow-up study indicating that liver damage in humans was likely through PCB contact with human skin. By 1937 the adverse health effects of PCBs were becoming so concerning that the Harvard School of Public Health sponsored a one-day conference on PCBs, the attendees of which included Monsanto (which had purchased the Anniston Ordnance Company), General Electric, the US Public Health Service, and representatives from two states in which PCBs were being manufactured. General Electric's representative claimed that having witnessed the pain and disfigurement of the workers exposed to PCBs, the company's initial reaction was to remove PCBs from General Electric's plant, but due to inadequate substitutes continued to use them. The president of another company attending the conference opined that the health problems associated with PCB exposure were likely to continue for years.[7]

Throughout the 1940s and 1950s, evidence of the harmfulness of PCBs continued to grow, while the use of PCBs began to infiltrate new consumer and agricultural markets, which opened new avenues of legal liability for Monsanto, the exclusive manufacturer of PCBs in the United States. Up to this point, PCBs had been used almost exclusively in closed applications in tightly controlled manufacturing settings, where harm to manufacturing plant workers could be tracked and measured carefully. The qualities that made PCBs so valuable for industrial applications, however, also proved advantageous to a bevy of new products, and PCBs found their way into a wide array of consumer products, including carbon paper, latex paints,[8] heating systems for fried foods, insecticides and pesticides, and as a plasticizer in Sarah Wrap, among the most popular.[9] While these new markets were financially lucrative for Monsanto, they also placed PCB-laden products in the hands of many people who either were unaware of the health dangers posed by PCBs or had little training in how to protect themselves from PCB exposure. At the same time, an ever-expanding chorus of experts continued to voice warnings about the health effects of PCBs. Cecil Drinker, the Dean of the Harvard School of Public Health, wrote that PCBs were "definitely toxic" at "such low concentrations" that even airborne concentrations should be kept at extremely low levels. An investigation by New York State's Division of Industrial Hygiene concluded that PCBs are "highly toxic compounds and must be used with extreme care." A major industrial toxicology text warned of severe damage and systemic poisoning following the inhalation of PCB fumes. The US Navy, which was considering using Pydraul 150, one of Monsanto's PCB-laden hydraulic fluids for use in its submarines, conducted independent animal studies on the hydraulic fluid and found that Pydraul 150 killed all the rabbits used in the test. The Navy not only declined to purchase any Pydraul 150, but it also refused even to consider purchasing any of Monsanto's other products containing PCBs.[10]

As PCBs found their way into an ever-expanding array of products, new classes of people emerged who were being harmed by these products, including end users and consumers, from the Frito company reporting a leak of PCBs into its cooking fat, to workers in Milwaukee being accidentally sprayed with a PCB-laden liquid, to concerns that pesticides containing PCBs were being accidentally sprayed on food or feed crops, despite not being approved for such use.[11] In addition to this expanding group of people harmed by PCBs, it was clear that PCBs were starting to find their way into ecosystems, either from accidental discharges or agricultural use or deliberate releases into the environment as a cost-saving solution to waste disposal. Scientists were particularly concerned about aquatic ecosystems, as PCBs are insoluble in water and heavier than water, which would cause them to sink to the bottom of streams, rivers, and lakes where they could be consumed by bottom feeders and potentially contaminate the entire aquatic ecosystem over long periods of time as they worked their way through the food chain.

A turning point in the story of PCBs occurred in 1964 when halfway around the world Sören Jensen, a Swedish chemist at the University of Stockholm who was hired by the Royal Swedish Commission on Natural Resources to study DDT levels in human fatty tissue and animal samples, started finding mysterious, unidentified substances in his samples.[12] DDT, a popular insecticide used worldwide to control mosquito populations, was known to bioaccumulate and increase in concentration and toxicity as it worked its way through the food chain, causing severe health problems for animals and humans high on the food chain. Jensen started expanding the animal species from which samples were taken and analyzed, and from this broader data set he was able to conclude that these mysterious compounds were found in every animal he tested, they did not occur naturally, and that concentrations were higher in animals connected to aquatic-based ecosystems than in land-based ecosystems, even though he could still not identify them. With the help of ecologists and some persistent sleuthing, over a period of two years Jensen was finally able to identify the mysterious compounds as PBCs, and his article in *New Scientist* in 1966,[13] alerting the world to the ubiquity of PCBs in the environment and our bodies, reverberated like a bombshell throughout the international community.

As countries became aware of the worldwide nature of the PCB contamination and the existing data on their human health effects, countries began banning the further manufacture of PCBs, with the United States being the first country in 1976 and Russia being the last country in 1990 to prohibit the new manufacture of PCBs, although many countries still allowed existing stockpiles of them to be used in select manufacturing processes, but were usually limited to "closed applications" in which the PCBs were encased in plastic or some other durable material to prevent their escape into the environment. Although estimates vary, a total of roughly 3.4 billion pounds of PCBs were produced in the period 1881–1990.

Several factors about PCBs make them a particularly pernicious environmental toxicant. First, they are highly stable and persistent in the environment and take decades if not centuries to degrade under natural conditions, which extends their chemical legacy and agency many generations into the future. This makes them nearly perfect for industrial applications, as there is virtually no way to destroy them, but it makes them an especially virulent environmental toxicant. Second, PCBs can assume liquid or gas form, which contributes to their quality as a world traveler, and it is virtually impossible to recall or control PCBs once they are released into the environment. Third, PCBs biomagnify as they work their way up the food chain, which means that animals and humans high on the food chain will accumulate a disproportionate amount of PCBs in their bodies. This is particularly bad news for apex predators in aquatic-based ecosystems, as there are typically seven links in aquatic-based ecosystems compared to five links in land-based ecosystems, and so the possibilities of bioaccumulation are much greater in the former. Especially when accounting for the marked longevity of many species in aquatic ecosystems, and thus the possibility to accumulate an unusually high level of PCBs in their bodies throughout their lifetimes, apex predators in aquatic ecosystems are the most contaminated beings on our planet. Concentrations of PCBs in polar bears, the Arctic's top predator, for instance, typically multiply three billion times as they move up the Arctic food chain, which means that the bodies of polar bears are simply littered with PCBs.[14] Fourth, PCBs are lipophilic and combine with or dissolve in fat, and as a consequence the two areas with the highest concentration of fat in the human body are the brain and female breasts. This bodes ill for breastfed babies, as the lifetime accumulation of PCBs in a woman's breasts are liquefied and transformed into milk when she breastfeeds her child, which means that a breastfed baby will start out life ingesting the highest concentration of PCBs that it ever will in his or her whole life, precisely at the time when it is undergoing sensitive developmental processes in the critical weeks after birth. According to international standards for PCB ingestion, a newborn infant gets five times the allowable daily level of PCBs for a 150 lb. adult—a truly staggering amount, which if adjusted for weight means that a typical breastfed baby ingests seventy-five times the level of PCBs allowable under international standards![15]

The data suggest a wide array of negative health effects from prenatal exposure to PCBs. Accidental contamination of mothers who gave birth subsequently showed a number of maladies in their children. The most comprehensive study, which examined the health effects on children whose mothers had ingested Great Lakes fish contaminated by PCBs, found that PCB exposure in utero caused lower birth weight, smaller head circumference at birth, weaker reflexes, impaired cognitive functioning, significantly lower scores on verbal and memory tests, poorer word and reading comprehension, deficits in short- and long-term memory, poorer gross and fine motor coordination, and hyperreactivity to negative stimuli.[16] Other studies have linked prenatal PCB exposure to impaired neurological development later in life;[17] a wide array of effects on sexual maturation and reproductive function;[18] and a number of immunological effects including a higher incidence of respiratory ailments, increased acute ear infections, and a higher prevalence of negative responses to childhood vaccinations.[19] Yet, as one researcher laments, there are still "significant gaps" in our scientific understanding of the cause-effect relationship between prenatal PCB exposure and negative health outcomes.[20]

About the only positive thing that can be said about prenatal exposure to PCBs is that it typically does not kill. Yet it has a dastardly effect on the quality of life for exposed children, limiting their possibilities, imposing maddening burdens on the children and their families, diminishing critical cognitive and emotional skills, disrupting their endocrine system and the many hormonal responses it controls, and overall making life more difficult and arduous for these children than it should have been absent exposure to PCBs.

The "Body Burden Report" (2005)

At one time, medical doctors thought that the placenta was an impregnable fortress shielding the baby from anything potentially injurious or inimical to its development. Today scientists know that the placenta is a highly porous border, with a constant exchange between mother and child, so that whatever enters a mother's body will most likely end up in her baby's body as well. In fact, in some instances, the toxicity of some substances will actually be magnified as they cross the placenta and prove to be more injurious to the baby! This means practically that there is no such thing as an "external environment";[21] nor is the notion of living and moving and breathing within an environment accurate, either. Just as the placenta is a porous boundary, our bodies are also continually absorbing and ingesting elements from our lived environments, so that our bodies become a living testament to the history of where we have been and the things to which we have been exposed, whether advantageous to our health or not.

The "Body Burden Report," published by the Environmental Working Group (EWG) in 2005, is perhaps the clearest testimony to the truth that there is no escaping our lived environments, even when nestled comfortably inside our mother's body. The goal of the "Body Burden Report" was to ascertain whether synthetic chemicals that were known toxicants were crossing the placenta and infiltrating the bodies of babies before birth. At the time of this testing, there were roughly 75,000 synthetic chemicals being marketed commercially, with approximately 1000 new synthetic chemicals making their way into commercial products per year. Given the exorbitant cost of the tests to detect the presence of environmental toxicants coupled with the fact that existing technology often could not detect certain toxicants, the Environmental Working Group chose to focus on the 413 most injurious synthetic chemicals known to children at that time that could be detected. Cord blood, which moves back and forth from mother to baby, was extracted from the umbilical cords of ten randomly selected newborn babies in the United States, tested for the presence of these toxicants, and the results were simply astounding.

A total of 287 environmental toxicants were detected, with an average of 200 found in each sample. This was also the first detection ever reported in cord blood for 209 different compounds. Here are the findings, broken down into three groups of toxicants.[22] Chemicals banned or severely restricted in the United States represented the largest number of toxicants detected, with a total of 212 different chemicals in the ten cord blood samples. PCBs were the most ubiquitous, with a total of 147 different PCBs detected, followed by fifty different types of polychlorinated naphthalenes (PCNs), which are commonly found in broad use industrial chemicals such as flame retardants, electrical insulators, and pesticides. Fourteen different kinds of organochlorine pesticides (OCs), which had been phased out of use in the United States, were detected.

The next group, common consumer product chemicals, had a total of forty-seven chemicals detected, including seven OCs still actively being used commercially in the United States, eight perfluorochemicals (PFCs) that are commonly used as stain and grease resistant coatings on household carpeting and furniture, and thirty-two polybrominated diphenyl ethers (PBDEs) that function as flame retardants in televisions, computers, and household furniture.

The final group, waste byproducts, contained twenty-eight different toxicants. Eighteen polychlorinated and polybrominated dibenzo dioxins and furans (PCDD/F and PBDD/F) were detected, which are created through garbage incineration and the production of plastics. Rounding out this category were ten polynuclear aromatic hydrocarbons (PAHs), which are created during fossil fuel combustion, especially the driving of automobiles.

While the total number of chemicals in the EWG's "Body Burden Report" is an important category, a more relevant number is the range of toxicants found in individual babies. Environmental contamination can often be concentrated in certain geographical areas, with those living in these areas suffering contamination far beyond those in the general population. As a result, even though the total number of toxicants detected might be quite high, the contamination might be limited to a few subjects who live in these highly contaminated areas, and the one benefit (if it can be called that) of localized contamination is its ability to be isolated, contained, and eventually remediated.

An even more telling number is the range of toxicants found in individual babies, as this is a better indicator of the distribution of contamination throughout the population. Here are findings of the "Body Burden Report," broken down by the chemical family name and the range of toxicants found in the individuals sampled: PCBs, 65-134 (meaning that each cord blood sample contained between 65-134 different PCBs); PCNs, 22-40; OCs banned in the United States, 7-14; PBDEs, 13-29; PFCs, 4-8; OCs actively used in the United States, 2-6; PCDD/Fs and PBDD/Fs, 5-13; and PAHs, 1-10.

Even a cursory glance at these numbers reveals two shocking facts. First, environmental toxicants are ubiquitous. Nobody, anywhere, can escape their malignant presence, even the bodies of babies nestled inside the bodies of their mothers, which we would hope (erroneously) is a safe, protected haven for a baby in which to grow and flourish. Second, the bodies of babies are being literally doused with hundreds, if not thousands, of injurious toxicants before they are even born—remember that the EWG tested for the presence of only a small fraction (413 of 75,000+) of the potential toxicants being sold commercially. As the EWG states, "fetal exposure to industrial chemicals is quite literally out of control."[23]

The ubiquity of these environmental toxicants, however, is only one part of this story. The other part is the unique effects of each toxicant in the human body and the ways in which they can harm or injure those unfortunate enough to come into contact with them. To this end, let me construct a précis for a few of the most common toxicants that were detected in the cord blood and their likely effects on humans.

Organochlorine pesticides. These are some of the most popular pesticides used worldwide, with a number of different applications, including insecticides, fungicides, bactericides, herbicides, and rodenticides. The relatively long half-life of organochlorine pesticides (they are listed as a persistent organic pollutant (POP)) means that they stay active in topsoil, water, and the air for long periods of time, and coupled with their high lipophilicity and tendency to bioaccumulate, they are some of the more persistent and nefarious chemical threats to human health.[24] Many organochlorine pesticides are also listed as "highly hazardous" by the World Health Organization based on the LD_{50} test,[25] and many are known to be carcinogenic, neurotoxic, and endocrine disruptors.[26] Common health effects associated with these pesticides include hypertension, cardiovascular disorders,[27] abnormal thyroid hormone levels,[28] hormone related cancers (breast, stomach, prostate, and lung cancers),[29] autoimmune diseases such as multiple sclerosis and eczema,[30] learning disabilities and hyperreactivity disorder in children,[31] liver dysfunction,[32] Parkinson's Disease,[33] diabetes and insulin resistance,[34] early psychomotor development delays,[35] and a number of maladies associated with endocrine disruption. In addition to the human health effects, the organochlorine pesticide DDT is famous for thinning the eggshells of bald eagles and taking our national bird to the brink of extinction before the ban of DDT in 1972 in the United States.

Polybrominated Diphenyl Ethers (PBDEs). Similar to PCBs, the commercial success of PBDEs was associated with their flame retardant capabilities,[36] which meant that the main route of human exposure occurred through the inhalation of house dust[37] as PBDEs saw a great deal of domestic applications including fire proofing substances on furniture, upholstery, carpeting, and flooring.[38] The documented human health effects of PBDEs are legion. PBDEs have a disruptive influence on a baby's endocrine system, primarily on the thyroid function, but neurodevelopment and reproductive functions are also affected.[39] In children, exposure to PBDEs has been linked to increased anxiety and social withdrawal,[40] adverse birth outcomes such as preterm birth and low birth weight,[41] deficits in attention, fine motor coordination, and cognitive functioning, lower scores on standardized tests for verbal comprehension, perceptual reasoning, and mental processing speed, and increased incidence of hyperactive and impulsive behavior.[42] PBDEs are also associated with altered thyroid functioning in pregnant women, a number of endocrine disrupting activities, and increased risk of miscarriage. Unfortunately for American women, a more permissive regulatory climate means that concentrations of PBDEs in their bodies can be upwards of twenty times higher than in the bodies of European or Asian women.[43]

Polychlorinated and Polybrominated dibenzo dioxins and furans (PCDD/F and PBDD/F). These chemicals are typically associated with industrial and thermal processes, garbage incineration, or the production of industrial plastics, and concentrations can be found in ambient air, fly ash, sediments, fish and shellfish, plastics, human milk, adipose tissue, and the blood of manufacturing workers.[44] Chlorinated and brominated dioxins are considered some of the most toxic human-made substances due to the low doses necessary to be lethal, and they are associated with a number of serious health effects: severe wasting, immunotoxicity, thymic atrophy, reproductive deficiencies, teratogenesis, chloracne, altered metabolism and homeostasis, altered growth, and decreases in T4 and vitamin A.[45] Long-term exposure has been linked to immune system dysfunction, nervous system deficiencies, endocrine system disruption, and various reproductive issues.[46]

From this brief survey alone of the most common toxicants found in the cord blood of babies who were subjects of the Environmental Working Group study, there is an almost mind-boggling array of health effects associated with exposure to these toxicants, ranging from minor harms that make life more difficult for those affected to grievous harms that are life altering and could adversely affect a child for the rest of his or her life. Keep in mind that we surveyed only the known health effects of the most common toxicants found in the cord blood, which represents a minute fraction of the potential toxicants and their health effects that could be making their way into babies' bodies before they are born. So while there is much that remains unknown about the actual effects of environmental toxicants and children, what we do know is that babies' bodies are being bombarded with environmental toxicants in utero and the health effects of this exposure are wide ranging, sometimes highly debilitating, and terrifying to anyone intent on raising happy and healthy children.

Drawing Some Conclusions

The two stories of PCB contamination and the findings of the Environmental Working Group's "Body Burden Report" reveal a number of features about the chemicalization of our lives and the ethical dimension of this issue. Some of these features pose unique challenges to constructing an ethical assessment of what has transpired, as they often require factual information that cannot be known or there are few precedents within the Catholic moral tradition to render them intelligible. Yet many of these challenging features will also be common to other large-scale, long-term environmental problems, and it behooves us to identify some of the conceptual challenges involved and to start rendering them intelligible. To this end, let me start with some salient facts that deserve mention.

First, the time scales for dealing with environmental contamination are expansive. For any one particular instance of contamination, the complete cycle from beginning to end would look something like this: (1) A compound is synthesized and marketed commercially; (2) the use of the compound becomes widespread enough to create a certain level of exposure; (3) a sufficient level of exposure in enough people causes identifiable symptoms in humans that get noticed by parents, nurses, doctors, and public health officials; (4) a consensus emerges over time that a synthetic compound is a "problem"; (5) there emerges a political consensus about a viable "solution" to the problem; (6) actions are taken to implement the solution; (7) over time, the effectiveness of these actions are assessed; (8) if the actions are deemed to be "effective," then the "end" of the problem is declared; (9) if the actions are deemed to be "ineffective," then officials go back to (6) and try a different strategy and go through the succeeding steps until some satisfactory solution to the problem is reached. What constitutes an "end" to a problem or a "satisfactory solution" is, of course, always a political judgment that can mean a number of different things, ranging from no further exposure to the injurious compound to acceptable levels of exposure to a tolerable level of deaths or harms associated with exposure to that particular compound.

For persistent, bioaccumulative, and dangerous pollutants (PBDs) like PCBs, which can remain intact in sediment and human and animal fat for very long periods of time, the contamination might span multiple generations and take decades if not centuries before an acceptable conclusion to the contamination is reached. PCBs were first marketed commercially in 1881, the first national ban on their further production occurred in 1976, with the last country to ban production in 1990, and yet twenty-five years later in 2005 they were still one of the most prevalent environmental toxicants in the bodies of babies—and it is anyone's guess as to how long PCBs will continue to be a legitimate threat to the health and safety of children.

These expansive time scales suggest that, at the very least, considerable forethought and planning are required to protect public health. With threats such as the contamination of the food supply or dangerous consumer products, unsafe conditions are recognized quickly as consumers are sickened or injured, recalls are issued, products are promptly removed from the market, and the problem quickly comes to a determinate end. This is certainly not the case with environmental toxicants, with extraordinarily long time periods required to deal with their nefarious health effects being the norm rather than the exception, which suggests that a robust dose of deliberation, foresight, and institutional planning for worst case scenarios ought to be woven into the regulatory process. As in life generally, when contemplating options that might have serious, long-term consequences for scores of people for generations to come, extreme care and extensive deliberation ought to characterize such decision-making processes.

In addition, the PCB story also illustrates vividly the almost inherently trans-national character of environmental contamination and the thorny issues raised by the inability to contain toxicants. Like many environmental toxicants that assume different forms or bioaccumulate, once released into the environment many environmental toxicants become world travelers and are very difficult to contain. Moreover, most environmental toxicants are invented and produced in highly industrialized countries by corporations that have high levels of capital, both financial and intellectual, which gives them a considerable advantage in being able to understand, monitor, and protect their interests from the adverse outcomes of chemical contamination. Yet as environmental toxicants transgress national boundaries and begin traipsing across our planet, it is often the poorest people in the poorest countries who have virtually no institutional resources to protect themselves from the contamination who suffer the most. Stated a bit differently, it is often the poorest who benefit the least from the production and use of environmental toxicants, yet they frequently bear the brunt of the pollution and the manifold nefarious health effects associated with the contamination. As Pope Francis repeats frequently in his encyclical *Laudato Si'*, we live in an interconnected world[47] in which every action, policy, and behavioral pattern will unquestionably affect many others, some near and dear to us and readily known and others nameless and faceless and sometimes halfway across the planet, but each affected in some way by our individual actions and choices, and this interconnection with everything that exists becomes readily apparent when dealing with environmental toxicants.

Second, the chemical industry has a robust financial incentive to present its products in the best light possible, to resist any attempt to impose governmental regulation on its products, and to create a secure and stable market for its products by fostering a receptive environment in which to do business. Of course, the chemical industry is probably not unique in its desire to make a profit and not to experience a contraction in the market for its products. Yet, if the behavior of Monsanto is indicative of what should be expected from the chemical industry, then any kind of effective internal policing behavior by the chemical industry should not be expected. Monsanto knew for decades about a multitude of negative health effects of its PCB-laden products, and despite this knowledge continued to search for new markets and opportunities to expand sales of its PCB products. In practice, this means that if it is determined that some type of restraint needs to be exercised regarding the production or distribution of any potential environmental toxicant, it should be assumed that those with a financial interest in the sale of the toxicant should not be expected to implement adequate safeguards and that an external authority will have to set safety standards in order to protect public health.

Third, human knowledge is fragmentary and limited, which means that there will always be an element of unpredictability when developing new technologies. Environmental history is replete with illustrations of technologies being deployed and adopted that turned out to have quite consequential, and sometimes large-scale, effects that were neither intended nor foreseen. From the internal combustion engine that is now complicit in a sizable percentage of greenhouse gas emissions worldwide every year, to the widespread use of chlorofluorocarbons (CFCs) in refrigerants and propellants that caused the thinning of our planet's ozone layer, to the use of DDT to control mosquito populations that caused precipitous declines of many bird species due to the thinning of their eggs, our ability to foresee the manifold effects of our technologies is partial, at best, even though as a species we are notably self-congratulatory about our purported intellectual prowess.

Fourth, scientists have noted that the expected 1:1 correspondence between exposure to an environmental toxicant and an illness, which assumes that more exposure is worse for one's health, is dubious at best and can unwittingly have grave effects on the health of children. For adults, this assumption is often true, so that the best policy is to limit the amount of exposure to environmental toxicants. In turn, this assumption is often the basis for legislation intended to limit exposure by setting safety thresholds for the ingestion of environmental toxicants. Fetuses and children, however, are uniquely vulnerable to environmental toxicants for a number of different reasons. The immature and porous blood–brain barrier of a baby allows greater exposure of the brain in utero to environmental toxicants. Children also have lower levels of certain chemical binding protective proteins, which allows more environmental toxicants to reach organ systems and to do damage there. Detoxification and excretion systems of children are undeveloped compared to adults, which means that toxicants typically remain in the bodies of children for longer periods of time. Yet most importantly, the most critical developmental stages in any person's life are the early years when all major organs and systems are developing rapidly and undergoing constant changes, which makes the bodies of babies and children far more vulnerable to the nefarious effects of exposure to environmental toxicants than adults. The practical upshot is that quantity turns out to be a far less important consideration than timing, as it has become clear that there are critical developmental windows in which the bodies and organs of babies and children are highly vulnerable to even the slightest perturbation, and during these critical windows even the most minute exposures to certain environmental toxicants could have potentially devastating consequences.[48]

This poses a number of challenges for regulators and parents who are charged with the responsibility for keeping children safe from environmental toxicants. Given the unique susceptibility of babies and children, data gained from studying the health effects of environmental toxicants on adults is not only inapplicable to babies and children, but using such data to set safety standards could actually be injurious to them, insofar as they could specify threshold levels far above those required to keep babies and children safe. In order to be accurate, scientific data would have to be generated by studies on babies and children, rather than by studies on adults.

Fifth, regulatory tools such as setting threshold levels often do not account for the synergistic or cumulative effects of multiple environmental toxicants in a child's body, which individually might be benign but in combination might lead to a number of deleterious health effects. Setting threshold levels is always a tenuous process, as many assumptions have to be made about the typical ways an "average" human body responds to exposure to environmental toxicants and the chemicals likely to be encountered by a typical child. Of course, each child's body is unique and each child is going to be exposed to different chemicals in different quantities at different times during his or her development, so the assumptions that are at the heart of setting threshold levels are, at best, rough approximations that might frequently fail to protect children, to the extent that the actual lives and bodies of children do not adhere to those assumptions.[49] Setting threshold levels could be much better tool if they were based on a more holistic evaluation of cumulative exposures over time and their synergistic effects, but this is a far more painstaking and resource intensive process than simply making some critical assumptions.

There are a few more reasons why the common practice of establishing threshold levels might fail to protect fetuses and children. Threshold levels are typically based on a 150 pound adult, and most children weigh far less, which means that even if threshold levels are observed assiduously and great care is taken to keep children from ingesting environmental toxicants above known threshold levels, this still might entail children getting harmful levels of toxicants into their bodies. Furthermore, threshold levels are established for each environmental toxicant individually, yet it is entirely possible that children frequently ingest many potential sources of the same toxicant (pesticides on fruits are the classic example of this). In addition, children are highly specialized eaters and drinkers and will binge on their favorite foods and drinks all day long, sometimes for months on end. When my daughter, Hannah, was two years old she went through a six-month period during which she wanted to eat fresh blueberries exclusively. While a parent might be inclined to jump for joy at the thought of his daughter gorging herself on a popular "superfood," which is chock full of vitamins and nutrients and antioxidants, blueberries, like many other fruits, often have a number of pesticide residues on them. The United States Department of Agriculture's "Pesticide Data Program,"[50] for instance, has found fifty-two pesticide residues on blueberries, ranging from carcinogens to hormone disruptors to neurotoxicants and developmental and reproductive toxicants[51]—and blueberries are typically regarded as one of the cleaner fruits to consume! The Environmental Working Group's infamous annual "Dirty Dozen" list, which identifies the fruits and vegetables most contaminated by pesticide residues, recently found that nearly 70 percent of the non-organic produce sold in the United States contains potentially harmful pesticide residues, and a number of those making the "Dirty Dozen" list this year are the foods that children will eat and drink excessively: strawberries, apples, grapes, cherries, peaches, and pears.[52]

The disquieting insight is that the dominant model of ensuring safety by limiting exposure to environmental toxicants via threshold levels is ineffective for all the aforementioned reasons and needs to be jettisoned in the case of babies and children, as the relevant question often is not, How much exposure is safe? but Is **any** exposure safe? While well intentioned and perhaps the best current regulatory tool to keep most average adults safe from environmental toxicants, threshold levels, in turns out, are dubious in their ability to protect children from harmful environmental toxicants, as they were not designed with their unique vulnerabilities in mind.

The regulatory approach in the United States for protecting children from environmental toxicants consists of two major pieces of federal legislation, the Toxic Substances Control Act (TSCA) in 1976 and the Frank Lautenberg Chemical Safety for the 21st Century Act in 2016. The post-Second World War era saw an enormous surge in new chemical products entering the commercial market, which were variants of chemicals that had found use during the war and now enjoyed various commercial applications. This deluge and the mounting scientific data during this period of the harm resulting from exposure to these chemicals prompted Congress to pass TSCA, which partitioned chemicals into two categories, new chemicals and those already present on the commercial market. For the latter, the Environmental Protection Agency (EPA) was not statutorily mandated to assess this group of chemicals, and even if the EPA suspected that a chemical commercially available did pose a threat to human health or safety, it faced a Catch 22 when attempting to gather the requisite data to determine whether such a standard of risk was present, as the EPA needed scientific data in order to compel testing of a particular chemical, but testing was required in order to generate the necessary scientific data. As a result, TSCA proved to be remarkably inept and "glacially slow"[53] at regulating chemicals that were marketed commercially before the passage of the act and effectively grandfathered in approximately 62,000 chemicals as safe for their intended purposes.[54]

The focus of TSCA, however, was on new chemicals, and the EPA was mandated to conduct a review of each new chemical before it was approved for commercial application. From the time that a premanufacture notice was submitted, the EPA had ninety days to collect information and make a determination on whether the new chemical posed an unreasonable risk to human health or safety. Those privy to the mechanics of scientific studies know that ninety days is hardly enough time to collect any meaningful data, which meant that the principal source of information upon which the EPA relied to make this assessment was industry data, which were often blatantly skewed to show the benign nature of the chemical. In addition, TSCA's broad notion of proprietary information, which no company was legally bound to divulge to the EPA, meant that companies often shared very little information with the EPA. Once again, the EPA's oversight and ability to protect the health of Americans was severely undercut by limited statutory powers that prevented it from keeping dangerous chemicals off the commercial market and commentators almost universally agree that TSCA was "notoriously ineffective"[55] in realizing its intended purpose of protecting public health. So ineffective, in fact, that only five chemicals were either limited or banned for use by the EPA during the entire lifespan of TSCA—a small fraction of the chemicals that many considered to be highly toxic to human health.[56]

Widespread dissatisfaction with TSCA was the impetus behind the passage of the Frank Lautenberg Chemical Safety for the 21st Century Act (FLCSA) in 2016, which considerably expanded the EPA's regulatory powers and was intended to give the EPA sufficient tools to become more effective at regulating potentially dangerous chemicals. In order to address the tens of thousands of chemicals grandfathered in under TSCA with little to no review of their potential toxicity, FLCSA mandated that the EPA establish a new priority schema for reviewing existing chemicals, with those determined to be in the high priority category due to their potential toxicity triggering an automatic deadline for the EPA to have completed its risk assessment for these chemicals, which can be renewed if the EPA thinks that more time will yield more accurate safety data. In addition, the EPA is mandated to have an assessment pipeline, with ten ongoing evaluations in the first 180 days after the passage of FLCSA and twenty ongoing evaluations within 3.5 years of its passage.[57]

For new chemicals, the FLCSA essentially doubles the amount of time (from ninety days under TSCA to 180 days) the EPA has to collect and study scientific data and to make a determination about a chemical's safety, and the EPA is mandated at the end of this process to make one of three specific determinations: that a new substance presents an unreasonable risk to human health, which the EPA must then regulate; that it is not likely to present an unreasonable risk, which forbids the EPA from regulating; or that it lacks sufficient evidence to make a determination, which allows the EPA to request more time to collect data and to regulate it in the interim. The EPA also has considerably more flexibility in ordering additional data to be generated by manufacturers, as well as tighter regulations surrounding claims of proprietary business information, which industry has used in the past to limit the amount of information that it was legally required to share with the EPA.

The FLCSA also mandates that companies be responsible for 50 percent or 100 percent of the costs necessary for safety testing, which greatly insulates the EPA against the unpredictable vicissitudes of changing administrations and fluctuations in funding,[58] which could have a significant impact on the EPA's ability to fulfill the FLCSA's legal mandates. In addition, the FLCSA prohibits traditional cost-benefit analysis, which requires that all the benefits and burdens associated with a regulatory decision be part of the assessment process. In practice, this often leads to economic considerations of industry being given priority over the health and safety of citizens. Under FLCSA, however, only health effects are germane to the judgment of a chemical's safety.

Perhaps most important for our purposes, though, is the recognition that various groups ought to be the subject of special protections by the EPA with "infants, children, pregnant women, workers, [and] the elderly" being explicitly mentioned as common groups that are uniquely vulnerable to the deleterious health effects of environmental toxicants either due to their unique susceptibility or their greater exposure to a toxicant. Furthermore, the EPA is also legally mandated under FLCSA to use its regulatory powers to protect these vulnerable groups.[59] Thus, for the first time in American history, federal legislation enshrines legal protection for the weakest and most vulnerable among us—a cause for hearty celebration!

While FLCSA is a considerable improvement upon TSCA and in many ways rectifies its obvious shortcomings, the critical question is whether FLCSA does what it promises—and is legally mandated to do—and actually protects these vulnerable populations of people from the negative health effects of environmental toxicants? Unfortunately, according to most commentators the answer is a resounding "No!" This is not attributable specifically to the contents of FLCSA, but rather to chronic issues with chemical regulation in the United States. One issue is that the chemical industry in the United States is simply too vast and its products too numerous for the resources of the EPA to manage effectively. Valerie Watnick offers an eye-opening assessment of the magnitude of this undertaking:

> While [F]LCSA was designed to be more health-protective and, for the first time, requires EPA to review existing chemicals, the exceedingly slow process of review makes this a bureaucratic nightmare, with little potential to achieve [F]LCSA's goals. There are over 87,000 existing chemicals potentially on the market today and over 60,000 without safety data on

file. Yet [F]LCSA calls for EPA to review just twenty existing high-priority chemicals within three and a half years of its enactment.

Nor does the Act provide any requirements or mechanisms for EPA to work quickly enough through existing chemical reviews to protect human health. One report has suggested that, even considering only the ninety high priority existing chemicals listed in the "Work Plan" established in 2014 pursuant to the old TSCA, it will take EPA twenty-eight years to complete initial risk evaluations, thirty years to finalize regulations, and thirty-five years to implement the rules. Other reports are even less sanguine. Sheldon Krimsky has stated that it would take EPA 1,500 years to prioritize and evaluate 8,500 existing chemicals—just ten percent of those on the market today. If the list were reduced to just 500 chemicals, with a three-year completion time to evaluate and establish rules on each chemical, the task would take fifty years.[60]

Critics also contend that limitations inherent to the EPA's current testing regime prevent it from generating accurate scientific data. The principal tool for generating data is animal toxicology tests, which expose animals to high doses of chemicals in order to determine the level at which a particular chemical becomes dangerous. There are two critical problems with this approach. First, animal physiology is often very different from human physiology, and as a result the findings of animal experiments often are inapplicable to humans. Insofar as these findings become the basis for regulation decisions by the EPA, this could result in dangerous chemicals not being regulated, or benign chemicals being the subject of strict regulations—neither of which is a desirable outcome. Furthermore, human exposure to environmental toxicants typically occurs at low doses over extended periods of time, which means that the EPA's preferred method of ascertaining toxicity via high doses on animals over short periods of time is likely to be a highly inaccurate method for determining toxicity and deleterious health effects.[61]

Yet even if these two limitations could be surmounted, critics still contend that the testing regime mandated by the FLCSA still fails to protect children, as it grossly underestimates real-life risk to injurious chemicals. In gathering toxicological data, the EPA only requires that it consider exposure pathways in isolation, which means that it does not consider aggregate exposures over time, which are the combined exposures to a person across multiple pathways (air, water, food, skin contact) throughout a person's life. Given the fact that exposure to common chemicals can often occur through multiple sources, it only makes sense to set safety thresholds based on aggregate exposures, as these represent the most realistic real-life scenarios, and by failing to do so the EPA systematically underestimates risk.[62] In addition, the EPA is also charged with protecting vulnerable populations, and in many cases certain populations become more vulnerable through repeated exposure to a harmful chemical, which means that the EPA cannot fulfill its legally mandated requirement without moving to a testing regime that identifies vulnerable populations by taking account of aggregate exposures over time.

Finally, but no less importantly, the EPA does not consider interactions among chemicals, nor does it consider potentially synergistic relationships between chemicals, which magnifies the injurious potential of combinations of chemicals.[63] Especially when dealing with children, who have a much greater likelihood of being harmed by low doses of chemicals during critical developmental windows, it becomes incumbent upon the EPA, if it is interested in actually protecting our most vulnerable populations and their real life risks, to adopt a different testing regime that more closely approximates what is actually happening in the bodies of people as they live their lives.

The practical upshot of the current regulatory apparatus in the United States is that it is very well intentioned yet, by almost all accounts, remarkably unsuccessful at protecting children and other vulnerable populations from the deleterious health effects of environmental toxicants. There are upwards of 90,000 chemicals currently being marketed commercially, with another 1000 new chemicals being introduced to the commercial market every year, and we know next to nothing about them, who is ingesting them and at what rates, whose health is being affected adversely, what synergistic effects are occurring, what kind of damage they are doing, and what level of exposure is injurious for the most vulnerable segments of our population. As one commentator notes, even though widespread exposure to environmental toxicants is probably a more ominous long-term threat to humankind than global warming, the current state of chemical regulation is comparable to a grand experiment insofar as we know that millions of vulnerable children are coming into frequent contact with scores of potentially injurious environmental toxicants, yet we are unsure about who will be affected and how.[64] Knowing so little when the stakes are so high for our children is enough to make one nauseous.

Our entire regulatory structure is organized around the assumption that a chemical should be proven to be dangerous before it is subject to governmental regulation, yet Pope Francis in *Laudato Si'* chides this particular approach and urges nations to embrace the precautionary principle and to make it a bedrock of the legal approach surrounding environmental safety. He writes,

> The Rio Declaration of 1992 states that 'where there are threats of serious or irreversible damage, lack of full scientific certainty shall not be used as a pretext for postponing cost-effective measures which prevent environmental degradation.' This precautionary principle makes it possible to protect those who are most vulnerable and whose ability to defend their interests and to assemble incontrovertible evidence is limited. If objective information suggests that serious and irreversible damage may result, a project should be halted or modified, even in the absence of indisputable proof. Here the burden of proof is effectively reversed, since in such cases objective and conclusive demonstrations will have to be brought forward to demonstrate that the proposed activity will not cause serious harm to the environment or to those who inhabit it.[65]

Pope Francis notes that embracing the precautionary principle entails neither a recalcitrant attitude toward technological innovation nor a dismissal of profitability as a legitimate end to be pursued by industry, but it does entail several seismic shifts in the regulatory criteria applicable to the chemical industry. First, according to Pope Francis the appropriate level of epistemic certainty should not be the traditional scientific "proof," but something along the lines of "objective information" suggesting a cause-effect link, which is a far weaker standard. This criterion would require far less time and data to establish. Second, Pope Francis is placing the burden on industry—not on the government—to generate the necessary data on its products to make a safety determination. Third, he is changing the end that must be achieved from harm to safety; in other words, it is industry's job to show that its products are safe, not the government's job to show that industry's products are dangerous. In essence, Pope Francis endorsement of the precautionary principle is another way of saying, if we are to err, we ought to do so on the side of safety, as the lives of our most vulnerable and helpless populations potentially hang in the balance.

Should Pope Francis's version of the precautionary principle become enshrined in federal legislation, there is every reason to believe that babies and children would be better protected from the negative health effects of harmful chemicals. But there is also good reason to believe that we live in a system in which federal legislation can be only marginally effective at protecting the vulnerable in our midst. With 90,000 chemicals on the commercial market and scores of new chemicals being patented in the Unites States every year, with probably 95 percent of the chemicals in our national inventory never having sufficient safety data generated on them, the chemical system in the United States is so vast and the amount of time, resources, and energy necessary to gain relevant safety data on them is so cumbersome and lengthy that our federal government will probably never be doing much more than playing an endless catch up game with the most egregious chemical manufacturers.

This should not obviate the fact that Pope Francis's endorsement of the precautionary principle is right on target, and that as Catholics whose bedrock moral identity is being agents of love and compassion, the chemicalization of our lives represents one of the most insidious realities of our time, affecting a class of people—babies and children—who are the most vulnerable and because of this ought to be given robust preference when it comes to policies and behaviors that are designed to protect humans. They are vulnerable, as Pope John Paul II points out, because they are voiceless and powerless and they necessarily depend on others to protect their health and to secure their well-being.[66] Yet they are also vulnerable in the sense that their bodies are literally being fashioned in the womb, and the quality and texture of the rest of their lives depend on the conditions at the beginning, and we as an advanced industrial society have greatly increased the risk that this fragile beginning will go terribly awry and they will have to spend their entire lives either chronically underperforming, or dealing with unnecessary adversity, or suffering from cognitive deficits, or experiencing sexual health issues, or being hampered by emotional volatility, or struggling in school, or suffering from any one of literally hundreds of other psychological, mental, or physical health maladies associated with exposure to environmental toxicants at an early stage in life. The stakes are exceptionally high at the beginning of life, and if John Paul II's admonition that the way in which we treat children is a measure of our fidelity to God is correct, we ought to be open to the possibility that the quality of our moral lives before God is seriously wanting.

Indeed, the contrast between the ethical substance of the parables that have sculpted our understanding of compassion and the way in which we currently act toward children is stark. The parables consistently drive home the point that compassion impels us to struggle against the all-too-human temptation to render the weak and vulnerable and defenseless invisible, and thereby to absolve ourselves of any responsibility to care for and to protect them from harm. In the Parable of the Good Samaritan (Luke 10:25-37), when coming across a man beaten unmercifully and left for dead in a ditch, a priest and Levite attempt to make the man invisible by crossing to the other side of the road and putting physical distance between themselves and the man—out of sight, out of mind—despite their religious obligation to render aid or to bury the corpse. The Samaritan, on the other hand, who hailed from a tribe with a fair amount of antipathy toward Jews, does the opposite of rendering the man in the ditch invisible. He jumps down into the ditch, draws himself into the full, horrifying reality of man beaten and bloody and swollen and in awful pain, and then not only renders aid but takes him to a place where longer term care can be administered and then pays for that care!

The Parable of Lazarus and the Rich Man (Luke 16:19-31) is perhaps the most vivid illustration of chronic invisibility. Luke's rendition of this story is intended to illustrate the almost fantastically different social locations of the rich man and Lazarus. The rich man is wealthy beyond belief, and Lazarus is in horrible shape—malnourished, sick, alone, frail, suffering from neglect, tormented by aggressive wild dogs that want to eat him. Lazarus is lying right outside the rich man's front gate, which means that the rich man would be passing right by Lazarus multiple times per day, yet there is never any indication that the rich man ever reached out to help Lazarus—no food, no money, no kind words, not even the slightest recognition that Lazarus existed. Like a rock or a curb or a dog sleeping on the sidewalk, Lazarus was nothing more than an inconvenient physical object around which the rich man had to maneuver in order not to trip and fall and hurt himself. Day after day, week after week, stepping over or around Lazarus multiple time per day and nothing in the parable indicates that the rich man ever interacted with Lazarus. No greeting, no smile, no offer of kindness. Nothing. This is perhaps the height of invisibility, where the rich man could literally stumble and fall over Lazarus, or smell the stench of his open festering sores, or touch the tattered threads of his soiled garment, and yet the rich man functions as if Lazarus is not even there. Had the rich man shown compassion once toward Lazarus, this parable probably never would have been written, as the whole point is to offer the reader a vivid, gut-wrenching description of the type of person that one ought **not** to become.

The Parable of the Sheep and the Goats (Matt. 25:31-46), the context for which is the final judgment where the sheep are welcomed into God's kingdom and the goats are sent to a place of eternal fire, is elegant in its simplicity. The difference between the sheep and goats is that the former fed the hungry, clothed the naked, provided water to the thirsty, and visited the sick or those in prison while the latter did not. It is difficult to find a simpler, more straightforward moral equation that defines one's standing before God in Scripture than this parable: pedestrian and mundane acts of compassion toward the vulnerable are a necessary prerequisite for eternal life with God and rendering them invisible and not tending to their needs is grounds for eternal separation from God.

The lessons from these parables are instructive. First, it is very easy to succumb to the temptation to render the vulnerable invisible and to make their needs and struggles seem trivial, inconsequential, and unimportant—to the point where they completely recede into the background of our awareness. Nor is there a surefire antidote to this temptation, as neither a deep religiosity nor close physical proximity to those suffering seems sufficient to guarantee a compassionate response. Second, our actions are important in defining our status before God, but so are our inactions. This is an especially difficult claim for Catholics to accept, as the entire superstructure of the Catholic moral life centers around the discrete, individual action and the conceptual tools that the Catholic Church has erected to assess actions morally are extensive. On the other hand, inactions or "omissions" as they are commonly called in Catholic moral theology receive scant attention. In the *Catechism of the Catholic Church*, for instance, literally hundreds of sections are devoted to clarifying the assessment of actions and the direct and indirect causes, limitations, and precursors necessary for evaluating actions, such as freedom, the virtues, conscience, types of law, and sin. Omissions or inactions, in contrast, are largely ignored in the *Catechism of the Catholic Church*, and when they are mentioned the treatment is cryptic and bland.[67] It is clear that for Catholics the paramount question is, "Is my action morally right?"

rather than "Am I not doing something that I should be doing?"—and if the message in the parables is correct, such mental habituation might be a formidable obstacle to becoming the agents of compassion that the Catholic moral imagination requires. Third, rendering the vulnerable invisible and thereby making them objects of nonchalant avoidance not only stunts our moral growth and impedes our goal to become faithful disciples of Jesus, but it also has eternal implications for each Catholic.

If rendering the vulnerable invisible was a problem in the ancient Jewish world and the early Christian Church to the extent that it needed to be highlighted over and again in the Jewish and Christian scriptures, the problem is even more acute today. We no longer inhabit small villages in which intimacy reigns through the bonds of blood or familiarity and where the consequences of making the vulnerable invisible are seen and experienced directly and perhaps even daily. We now live in a world in which urban centers have emerged and dominate the geopolitical landscape. According to the United Nations, 2007 represented the tipping point where, for the first time in human history, more people lived in urban centers than in rural areas, and by 2050 the UN estimates that two-thirds of all humans on Earth will live in an urban center. Asia currently has a staggering 89 percent of its population living in urban centers, with North American not far behind at 73 percent.[68] Now, more than ever before in human history, it is possible to live, work, recreate, exercise, travel, play, and raise a family around strangers, and being a citizen of this culture of anonymity has produced widespread feelings of loneliness and isolation and increasing incidences of depression and other psychological problems.[69] In this context, in which the lives of many people with whom we come into contact every day remain invisible, it becomes awfully easy to remain oblivious to the suffering of those on the periphery of our social order whose unobtrusive hardships are rarely noticed.

Yet apart from shifting population dynamics and accompanying psychological pressures, the phenomenon of invisibility remains a potent obstacle to grasping the moral import of the effect of environmental toxicants on children in another distinct way. The easiest moral situations to render intelligible are those in which the entire scope of factual information is abundantly clear. The agent is known, as well as his or her intention and motivation. The specific circumstances surrounding the action are known, which gives every moral situation a different texture and nuance. The specific people affected by the agent's action can be readily identified, and the effect of the agent's action on them can be discerned, whether beneficial or harmful, both in the short-term and long-term. As the renowned Christian ethicist Daniel Maguire once quipped, insufficient factual information is the bane of ethics, and it behooves us to make sure that adequate factual information is known before making any moral judgment.[70]

One of the intractable problems with the issue of environmental toxicants and children is that factual information is frequently partial, incomplete, and sometimes unobtainable, and often it can take many years if not decades to amass the knowledge necessary to be able to know with sufficient precision the harms involved and the children affected and in what way in order to implement policy decisions or to make choices intended to protect one's own children. Scientific "proof" is a phantom, and the best knowledge that policy makers often have upon which to make major regulatory decisions is a schedule of probabilities that exposure to chemical A in X amount over a period of Z years is likely to produce a certain health effect here—which, of course, does not take into account the unique windows of vulnerability specific to babies and children. Moreover, it is nearly impossible to ascertain accurately any particular child's prior exposure to an environmental toxicant, or the potential multiple sources from which a child might be exposed to a toxicant, or the possible synergistic effects on a child's body from exposure to multiple toxicants, all of which means that rough approximations of risk assessments are probably the best that can be done in our circumstances.

Literally hundreds (and perhaps thousands) of toxicants are crossing the placenta and getting into the bodies of babies throughout all gestational phases and there is nothing to suggest that this number decreases after children are born. We have extensive data on the health effects of a handful of the most injurious chemicals, yet very little on the other 90,000 chemicals on the commercial market. Federal legislation and the regulatory agency tasked to enforce environmental laws, the EPA, seem remarkably impotent either to curb the deluge of new chemicals that find their way to the commercial marketplace every year or to get accurate data on the thousands of chemicals to which children have been exposed since the Second World War. The most generous characterization of this situation is that we are playing fast and loose with the health and safety of our children; a less generous one would be that we are demonstrating a morally condemnable callousness and indifference to our little ones;

and the worst would be that this resembles a cruel and borderline brutal experiment that is fodder for a horror movie. Whichever characterization is most apt, please remember that these are our children, to which our emotional attachment and protective instincts ought to be naturally fierce and unrelenting, who depend on our vigilance and love and practical wisdom in order to flourish, and whose quality of life hinges on our choices and policies.

We are faced with perhaps the perfect moral storm. Our children's health is being undermined, probably on a widespread basis, yet the actual harms remain cloaked in obscurity. We know that harm is occurring, that we are creating a massive risk for our young ones with our increasingly chemicalized world and our government institutions seem incapable of actually protecting our children through regulatory frameworks. Even if the recommendation of Pope Francis is followed, namely, that governments implement the precautionary principle and base their regulatory efforts on its stringent standards, the effectiveness of such an approach is still questionable given the magnitude of the issue. Also there is currently no widespread public interest in placing this issue front and center on our national radar screen and sculpting a more effective strategy for protecting our children, which means that implementing more robust protectionary measures on the federal or state level is not likely to happen any time soon.

Yet perhaps the most foundational dictum of Catholic ethics—to protect the helpless, vulnerable, and defenseless—clearly warrants something akin to a revolution in our moral awareness and efforts to protect children from the nefarious effects of environmental toxicants. So we are left in moral quagmire: A clear mandate—to love and to be compassionate— foundational to the Catholic moral identity that is being violated every single day, with no effective large-scale remedy in sight to prevent our children from being brutalized by the chemical regime we have created. Especially given the robust pro-natal sentiment of the Catholic Church, which prides itself on protecting and defending every human life from conception to natural death, this seems to be an issue that would naturally pique the interest of Catholics and could easily lead to some organized action and resistance.

In our current context, the most feasible way to protect our children from environmental toxicants is through vigilant parents and industry representatives who are committed to making products as benign as possible. Chemists, chemical engineers, and others who represent the upstream section of the production process occupy an ideal location from which to prevent harm to children, as they can make entire lines of products safer from the very beginning either by substituting more benign individual components, or by using components in the manufacturing process that are better understood, or by using components that biodegrade quicker, or by doing an inventory wide audit and attempting to find manufacturing substitutes that are more benign. There are a number of ways to make commercial products gentler on our children, and if companies could manufacture products that are safe for children at all stages of their life, they could usher in an era of product safety the likes of which have not been seen since the Second World War. This is precisely why a cadre of deeply committed product development professionals are needed who can muster the creativity, originality, and doggedness to rid our world of environmental toxicants. If dangerous products never get created in the first place, the enormous problem of environmental toxicants harming our children simply evaporates.

Until this occurs, the best chance of protecting children from the effects of harmful chemicals is for parents to be robustly proactive in creating hospitable environments for our children by shielding them from environmental toxicants. Fortunately, information and education are formidable allies in this regard and there are many beneficial steps that can be taken to make a practical difference. Since the most vulnerable phases of a child's development occur in utero, it is imperative for all women who are planning to get pregnant or who are pregnant to limit their exposure to toxicants, especially in their home environment. Often small changes in one's lived environment can make a big difference in terms of reducing exposure to some of the most harmful toxicants, and there are a number of resources that provide a checklist of important things to do.[71] After babies are born, a different set of concerns arise, particularly concerning plastics for bottle-fed infants, household dust when they start crawling, and pesticide residues when children start the highly predictable pattern of specialized eating and drinking of fruits and fruit juices.[72] The good news is that there are many practical and relatively inexpensive ways to reduce a child's exposure to environmental toxicants, given an investment of time and the acquisition of accurate information.

If, as Pope John Paul II claims, our treatment of children is a measure of our fidelity to God,[73] our recent track record on protecting children from environmental toxicants is perhaps more indicative of a band of golden calf worshippers (Ex. 32:1–35) than of faithful and compassionate followers of Jesus. Let us hope that Pope Francis's call to ecological conversion in *Laudato Si'* reaches more Catholics and as it moves deeper into the implementation phase will prompt Catholic leaders to construct a world friendlier to the health of our beloved children.

Notes

1. Florence Williams, "Toxic Breast Milk?" *The New York Times Magazine* (January 9, 2005), https://www.nytimes.com/2005/01/09/magazine/toxic-breast-milk.html (accessed November 27, 2025).
2. https://www.mayoclinic.org/healthy-lifestyle/infant-and-toddler-health/in-depth/breast-feeding/art-20047898#:~:text=Commercial%20infant%20formulas%20don't,who%20have%20typical%20dietary%20needs; https://kidshealth.org/en/parents/breast-bottle-feeding.html; https://www.webmd.com/baby/breastfeeding-vs-formula-feeding#1; and https://www.cdc.gov/breastfeeding/php/faq/faq.html (accessed November 27, 2025).
3. "The History of PCBs," http://www.americaunites.com/the-history-of-pcbs (accessed November 27, 2025).
4. Bart Hens and Luc Hens, "Persistent Threats by Persistent Pollutants: Chemical Nature, Concerns and Future Policy Regarding PCBs—What Are We Heading For?" *Toxics* 6 (1) (2018): 1–2.
5. Gerald Markowitz, "From Industrial Toxins to Worldwide Pollutants: A Brief History of Polychlorinated Biphenyls," *Public Health Reports* 133 (6) (2018): 722.
6. "The History of PCBs."
7. "The History of PCBs."
8. Markowitz, "From Industrial Toxins to Worldwide Pollutants," 722.
9. Gerald Markowits and David Rosner, "Monsanto, PCBs, and the creation of a 'world-wide ecological problem," *Journal of Public Health* 39 (2018): 472–5.
10. Markowitz and Rosner, "Monsanto, PCBs, and the creation of a 'world-wide ecological problem," 477.
11. Markowitz, "From Industrial Toxins to Worldwide Pollutants," 723.
12. Soren Jansen, "The PCB Story," *Ambio* 1(4) (1972): 124–5.
13. Soren Jansen, "Report of a new chemical hazard," *New Scientist* 32 (1966): 612.

14. Theo Colborn, Dianne Dumanoski, and John Peterson Myers, *Our Stolen Future: Are We Threatening Our Fertility, Intelligence, and Survival?—A Scientific Detective Story* (New York: Plume, 1997), 104.

15. Colborn, et al., *Our Stolen Future*, 106-7.

16. Joseph L. Jacobson and Sandra W. Jacobson, "Intellectual Impairment in Children Exposed to Polychlorinated Biphenyls in Utero," *New England Journal of Medicine* 335 (11) (1996): 783-9.

17. W. J. Rogan and B. C. Gladden, "PCBs, DDE, and child development at 18 and 24 months," *Annals of Epidemiology* 1 (5) (Aug. 1991): 407-13.

18. H. Tsukamoto. S. Makisumi, and H. Hirose, "The chemical studies on detection of toxic compounds in the rice bran oils used by the patients of Yusho," *Fukuoka Acta Medica* 60 (1969): 496-512.

19. C. Heilmann, P. Grandjean, P. Weihe, E. Neilsin, and E. Budtz-Jorgensen, "Reduced antibody responses to vaccinations in children exposed to polychlorinated biphenyls," *PLOS Medicine* 3 (8) (Aug. 2006): 311.

20. Muktar H. Aliyu, Amina P. Alio, and Hamisu M. Salihu, "To Breastfeed or Not to Breastfeed: A Review of the Impact of Lactational Exposure to Polychlorinated Biphenyls (PCBs) on Infants," *Journal of Environmental Health* 73 (3) (Oct. 2010): 10.

21. Eva Marie Simms, "Eating One's Mother: Female Embodiment in a Toxic World," *Environmental Ethics* 31 (3) (2009): 263-77.

22. This is a synopsis of the graph taken from https://www.ewg.org/research/body-burden-pollution-newborns (accessed November 28, 2025).

23. Environmental Working Group, "Body Burden: The Pollution in Newborns," (July 14, 2005), https://www.ewg.org/research/body-burden-pollution-newborns (accessed November 28, 2025).

24. Jayaraj Ravindran, Megha Pankajshan, and Sreedev Puthur, "Organochlorine pesticides, their toxic effects on living organisms and their fate in the environment," *Interdisciplinary Toxicology* 9 (3-4) (2017): 91.

25. Ravindran, et al., "Organochlorine pesticides," 92-3. The LD_{50} test stands for lethal dose in 50 percent of the subjects and is usually used to determine levels of acute toxicity.

26. J. Kaiser, "Endocrine disrupters: Panel cautiously confirms low-dose effects," *Science* 290 (2000): 695-7.

27. Waseem E. Sohail, W. L. Chae, J. L. Jong, and H. Imitiaz, "Endocrine Disrupting Pesticides: A Leading Cause of Cancer among Rural People in Pakistan," *Experimental Oncology* 26 (2) (2004): 98-105.

28. J. D. Meeker, L. Altshul, and R. Hauser, "Serum PCBs, DDE and HCB predict thyroid hormone levels in men," *Environmental Research* 104 (2007): 296-304.

29. M. S. Wolff, P. G. Toniolo, E. W. Lee, M. Rivera, and N. Dubin, "Blood levels of organochlorine residues and risk of breast cancer," *Journal of the National Cancer Institute* 21 (1993): 648-52.

30. N. Sinaii, S. D. Cleary, M. L. Ballweg, L. K. Niewman, and P. Stratton, "High rates of autoimmune and endocrine disorders, fibromyalgia, chronic fatigue syndrome and atopic disease among women with endometriosis: A survey analysis," *Human Reproduction* 17 (10) (2002): 2715-24.

31. S. K. Sagiv, S. W. Thurston, D. C. Bellinger, P. E. Tolbert, L. M. Altshul, and S. A. Korrick, "Prenatal organochlorine exposure and behaviours associated with attention deficit hyperactivity disorder in school-aged children," *American Journal of Epidemiology* 171 (5) (2010): 593–601.

32. J. Kumar, L. Lind, S. Salihovic, B. van Bavel, E. Ingelsson, and P. M. Lind, "Persistent organic pollutants and liver dysfunction biomarkers in a population based human sample of men and women," *Environmental Research* 134 (2014): 251-6.

33. K. Steenland, A. M. Mora, D. B. Barr, J. Juncos, N. Roman, and C. Wesseling, "Organochlorine chemicals and neurodegeneration among elderly subjects in Costa Rica," *Environmental Research* 134 (2014): 205-9.

34. J. P. Arrebola, A. González-Jiménez, C. Fornieles-González, F. Artacho-Cordón, N. Olea, F. Escobar-Jiménez, and M. L. Fernández-Soto, "Relationship between serum concentrations of persistent organic pollutants and markers of insulin resistance in a cohort of women with a history of gestational diabetes mellitus," *Environmental Research* 136 (2015): 435-40.

35. J. Forns, N. Lertxundi, A. Aranbarri, M. Murcia, M. Gascon, D. Martinez, J. Grellier, A. Lertxundi, J. Julvez, E. Fano, F. Goñi, J. O. Grimalt, F. Ballester, J. Sunyer, and J. Ibarluzea, "Prenatal exposure to organochlorine compounds and neuropsychological development up to two years of life," *Environment International* 45 (2012): 72-7.

36. V. Linares, B. Montserrat, and J. Domingo, "Human exposure to PBDE and critical evaluation of health hazards," *Archives of Toxicology* 89 (2015): 335-56.

37. Matthew Lorber, "Exposure of Americans to polybrominated diphenyl ethers," *Journal of Exposure Science and Environmental Epidemiology* 18 (2008): 2-19.

38. United States Environmental Protection Agency, "Technical Fact Sheet—Polybrominated Diphenyl Ethers (PBDEs)," (Nov. 2017), https://19january2017snapshot.epa.gov/sites/production/files/2014-03/documents/ffrrofactsheet_contaminant_perchlorate_january2014_final.pdf (accessed November 28, 2025).

39. Shanna H. Swan, *Countdown: How Our Modern World is Threatening Sperm Counts, Altering Male and Female Reproductive Development, and Imperiling the Future of the Human Race* (New York: Scribner, 2020), 119–20.

40. M. A. Adgent, K. Hoffman, B. D. Goldman, A. Sjödin, and J. L. Daniels, "Brominated Flame Retardants in Breast Milk and Behavioural and Cognitive Development at 36 Months," *Paediatric and Perinatal Epidemiology* 28 (2014): 48–57.

41. J. P. Wu, X. J. Luo, Y. Zhang, M. Yu, S. J. Chen, B. X. Mai, and Z. Y. Yang, "Biomagnification of polybrominated diphenyl ethers (PBDEs) and polychlorinated biphenyls in a highly contaminated fresh water food web from South China," *Environmental Pollution* 157 (2009): 904–9.

42. B. Eskenazi, L. Fenster, R. Castorina, A. R. Marks, A. Sjödin, and L. G. Rosas, "A comparison of PBDE serum concentrations in Mexican and Mexican-American children living in California." *Environmental Health Perspectives* 119 (2011): 1442–-8.

43. Swan, *Countdown*, 120.

44. Filip Bjurlid, *Polybrominated dibenzo-p-dioxins and furans: from source of emission to human exposure* (Örebro University, 2018), 24.

45. Bjurlid, *Polybrominated dibenzo-p-dioxins and furans*, 28.

46. World Health Organization, "Dioxins and their effects on human health," (October 4, 2016), https://www.who.int/news-room/fact-sheets/detail/dioxins-and-their-effects-on-human-health (accessed November 28, 2025).

47. Pope Francis, *Laudato Si'*, #70, #92, and #138.

48. National Research Council, *Pesticides in the Diets of Infants and Children* (Washington, DC: National Academy Press, 1993), 23-47.

49. Valerie J. Watnick, "The Lautenberg Chemical Safety Act of 2016: Cancer, Industry Pressure, and a Proactive Approach," *Harvard Environmental Law Review* 43 (July 3, 2019): 381-2.

50. US Department of Agriculture, "Pesticide Data Program," https://www.ams.usda.gov/datasets/pdp (accessed November 28, 2025).

51. Pesticide Action Network North America, "What's On My Food?" https://www.panna.org/resources/do-you-know-whats-in-your-food (accessed December 24, 2025).

52. Environmental Working Group, "2021 Shopper's Guide to Pesticides in Produce," https://www.ewg.org/foodnews/summary.php (accessed November 28, 2025).
53. David Goldston, "Not 'Til the Fat Lady Sings: TSCA's Next Act," *Issues in Science and Technology* (Fall 2016): 73.
54. Sheldon Krimsky, "The Unsteady State and Inertia of Chemical Regulation Under the US Toxic Substances Control Act," *PLOS Biology* 15 (12) (December 18, 2017): 3.
55. P. D. Koman, V. Singla, J. Lam, and T. J. Woodruff, "Population Susceptibility: A Vital Consideration in Chemical Risk Evaluation Under the Lautenberg Toxic Substances Control Act," *PLOS Biology* 17 (8) (August 29, 2019): 2.
56. Krimsky, "The Unsteady State," 4.
57. United States Environmental Protection Agency, "Highlights of Key Provisions in the Frank R. Lautenberg Chemical Safety for the 21st Century Act," https://www.epa.gov/assessing-and-managing-chemicals-under-tsca/highlights-key-provisions-frank-r-lautenberg-chemical (accessed November 28, 2025).
58. Krimsky, "The Unsteady State," 5.
59. Koman, et al., "Population Susceptibility," 11.
60. Watnick, "The Lautenberg Chemical Safety Act," 404.
61. Krimsky, "The Unsteady State," 6.
62. Koman, et al., "Population Susceptibility," 6.
63. Alissa Cordner, *Toxic Safety: Flame Retardants, Chemical Controversies, and Environmental Health* (New York: Columbia University Press, 2016), 202.
64. Cordner, *Toxic Safety*, 202.
65. Pope Francis, *Laudato Si'*, #186.
66. Pope John Paul II, "Letter to the Secretary General of the United Nations Organization on the Occasion of the World Summit for Children," 2.
67. See, for instance, *Catechism of the Catholic Church*, #1853, 2326, and 2284.
68. Hannah Ritchie and Max Roser, "Urbanization," (Sept. 2018), https://ourworldindata.org/urbanization#number-of-people-living-in-urban-areas (accessed November 28, 2025).
69. Emma Harries, "Social Isolation and its Relationship to the Urban Environment," 3, https://www.socialconnectedness.org/wp-content/uploads/2019/12/Emma-Harries-Social-Isolation-and-its-Relationship-to-the-Urban-Environment.pdf (accessed November 28, 2025).

70. Daniel C. Maguire, *Ethics: A Complete Method for Moral Choice* (Minneapolis: Fortress Press, 2009).

71. https://www.epa.gov/children/what-you-can-do-protect-children-environmental-risks; https://toxicfreefuture.org/healthy-living/healthy-kids; https://www.edf.org/health/chemicals; https://www.health.state.mn.us/communities/environment/childenvhealth/chemicals.html; https://cehn.org/resources/#blueprint; https://www.atsdr.cdc.gov/index.html (all accessed December 24, 2025); Swan, *Count Down*, chaps. 11 and 12; Dona Schneider and Natalie Freeman, *Children's Environmental Health: Reducing Risk in a Dangerous World* (Washington, DC: American Public Health Association, 2000), 131–49; Nena Baker, *The Body Toxic: How the Hazardous Chemistry of Everyday Things Threatens Our Health and Well-being* (New York: North Point Press, 2008); Melody Milam Potter and Erin E. Miliam, *Healthy Baby, Toxic World: Practical Ways to Protect Your Baby During Pregnancy and Infancy* (Oakland: New Harbinger Publications, 1999); Philip J. Landrigan and Mary M. Landrigan, *Children and Environmental Toxins: What Everyone Needs to Know* (New York: Oxford University Press, 2018); Libby McDonald, *The Toxic Sandbox: The Truth About Environmental Toxins and Our Children's Health* (New York: Penguin, 2007); and Sophia Ruan Gushee, *A to Z of D-Toxing: The Ultimate Guide to Reducing our Toxic Exposures* (New York: S File Publishing, 2015).

72. Special notice should be given to the United States Conference of Catholic Bishops' work on this topic, which includes a 2007 conference on "Protecting Human Life and Caring for Creation: Why Protecting Unborn Children in Their First Environment Matters," a study guide from which was issued and can be found here: https://www.usccb.org/upload/Protecting-human-life-and-caring-for-creation-why-protecting-unborn-children-in-their-first-environment-matters-2.pdf (accessed November 28, 2025).

73. Pope John Paul II, "Letter to the Secretary General of the United Nations Organization on the Occasion of the World Summit for Children," (September 22, 1990), 2, https://www.vatican.va/content/john-paul-ii/en/letters/1990/documents/hf_jp-ii_let_19900922_de-cuellar.html (accessed December 24, 2025).

Bibliography

Adgent, Margaret A., Kate Hoffman, Barbara Davis Goldman, Andreas Sjödin, and Julie L. Daniels. "Brominated Flame Retardants in Breast Milk and Behavioural and Cognitive Development at 36 Months." *Paediatric and Perinatal Epidemiology* 28 (1) (January 2014): 48-57.

Albrecht, Glenn A. *Earth Emotions: New Words for a New World*. Ithaca, NY: Cornell University Press, 2019.

Aliyu, Muktar H., Amina P. Alio, and Hamisu M. Salihu. "To Breastfeed or Not to Breastfeed: A Review of the Impact of Lactational Exposure to Polychlorinated Biphenyls (PCBs) on Infants." *Journal of Environmental Health* 73 (3) (October 2010): 8–14.

Allen, Joseph L. *Love & Conflict: A Covenantal Model of Christian Ethics*. Nashville, TN: Abingdon Press, 1984.

Alli, Renee A. "Breastfeeding vs. Formula Feeding." WebMD, https://www.webmd.com/baby/breastfeeding-vs-formula-feeding#1 (accessed November 28, 2025).

America Unites for Kids. "The History of PCBs." http://www.americaunites.com/the-history-of-pcbs (accessed November 28, 2025).

Arrebola, Juan P., Amalia González-Jiménez, Constanza Fornieles-González, Francisco Artacho-Cordón, Nicolás Olea, Fernando Escobar-Jiménez, and María Luisa Fernández-Soto. "Relationship between Serum Concentrations of Persistent Organic Pollutants and Markers of Insulin Resistance in a Cohort of Women with a History of Gestational Diabetes Mellitus." *Environmental Research* 136 (January 2015): 435–40.

Ashley, Mary A. "In Communion with God's Sparrow: Incorporating Animal Agency into the Environmental Vision of Laudato Sí." *Sophia* 57 (2018): 103-18.

Baker, Lauren, Jin Huh, and Anne Marie Brose. "Rich Harvest." *Alternatives Journal* 29 (2003): 21-5.

Baker, Nena. *The Body Toxic: How the Hazardous Chemistry of Everyday Things Threatens Our Health and Well-Being*. New York: Farrar, Straus and Giroux, 2008.

Ballew, Matthew T., and Allen M. Omoto. "Absorption: How Nature Experiences Promote Awe and Other Positive Emotions." *Ecopsychology* 10 (1) (March 1, 2018): 26–35.

Bar-On, Yinon. M., Rob Phillips, and Ron Milo. "The biomass distribution on Earth." *Proceedings of the National Academy of Sciences of the United States of America* 115 (25) (2018): 6506–11.

Benedict XVI, Pope. "Caritas in Veritate." June 29, 2009, https://www.vatican.va/content/benedict-xvi/en/encyclicals/documents/hf_ben-xvi_enc_20090629_caritas-in-veritate.html (accessed November 28, 2025).

Benedict XVI, Pope. "Deus Caritas Est." December 25, 2005, https://www.vatican.va/content/benedict-xvi/en/encyclicals/documents/hf_ben-xvi_enc_20051225_deus-caritas-est.html (accessed November 28, 2025).

Benedict XVI, Pope. *The Garden of God: Toward a Human Ecology*. Edited by Maria Milvia Morciano. Washington, DC: The Catholic University Press of America, 2014.

Benedict XVI, Pope. "Message of His Holiness Pope Benedict XVI for the Celebration of the World Day of Peace." January 1, 2010, https://www.vatican.va/content/benedict-xvi/en/messages/peace/documents/hf_ben-xvi_mes_20091208_xliii-world-day-peace.html (accessed November 28, 2025).

Ben-Joseph, Elana Pearl, ed. "Breastfeeding vs. Formula Feeding (for Parents) - Nemours Kidshealth." *The Nemours Foundation*. June 2018, https://kidshealth.org/en/parents/breast-bottle-feeding.html (accessed November 28, 2025).

Berg, Agnes E. van den, Sander L. Koole, and Nickie Y. van der Wulp. "Environmental Preference and Restoration: (How) Are They Related?" *Journal of Environmental Psychology* 23 (2) (2003): 135–46.

Berman, Marc G., Ethan Kross, Katherine M. Krpan, Mary K. Askren, Aleah Burson, Patricia J. Deldin, Stephen Kaplan, Lindsey Sherdell, Ian H. Gotlib, and John Jonides. "Interacting with Nature Improves Cognition and Affect for Individuals with Depression." *Journal of Affective Disorders* 140 (3) (November 2012): 300–5.

Berry, Thomas. *Befriending the Earth: A Theology of Reconciliation Between Humans and the Earth*. Mystic, CT: Twenty-Third Publications, 1991.

Berry, Thomas. *The Dream of the Earth*. San Francisco: Sierra Club Books, 1988.

Berry, Thomas. "Ethics and Ecology." In *Educating for Humanity: Rethinking the Purposes of Education*. Edited by Mike Seymour, 145–54. New York: Routledge, 2004.

Berry, Thomas. *The Great Work: Our Way into the Future*. New York: Three Rivers Press, 1999.

Berry, Thomas, and Brian Swimme. *The Universe Story: From the Primordial Flaring Forth to the Ecozoic Era*. San Francisco: Harper Collins, 1992.

Bjurlid, Filip. "Polybrominated Dibenzo-p-Dioxins and Furans: from Source of Emission to Human Exposure." PhD diss., Orebro University, 2018.

Bonneuil, Christophe, and Jean-Baptiste Fressoz. *The Shock of the Anthropocene: The Earth, History and Us.* Translated by David Fernbach. Brooklyn, NY: Verso Books, 2016.

Boulting, Noel E. "Between Anthropocentrism and Ecocentrism." *Philosophy in the Contemporary World* 2 (4) (November 1, 1995): 1–8.

Bulliet, Richard W. *Hunters, Herders, and Hamburgers: The Past and Future of Human-Animal Relationships.* New York: Columbia University Press, 2005.

Callicott, J. Baird. "Non-Anthropocentric Value Theory and Environmental Ethics." *American Philosophical Quarterly* 21 (4) (1984): 299–309.

Carmody, John. *Ecology and Religion: Toward a New Christian Theology of Nature.* New York: Paulist Press, 1983.

Catechism of the Catholic Church, 2nd edition. 1997, https://www.usccb.org/beliefs-and-teachings/what-we-believe/catechism/catechism-of-the-catholic-church (accessed November 28, 2025).

Cates, Diana Fritz. *Choosing to Feel: Virtue, Friendship, and Compassion for Friends.* Notre Dame, IN: University of Notre Dame Press, 1997.

Catholic Bishops of the Columbia River Watershed Region. "The Columbia River Watershed: Caring for Creation and the Common Good." January 8, 2001, https://www.wacatholics.org/stay-informed/the-columbia-river-watershed-caring-for-creation-and-the-common-good (accessed November 28, 2025).

Cauthen, Kenneth. "The Churches and the Future: A Utopian Proposal." *Zygon* 6 (December 15, 2005): 311–29.

Centers for Disease Control and Prevention. "Case Studies in Environmental Medicine." September 9, 2022, https://www.atsdr.cdc.gov (accessed December 24, 2025).

Centers for Disease Control and Prevention. "Frequently Asked Questions: What Are the Benefits of Breastfeeding?" December 18, 2023, https://www.cdc.gov/breastfeeding/php/faq/faq.html?CDC_AAref_Val=https://www.cdc.gov/breastfeeding/faq/index.html (accessed November 28, 2025).

Chawla, Louise. "Childhood Experiences Associated with Care for the Natural World: A Theoretical Framework for Empirical Results." *Children, Youth, and Environments* 17 (4) (2007): 144–70.

Children's Environmental Health Network. "A Blueprint for Protecting Children's Environmental Health." October 2015, https://cehn.org/a-blueprint-for-protecting-childrens-environmental-health-2015 (accessed November 28, 2025).

Christiansen, Drew, and Walter E. Grazer. *And God Saw That It Was Good: Catholic Theology and the Environment*. Washington, DC: United States Catholic Conference, 1996.

Colborn, Theo, Dianne Dumanoski, and John Peterson Myers. *Our Stolen Future: Are We Threatening Our Fertility, Intelligence, and Survival? A Scientific Detective Story*. New York: Penguin Publishing Group, 1997.

Conference of the Parties to the Convention on Biological Diversity, 15th Meeting. "Kunming-Montreal Global Biodiversity Framework." December 2022, https://www.cbd.int/doc/c/e6d3/cd1d/daf663719a03902a9b116c34/cop-15-l-25-en.pdf (accessed November 28, 2025).

Cordner, Alissa. *Toxic Safety: Flame Retardants, Chemical Controversies, and Environmental Health*. New York: Columbia University Press, 2016.

Crist, Eileen, and Helen Kopnina. "INTRODUCTION: Unsettling Anthropocentrism." *Dialectical Anthropology* 38 (4) (2014): 387–96.

Darnell, Rezneat M. "Morality and the Ecological Crisis." *BioScience* 17 (10) (October 1, 1967): 685–6.

Davidson, Debra. "Rethinking Adaptation." *Nature and Culture* 13 (December 1, 2018): 378–402.

Davis, Henry. *Moral and Pastoral Theology*, 4 volumes. London: Sheed and Ward, 1935.

Derr, Thomas S. "Religion's Responsibility for the Ecological Crisis: An Argument Run Amok." *Worldview* 18 (1) (January 1975): 39–45.

De Vos, J. M., L. N. Joppa, J. L. Gittleman, P. R. Stephens, and S. L. Pimm. "Estimating the Normal Background Rate of Species Extinction." *Conservation Biology* 29 (2) (2015): 452–62.

Diamond, Jared M. *Collapse: How Societies Choose to Fail or Succeed*. New York: Penguin, 2005.

DiLeo, Daniel R. "Introduction: The 'Climate Emergency' and US Catholic Responses to Laudato Si." *Journal of Moral Theology* 9(1) (2020): 1-18.

Doyle, Eric. "Ecology and the Canticle of Brother Sun." *New Blackfriars* 55 (652) (1974): 392–402.

Edwards, Denis. "Earth as God's Creation: The Theology of the Natural World in Pope Francis's *Laudato Si.*" *Phronema* 31 (2) (2016): 1-16.

Edwards, Denis. "'Sublime Communion': The Theology of the Natural World in *Laudato Si.*" *Theological Studies* 77 (2) (2016): 377-91.

Edwards, Steven A. "Our bodies as ecosystems." *American Association for the Advancement of Science*. November 29, 2012, https://www.aaas.org/

taxonomy/term/10/our-bodies-ecosystems (accessed November 28, 2025).

Ejaz, Sohail, Waseem Akram, Chae Woong Lim, Jong Jin Lee, and Imtiaz Hussain. "Endocrine Disrupting Pesticides: A Leading Cause of Cancer among Rural People in Pakistan." *Experimental Oncology* 26 (2) (June 2004): 98–105.

Engemann, Kristine, Carsten Bøcker Pedersen, Lars Arge, Constantinos Tsirogiannis, Preben Bo Mortensen, and Jens-Christian Svenning. "Residential Green Space in Childhood Is Associated with Lower Risk of Psychiatric Disorders from Adolescence into Adulthood." *Proceedings of the National Academy of Sciences* 116 (11) (March 12, 2019): 5188–93.

Environmental Defense Fund. "Safer Chemicals." https://www.edf.org/health/chemicals (accessed November 28, 2025).

Environmental Working Group. "Body Burden: The Pollution in Newborns." July 14, 2005, https://www.ewg.org/research/body-burden-pollution-newborns (accessed November 28, 2025).

Environmental Working Group. "EWG's 2025 Shopper's Guide to Pesticides in Produce." June 11, 2025, https://www.ewg.org/foodnews/summary.php (accessed November 28, 2025).

Eskenazi, Brenda, Laura Fenster, Rosemary Castorina, Amy R. Marks, Andreas Sjödin, Lisa Goldman Rosas, Nina Holland, Armando Garcia Guerra, Lizbeth López-Carillo, and Asa Bradman. "A Comparison of PBDE Serum Concentrations in Mexican and Mexican-American Children Living in California." *Environmental Health Perspectives* 119 (10) (October 1, 2011): 1442–48.

Forns, Joan, Nerea Lertxundi, Aritz Aranbarri, Mario Murcia, Mireia Gascon, David Martinez, James Grellier, Aitana Lertxundi, Jordi Julvez, Eduardo Fano, Fernando Goñi, Joan O. Grimalt, Ferran Ballester, Jordi Sunyer, and Jesus Ibarluzea. "Prenatal Exposure to Organochlorine Compounds and Neuropsychological Development up to Two Years of Life." *Environment International* 45 (September 15, 2012): 72–7.

Fox, Matthew. *Original Blessing: A Primer in Creation Spirituality*. Sante Fe, NM: Bear & Co., 1983.

Francis, Pope. *Laudate Deum*. October. 4, 2023, https://www.vatican.va/content/francesco/en/apost_exhortations/documents/20231004-laudate-deum.html (accessed November 28, 2025).

Francis, Pope. *Laudato Si'*. May 24, 2015, https://www.vatican.va/content/francesco/en/encyclicals/documents/papa-francesco_20150524_enciclica-laudato-si.html (accessed November 28, 2025).

Francis, Pope. *Misericordia et Misera*. November 20, 2016, https://www.vatican.va/content/francesco/en/apost_letters/documents/papa-francesco-lettera-ap_20161120_misericordia-et-misera.html (accessed November 28, 2025).

Francis, Pope. *Querida Amazonia*. February 2, 2020, https://www.vatican.va/content/francesco/es/apost_exhortations/documents/papa-francesco_esortazione-ap_20200202_querida-amazonia.html (accessed November 28, 2025).

Gabriel, Andrew K. "Beyond Anthropocentrism in Barth's Doctrine of Creation: Searching for a Theology of Nature." *Religious Studies and Theology* 28 (2) (March 30, 2010): 175–87.

Gallagher, James. "More than half your body is not human." *BBC*, April 9, 2018, https://www.bbc.com/news/health-43674270 (accessed November 28, 2025).

Galli, Alessandro, David Lin, Mathis Wackernagel, Michel Grissot, and Sebastian Winkler. "Humanity's Growing Ecological Footprint: Sustainable Development Implications." 2015, https://sustainabledevelopment.un.org/content/documents/5686humanitysgrowingecologicalfootprint.pdf (accessed November 28, 2025).

Gebara, Ivone. *Longing for Running Water: Ecofeminism and Liberation*. Minneapolis, MN: Fortress Press, 1999.

Geisler, Charles, and Ben Currens. "Impediments to inland resettlement under conditions of accelerated sea level rise." *Land Use Policy* 66 (2017): 322–30.

Goldston, David. "Not 'Til the Fat Lady Sings: TSCA's Next Act." *Issues in Science and Technology* 33 (1) (2016): 73–6.

Goodland, Robert and Jeff Anhang. "Livestock and climate change: what if the key actors in climate change are … cows, pigs, and chickens?" *World Watch* (November/December 2009): 10–19, https://awellfedworld.org/wp-content/uploads/Livestock-Climate-Change-Anhang-Goodland.pdf (accessed November 28, 2025).

Graham, Mark. "Catholic Act Analysis and Unintended Side Effects: Time for a New Tradition." *Studies in Christian Ethics* 18 (2) (2005): 67–88.

Graham, Mark. "James Keenan's Fundamental Moral Theology and Catholic Environmentalism." In *Bothering to Love: James F. Keenan's Retrieval and Reinvention of Catholic Ethics*. Edited by Christopher P. Vogt and Kate Ward, 47–56. Maryknoll, NY: Orbis Books, 2024.

Graham, Mark. "Pope Francis's *Laudato Si*: A Critical Response." *Minding Nature* 10 (2) (2017): 57–64.

Graham, Mark. *Sustainable Agriculture: A Christian Ethic of Gratitude.* Cleveland, OH: Pilgrim Press, 2005.

Graham, Mark. "The Unsavory Gamble of Industrial Agriculture." In *Just Sustainability: Technology, Ecology, and Resource Extraction.* Edited by Christiana Z. Peppard and Andrea Vicini, 105–16. Maryknoll, NY: Orbis Books, 2015.

Grey, William. "Environmental Value and Anthropocentrism." *Ethics and the Environment* 3 (1) (1998): 97–103.

Gullone, Eleonora. "The Biophilia Hypothesis and Life in the 21st Century: Increasing Mental Health or Increasing Pathology?" *Journal of Happiness Studies* 1 (September 1, 2000): 293–322.

Gushée, Sophia Ruan. *A to Z of D-Toxing: The Ultimate Guide to Reducing Our Toxic Exposures.* New York: S File Publishing, 2015.

Gustafson, James M. *Ethics from a Theocentric Perspective, Volume 1: Theology and Ethics.* Chicago: University of Chicago Press, 1983.

Gustafson, James M. *A Sense of the Divine: The Natural Environment from a Theocentric Perspective.* Cleveland, OH: Pilgrim Press, 1996.

Harries, Emma. "Social Isolation and Its Relationship to the Urban Environment." N.d., https://www.socialconnectedness.org/wp-content/uploads/2019/12/Emma-Harries-Social-Isolation-and-its-Relationship-to-the-Urban-Environment.pdf (accessed November 28, 2025).

Haught, Paul. "Hume's Knave and Nonanthropocentric Virtues." *Journal of Agricultural and Environmental Ethics* 23 (March 1, 2010): 129–43.

Heidegger, Martin. *The Question Concerning Technology, and Other Essays.* New York: Harper Collins, 1982.

Heilmann, Carsten, Philippe Grandjean, Pál Weihe, Flemming Nielsen, and Esben Budtz-Jørgensen. "Reduced Antibody Responses to Vaccinations in Children Exposed to Polychlorinated Biphenyls," *PLOS Medicine* 3 (8) (August 2006), https://journals.plos.org/plosmedicine/article?id=10.1371/journal.pmed.0030311 (accessed November 28, 2025).

Hens, Bart, and Luc Hens. "Persistent Threats by Persistent Pollutants: Chemical Nature, Concerns and Future Policy Regarding PCBs—What Are We Heading For?" *Toxics* 6 (1) (December 21, 2017): 1-21.

Hinds, Joe, and Paul Sparks. "The Affective Quality of Human-Natural Environment Relationships." *Evolutionary Psychology* 9 (3) (July 1, 2011): 451-69.

Hoffman, Andrew J., and Lloyd E. Sandelands. "Getting Right With Nature: Anthropocentrism, Ecocentrism, and Theocentrism." *Organization & Environment* 18 (2) (2005): 141–62.

Holmes, Steven Jon. *The Young John Muir: An Environmental Biography.* Madison, Wisconsin: University of Wisconsin Press, 1999.

Hopkins, David C. *The Highlands of Canaan: Agricultural Life in the Early Iron Age.* Decatur, GA: Almond, 1985.

Hulme, Mike. *Why We Disagree About Climate Change: Understanding Controversy, Inaction, and Opportunity.* New York: Cambridge University Press, 2009.

Intergovernmental Panel on Climate Change. *Climate Change 2021*, https://www.ipcc.ch/report/ar6/wg1 (accessed November 28, 2025).

Intergovernmental Panel on Climate Change. *Climate Change 2023*, https://www.ipcc.ch/report/ar6/syr (accessed November 28, 2025).

International Union for the Conservation of Nature. *State of the World's Amphibians: The Second Global Amphibian* Assessment. 2023, https://nc.iucnredlist.org/redlist/resources/files/1696400756-SOTWA_GAA2_04Oct2023.pdf (accessed November 28, 2025).

Islam, Mohammad Zahirul, Jessika Johnston, and Peter D. Sly. "Green Space and Early Childhood Development: A Systematic Review." *Reviews on Environmental Health* 35 (2) (June 25, 2020): 189–200.

Jacobson, J. L., and S. W. Jacobson. "Intellectual Impairment in Children Exposed to Polychlorinated Biphenyls in Utero." *The New England Journal of Medicine* 335(11) (September 12, 1996): 783–89, https://nejm.org/doi/full/10.1056/NEJM199609123351104 (accessed November 28, 2025).

Jayaraj, Ravindran, Pankajshan Megha, and Puthur Sreedev. "Organochlorine Pesticides, Their Toxic Effects on Living Organisms and Their Fate in the Environment." *Interdisciplinary Toxicology* 9 (3–4) (December 2016): 90–100.

Jenkins, Willis. *Ecologies of Grace: Environmental Ethics and Christian Theology.* New York: Oxford University Press, 2008.

Jensen, Sören. "The PCB Story." *Ambio* 1 (4) (1972): 123–31.

John XXIII, Pope. *Mater et Magistra.* May 15, 1961, https://www.vatican.va/content/john-xxiii/en/encyclicals/documents/hf_j-xxiii_enc_15051961_mater.html (accessed November 28, 2025).

John XXIII, Pope. *Pacem in Terris.* April 11, 1963, https://www.vatican.va/content/john-xxiii/en/encyclicals/documents/hf_j-xxiii_enc_11041963_pacem.html (accessed November 28, 2025).

John Paul II, Pope. *Evangelium Vitae.* March 22, 1995, https://www.vatican.va/content/john-paul-ii/en/encyclicals/documents/hf_jp-ii_enc_25031995_evangelium-vitae.html (accessed November 28, 2025).

John Paul II, Pope. "Homily of His Holiness John Paul II." October 1, 1979, https://www.vatican.va/content/john-paul-ii/en/homilies/1979/

documents/hf_jp-ii_hom_19791001_usa-boston.html (accessed November 28, 2025).

John Paul II, Pope. *Laborem Exercens*. September 14, 1981, https://www.vatican.va/content/john-paul-ii/en/encyclicals/documents/hf_jp-ii_enc_14091981_laborem-exercens.html (accessed December 24, 2025).

John Paul II, Pope. "Letter to the Secretary General of the United Nations Organization on the Occasion of the World Summit for Children." September 22, 1990, https://www.vatican.va/content/john-paul-ii/en/letters/1990/documents/hf_jp-ii_let_19900922_de-cuellar.html (accessed November 28, 2025).

John Paul II, Pope. "Message of His Holiness Pope John Paul II for the Celebration of the World Day of Peace." January 1, 1990, https://www.vatican.va/content/john-paul-ii/en/messages/peace/documents/hf_jp-ii_mes_19891208_xxiii-world-day-for-peace.html (accessed November 28, 2025).

John Paul II, Pope. *Redemptor Hominis*. March 4, 1979, https://www.vatican.va/content/john-paul-ii/en/encyclicals/documents/hf_jp-ii_enc_04031979_redemptor-hominis.html (accessed November 28, 2025).

John Paul II, Pope. *Sollictudo Rei Socialis*. December 30, 1987, https://www.vatican.va/content/john-paul-ii/en/encyclicals/documents/hf_jp-ii_enc_30121987_sollicitudo-rei-socialis.html (accessed November 28, 2025).

Kaiser, J. "Endocrine Disrupters. Panel Cautiously Confirms Low-Dose Effects." *Science* 290 (5492) (October 27, 2000): 695–7.

Kaplan, Rachel. "The Nature of the View from Home: Psychological Benefits." *Environment and Behavior* 33 (4) (July 1, 2001): 507–42.

Kaplan, Stephen. "The Restorative Benefits of Nature: Toward an Integrative Framework." *Journal of Environmental Psychology* 15 (September 1, 1995): 169–82.

Kellert, Stephen R., and Edward O. Wilson. *The Biophilia Hypothesis*. Washington, DC: Island Press, 1993.

Kellert, Stephen R., Case J. David, Daniel Escher, Daniel J. Witter, Jessica Mikels-Carrasco, and Phil T. Seng. *The Nature of Americans National Report*. April 2017, https://natureofamericans.org/sites/default/files/reports/Nature-of-Americans_National_Report_1.3_4-26-17.pdf (accessed November 28, 2025).

Kolbert, Elizabeth. *The Sixth Extinction*. New York: Picador, 2014.

Koman, Patricia D., Veena Singla, Juleen Lam, and Tracey J. Woodruff. "Population Susceptibility: A Vital Consideration in Chemical Risk

Evaluation under the Lautenberg Toxic Substances Control Act." *PLOS Biology* 17 (8) (August 2019): 1-11.

Krimsky, Sheldon. "The Unsteady State and Inertia of Chemical Regulation under the US Toxic Substances Control Act." *PLOS Biology* 15 (12) (December 2017): 1-10.

Kumar, Jitender, Lars Lind, Samira Salihovic, Bert van Bavel, Erik Ingelsson, and P. Monica Lind. "Persistent Organic Pollutants and Liver Dysfunction Biomarkers in a Population-Based Human Sample of Men and Women." *Environmental Research* 134 (October 2014): 251–6.

Kuo, Frances E., Magdalena Bacaicoa, and William Sullivan. "Transforming Inner-City Landscapes: Trees, Sense of Safety, and Preference." *Environment and Behavior* 30 (January 1, 1998): 28–59.

Landrigan, Philip J., and Mary M. Landrigan. *Children and Environmental Toxins: What Everyone Needs to Know*. New York: Oxford University Press, 2018.

Leakey, Richard A., and Roger Lewin. *The Sixth Extinction: Patterns of Life and the Future of Humankind*. New York: Anchor Books, 1996.

Lee, Elizabeth. "We're Only About 43% Human, Study Shows." *VOA News*. May 26, 2019, https://www.voanews.com/a/research-estimates-we-are-only-about-43-percent-human/4932876.html (accessed November 28, 2025).

Leo XIII, Pope. *Aeterni Patris*. August 4, 1879, https://www.vatican.va/content/leo-xiii/en/encyclicals/documents/hf_l-xiii_enc_04081879_aeterni-patris.html (accessed November 28, 2025).

Leo XIII, Pope. *Rerum Novarum*. May 15, 1891, https://www.vatican.va/content/john-paul-ii/en/encyclicals/documents/hf_jp-ii_enc_14091981_laborem-exercens.html (accessed December 24, 2025).

Leopold, Aldo. *A Sand County Almanac*. New York: Oxford University Press, 1949.

Lévi-Strauss, Claude. *Introduction to the Work of Marcel Mauss*. Translated by Felicity Baker. London: Routledge, 1987.

Linares, Victoria, Montserrat Bellés, and José L. Domingo. "Human Exposure to PBDE and Critical Evaluation of Health Hazards." *Archives of Toxicology* 89 (3) (March 2015): 335–56.

Lindsey, Rebecca. "Climate Change: Global Sea Level." January 25, 2021, https://www.climate.gov/news-features/understanding-climate/climate-change-global-sea-level (accessed November 28, 2025).

Linsey, Rebecca, and Dahlman, LuAnn. "Climate Change: Global Temperature." May 29, 2025, https://www.climate.gov/news-features/

understanding-climate/climate-change-global-temperature (accessed November 28, 2025).

Linzey, Andrew. *Animal Theology*. Champaign: University of Illinois Press, 1995.

Livingston, James C. "The Ecological Challenge to Christian Ethics." *The Christian Century* 88 (48) (December 1, 1971): 1409–12.

Looi, Mun-Keet. "The human microbiome: Everything you need to know about the 39 trillion microbes that call our bodies home." *BBC Science Focus Magazine*. July 14, 2020, https://www.sciencefocus.com/the-human-body/human-microbiome (accessed November 28, 2025).

Lorber, Matthew. "Exposure of Americans to Polybrominated Diphenyl Ethers." *Journal of Exposure Science & Environmental Epidemiology* 18 (1) (January 2008): 2–19.

Louv, Richard. *Last Child in the Woods: Saving Our Children From Nature-Deficit Disorder*. Chapel Hill, NC: Algonquin Books, 2008.

Louv, Richard. *The Nature Principle: Reconnecting with Life in a Virtual Age*. Chapel Hill, NC: Algonquin Books, 2012.

Luke, Timothy W. *Anthropocene Alerts: Critical Theory of the Contemporary as Ecocritique*. Candor, NY: Telos Press Publishing, 2019.

MacDonald, Nathan, Mark W. Elliott, and Grant Macaskill. *Genesis and Christian Theology*. Grand Rapids, MI: William. B. Eerdmans Publishing, 2012.

Macquarrie, John. "Creation and Environment." *Expository Times* 57 (2) (October 1971): 4–9.

Maguire, Daniel C. *Ethics: A Complete Method for Moral Choice*. Minneapolis, MN: Fortress Press, 2009.

Markowitz, Gerald. "From Industrial Toxins to Worldwide Pollutants: A Brief History of Polychlorinated Biphenyls." *Public Health Reports* 133 (6) (September 28, 2018): 721–5.

Markowitz, Gerald, and David Rosner. "Monsanto, PCBs, and the Creation of a 'World-Wide Ecological Problem.'" *Journal of Public Health Policy* 39 (4) (November 2018): 463–540.

Marselle, Melissa R., Terry Hartig, Daniel T. C. Cox, Siân de Bell, Sonja Knapp, Sarah Lindley, Margarita Triguero-Mas, Katrin Böhning-Gaese, Matthias Braubach, Penny A. Cook, Sjerp de Vries, Anna Heintz-Buschart, Max Hofmann, Katherine N. Irvine, Nadja Kabisch, Franziska Kolek, Roland Kraemer, Iana Markevych, Dörte Martens, Ruth Müller, Mark Nieuwenhuijsen, Jacqueline M. Potts, Jutta Stadler, Samantha Walton, Sara L. Warber, and Aletta Bonn. "Pathways Linking Biodiversity to Human Health: A Conceptual Framework." *Environment International* 150 (May 2021): 1-22.

Mayo Foundation for Medical Education and Research. "Get the Facts About Breast-Feeding and Formula-Feeding." April 7, 2020, https://www.mayoclinic.org/healthy-lifestyle/infant-and-toddler-health/in-depth/breast-feeding/art-20047898#:~:text=Commercial%20infant%20formulas%20don't,who%20have%20typical%20dietary%20needs (accessed November 28, 2025).

McCormick, Richard. "Notes on Moral Theology." *Theological Studies* 32 (1) (March 1971): 97–107.

McDonagh, Sean. *To Care for the Earth: A Call to a New Theology.* Santa Fe, NM: Bear & Company, 1987.

McDonald, Libby. *The Toxic Sandbox: The Truth About Environmental Toxins and Our Children's Health.* New York: Penguin, 2007.

McFague, Sallie. *Super, Natural Christians: How We Should Love Nature.* Minneapolis, MN: Fortress Press, 1997.

McKeown, James. *Genesis.* Grand Rapids, MI: William. B. Eerdmans Publishing, 2008.

McShane, Katie. "Anthropocentrism vs. Nonanthropocentrism: Why Should We Care?" *Environmental Values* 16 (2) (May 1, 2007): 169–86.

Meeker, John D., Larisa Altshul, and Russ Hauser. "Serum PCBs, p,p'-DDE and HCB Predict Thyroid Hormone Levels in Men." *Environmental Research* 104 (2) (June 2007): 296–304.

Middleton, Guy D. *Understanding Collapse: Ancient History and Modern Myths.* Cambridge: Cambridge University Press, 2017.

Minnesota Department of Health. "Chemicals of Special Concern to Children's Health." February 8, 2025, https://www.health.state.mn.us/communities/environment/childenvhealth/chemicals.html (accessed November 28, 2025).

Monbiot, George. "The Earth Is in a Death Spiral. It Will Take Radical Action to Save Us." *The Guardian.* November 14, 2018, https://www.theguardian.com/commentisfree/2018/nov/14/earth-death-spiral-radical-action-climate-breakdown (accessed November 28, 2025).

Moyer, Jeff, Andrew Smith, Yichao Rul, and Jennifer Hayden. *Regenerative Agriculture and the Soil Carbon Solution.* Kutztown, PA: Rodale Institute, 2020.

Murphy, Catherine. *Cultivating Havana: Urban Agriculture and Food Security in the Years of Crisis.* Oakland, CA: Food First, 1999.

Myers, Tim Christion. "Understanding Climate Change As an Existential Threat: Confronting Climate Denial As a Challenge to Climate Ethics." *De Ethica* 1 (1) (2014): 53–70.

Nash, James A. *Loving Nature: Ecological Integrity and Christian Responsibility*. Nashville, TN: Abingdon Press, 1991.

National Aeronautics and Space Administration. "2020 Tied for Warmest Year on Record, NASA Analysis Shows." January 14, 2021, https://climate.nasa.gov/news/3061/2020-tied-for-warmest-year-on-record-nasa-analysis-shows (accessed November 28, 2025).

National Institutes of Health. "NIH Human Microbiome Project defines normal bacterial makeup of the body." June 13, 2012, https://www.genome.gov/27549144/2012-release-nih-human-microbiome-project-defines-normal-bacterial-makeup-of-the-body (accessed November 28, 2025).

National Recreation and Park Association. "Children in Nature." N.d., https://www.nrpa.org/uploadedFiles/nrpa.org/Advocacy/Children-in-Nature.pdf (accessed November 28, 2025).

National Research Council Committee on Pesticides in the Diets of Infants and Children. *Pesticides in the Diets of Infants and Children*. Washington, D.C.: National Academies Press, 1993.

Nolt, John. "Anthropocentrism and Egoism." *Environmental Values* 22 (4) (2013): 441–59.

Northwest Power and Conservation Council. "Extinction." N.d., https://www.nwcouncil.org/reports/columbia-river-history/extinction (accessed November 28, 2025).

Nygren, Anders. *Agape and Eros*. Philadelphia, PA: Westminster, 1953.

Oceana, "Too Few Fish: A Regional Assessment of the World's Fisheries." May 2008, https://oceana.org/wp-content/uploads/sites/18/toofewfish41.pdf (accessed December 24, 2025).

Ogunrinola, Grace A., John O. Oyewale, Oyewumi O. Oshamika, and Grace I. Olasehinde. "The Human Microbiome and Its Impacts on Health." *International Journal of Microbiology* (June 12, 2020): 1–7, https://www.ncbi.nlm.nih.gov/pmc/articles/PMC7306068 (accessed November 28, 2025).

Ohlson, Kristin. *The Soil Will Save Us*. New York: Rodale, 2014.

Osborn, Liz. "Hundreds of Pacific Salmon Populations Now Extinct." N.d., http://www.currentresults.com/Wildlife/Endangered-Species/Endangered-Fish/hundreds-801101.php (accessed November 28, 2025).

Outka, Gene H. *Agape: An Ethical Analysis*. New Haven, CT: Yale University Press, 1972.

Passmore, Holli-Anne, and Andrew Howell. "Nature Involvement Increases Hedonic and Eudaimonic Well-Being: A Two-Week Experimental Study." *Ecopsychology* 6 (3) (September 1, 2014): 148–54.

Pesticide Action and Agroecology Network. "Do You Know What's In Your Food?" N.d., https://www.panna.org/resources/do-you-know-whats-in-your-food (accessed November 28, 2025).

Plumwood, Val. *Feminism and the Mastery of Nature.* New York: Routledge, 2002.

Ponting, Clive. *A New Green History of the World: The Environment and the Collapse of Great Civilizations.* New York: Vintage Books, 2007.

Post, Anne. "Why Fish Need Trees and Trees Need Fish." N.d., https://www.adfg.alaska.gov/index.cfm?adfg=wildlifenews.view_article&articles_id=407 (accessed November 28, 2025).

Potter, Melody Milam, and Erin E. Milam. *Healthy Baby: Toxic World.* Oakland, CA: New Harbinger Publications, 1999.

Preston, Noel. "The Great Work: Toward an Eco-Centric, Global Culture." *Social Alternatives* 26 (3) (2007): 5–9.

Rad, Gerhard Von. *Genesis: A Commentary.* Louisville, KY: Westminster John Knox Press, 1973.

Radford Ruether, Rosemary. "The Politics of God in the Christian Tradition." *Feminist Theology* 17 (3) (May 1, 2009): 329–38.

Ramsey, Paul. *Deeds and Rules in Christian Ethics.* New York: Charles Scribner's Sons, 1967.

Ratta, Annu, and Jac Smith. "Urban Agriculture: It's About Much More Than Food." *WHY Magazine* 13 (1993): 26–9.

Rees, William E. "Yes, the Climate Crisis May Wipe Out 6 Billion People." September 18, 2019, https://thetyee.ca/Analysis/2019/09/18/Climate-Crisis-Wipe-Out (accessed November 28, 2025).

Ritchie, Hannah, and Max Roser. "Urbanization." *Our World in Data.* June 13, 2018, https://ourworldindata.org/urbanization (accessed November 28, 2025).

Robertson, Ruairi. "How Does Your Gut Microbiome Impact Your Overall Health?" *Healthline.* Jan. 19, 2022, https://www.healthline.com/nutrition/gut-microbiome-and-health (accessed November 28, 2025).

Roewe, Brian. "The first green pope: How Benedict's eco-theology paved the way for Francis." *National Catholic Reporter* (January 4, 2023), https://www.ncronline.org/earthbeat/faith/first-green-pope-how-benedicts-eco-theology-paved-way-francis (accessed November 28, 2025).

Rogan, W. J., and B. C. Gladen. "PCBs, DDE, and Child Development at 18 and 24 Months." *Annals of Epidemiology* 1 (5)(August 1991): 407–13.

Rolston, Holmes. *Environmental Ethics*. Philadelphia, PA: Temple University Press, 2012.

Rosales, Judith. *Climate Change and Water Resources*. Oakville, Ontario: Delve Publishing, 2019.

Safina, Carl. *Beyond Words: What Animals Think and Feel*. London: Souvenir Press Limited, 2016.

Sagiv, Sharon K., Sally W. Thurston, David C. Bellinger, Paige E. Tolbert, Larisa M. Altshul, and Susan A. Korrick. "Prenatal Organochlorine Exposure and Behaviors Associated with Attention Deficit Hyperactivity Disorder in School-Aged Children." *American Journal of Epidemiology* 171 (5) (March 1, 2010): 593–601.

Santmire, Paul. "Reflections on the Alleged Ecological Bankruptcy of Western Theology." *Anglican Theological Review* 57 (2) (April 1975): 131–52.

Santurri, Edmund N., and William Werpehowski. *The Love Commandments: Essays in Christian Ethics and Moral Philosophy*. Eugene, OR: Wipf and Stock Publishers, 2009.

Schaefer, Jame. *Theological Foundations for Environmental Ethics: Reconstructing Patristic and Medieval Concepts*. Washington, DC: Georgetown University Press, 2009.

Scheid, Daniel P. *The Cosmic Common Good: Religious Grounds for Ecological Ethics*. New York: Oxford University Press, 2016.

Schneider, Dona, and Natalie Freeman. *Children's Environmental Health: Reducing Risk in a Dangerous World*. Washington, DC: American Public Health Association, 2000.

Schuller, Robert L. "Ecology—The New Religion?" *America* 122 (11) (March 21, 1970): 292–5.

Schumacher, E. F. *Small is Beautiful: Economics as if People Mattered*. New York: Harper Perennial, 2010.

Scranton, Roy. *We're Doomed. Now What?* New York: SoHo Press, 2018.

Scully, Matthew. *Dominion: The Power of Man, the Suffering of Animals, and the Call to Mercy*. New York: St. Martin's Griffin, 2002.

Secretariat of the Convention of Biological Diversity. "Sustaining Life on Earth: How the Convention on Biological Diversity Promotes Nature and Human Well-Being." 2000, https://www.forest-trends.org/wp-content/uploads/imported/27sustaining-life-on-earth-pdf.pdf (accessed November 28, 2025).

Simaika, John, and Michael Samways. "Biophilia as a Universal Ethic for Conserving Biodiversity." *Conservation Biology* 24 (3) (May 14, 2010): 903–6, https://doi.org/10.1111/j.1523-1739.2010.01485.x.

Simms, Eva. "Eating One's Mother: Female Embodiment in a Toxic World." *Environmental Ethics* 31 (3) (September 1, 2009): 263–77, https://doi.org/10.5840/enviroethics200931330.

Sinaii, N., S. D. Cleary, M. L. Ballweg, L. K. Nieman, and P. Stratton. "High Rates of Autoimmune and Endocrine Disorders, Fibromyalgia, Chronic Fatigue Syndrome and Atopic Diseases among Women with Endometriosis: A Survey Analysis." *Human Reproduction* 17 (10) (October 2002): 2715–24.

Singer, Peter. *Animal Liberation*. London: Pimlico, 1995.

Skylstad, William S. and Timothy W. Whitaker, "Heaven and Earth are Full of Your Glory. A United Methodist and Roman Catholic Statement on the Eucharist and Ecology." 2008, https://www.usccb.org/resources/heaven-and-earth-are-full-your-glory-united-methodist-and-roman-catholic-statement (accessed November 28, 2025).

Slater, Thomas. *A Manual of Moral Theology*. Volume 1. New York: Benzinger Brothers, 1908.

Smith, Laurence C. "More Time Out in Nature Is an Unexpected Benefit of the COVID-19 Sheltering Rules." *Scientific American Blog Network*. April 26, 2020, https://www.proquest.com/docview/2405303649?sourcetype=Scholarly%20Journals (accessed November 28, 2025).

Solomon, Robert C. *True to Our Feelings: What Our Emotions Are Really Telling Us*. New York: Oxford University Press, 2008.

South, Eugenia, Bernadette Hohl, Michelle Kondo, John MacDonald, and Charles Branas. "Effect of Greening Vacant Land on Mental Health of Community-Dwelling Adults: A Cluster Randomized Trial." *JAMA Network Open* 1 (July 20, 2018): 1-14.

Spezio, Michael. "The Neuroscience of Emotion and Reasoning in Social Contexts: Implications for Moral Theology." *Modern Theology* 27 (March 7, 2011): 339–56, https://doi.org/10.1111/j.1468-0025.2010.01680.x.

Spivak, Igor, Leviel Fluhr, and Eran Elinav. "Local and systemic effects of microbiome-derived metabolites." *EMBO Reports*. August 29, 2022, https://www.embopress.org/doi/full/10.15252/embr.202255664 (accessed November 28, 2025).

Stanhope, Jessica, Martin F. Breed, and Philip Weinstein. "Exposure to Greenspaces Could Reduce the High Global Burden of Pain." *Environmental Research* 187 (August 2020): 1-11, https://pmc.ncbi.nlm.nih.gov/articles/PMC7207132/pdf/main.pdf (accessed November 28, 2025).

Steenland, K., A. M. Mora, D. B. Barr, J. Juncos, N. Roman, and C. Wesseling. "Organochlorine Chemicals and Neurodegeneration among

Elderly Subjects in Costa Rica." *Environmental Research* 134 (October 2014): 205–9.

Stein, Rob. "Finally, A Map of All the Microbes on Your Body." *National Public Radio Online*. June 13, 2012, https://www.npr.org/sections/health-shots/2012/06/13/154913334/finally-a-map-of-all-the-microbes-on-your-body (accessed November 28, 2025).

Swan, Shanna H., and Stacey Colino. *Count Down: How Our Modern World Is Threatening Sperm Counts, Altering Male and Female Reproductive Development, and Imperiling the Future of the Human Race.* New York: Simon & Schuster, 2021.

Swanson, Tim, and Ben Groom. "Regulating Global Biodiversity: What Is the Problem?" *Oxford Review of Economic Policy* 28 (1) (2012): 114–38.

Swimme, Brian. *The Universe Story: From the Primordial Flaring Forth to the Ecozoic Era–A Celebration of the Unfolding of the Cosmos.* New York: Harper Collins, 1992.

Tainter, Joseph. *The Collapse of Complex Societies.* New York: Cambridge University Press, 1988.

Taylor, Paul W. *Respect for Nature: A Theory of Environmental Ethics – 25th Anniversary Edition.* Princeton, NJ: Princeton University Press, 2011.

The American Presidency Project. "The Biden Plan to Build a Modern, Sustainable Infrastructure and an Equitable Clean Energy Future." July 14, 2020, https://www.presidency.ucsb.edu/documents/biden-campaign-press-release-the-biden-plan-build-modern-sustainable-infrastructure-and (accessed December 24, 2025).

Thomas, Julia Adeney, Mark Williams, and Jan Zalasiewicz. *The Anthropocene: A Multidisciplinary Approach.* Hoboken, NJ: Wiley, 2020.

Toner, Jules J. *The Experience of Love.* Washington, DC: Corpus Books, 1968.

Trible, Phyllis. "Ancient Priests and Modern Polluters." *Foundations* 17 (2) (1974): 158–63.

Tucker, Evelyn, M., and John Grim, eds. *Thomas Berry: Selected Writings on the Earth Community.* Maryknoll: NY: Orbis Books, 2016.

Tull, Patricia K. *Inhabiting Eden: Christians, the Bible, and the Ecological Crisis.* Louisville, KY: Westminster John Knox Press, 2013.

Ulrich, R. S. "View through a Window May Influence Recovery from Surgery." *Science* 224 (4647) (April 27, 1984): 420–1.

Union of Concerned Scientists. "Climate Change and Agriculture: A Perfect Storm in Farm Country." March 20, 2019, https://www.ucsusa.org/resources/climate-change-and-agriculture (accessed November 28, 2025).

United Nations Conference on Trade and Development. *Wake Up Before It Is Too Late: Make Agriculture Truly Sustainable Now for Food Security in a Changing Climate.* March 2013, https://unctad.org/system/files/official-document/ditcted2012d3_en.pdf (accessed November 28, 2025).

United Nations, Department of Economic and Social Affairs, Population Division. *World Population Prospects, 2019,* https://population.un.org/wpp/assets/Files/WPP2019_Highlights.pdf (accessed November 28, 2025).

United Nations, Food and Agriculture Organization. *The State of Food and Agriculture, 2012,* https://www.fao.org/3/i3028e/i3028e00.htm (accessed November 28, 2025).

United States Conference of Catholic Bishops. "Renewing the Earth: An Invitation to Reflection and Action on Environment in Light of Catholic Social Teaching." November. 14, 1991, https://www.usccb.org/resources/renewing-earth (accessed November 28, 2025).

United States Department of Agriculture, Agriculture Marketing Service. "Pesticide Data Program," 2020, https://www.ams.usda.gov/datasets/pdp (accessed November 28, 2025).

United States Environmental Protection Agency. "Climate Change Impacts on Forests." N.d., https://www.epa.gov/climateimpacts/climate-change-impacts-forests (accessed November 28, 2025).

United States Environmental Protection Agency. "Global Greenhouse Gas Emissions Data." N.d., https://www.epa.gov/ghgemissions/global-greenhouse-gas-emissions-data#Sector (accessed November 28, 2025).

United States Environmental Protection Agency. "Highlights of Key Provisions in the Frank R. Lautenberg Chemical Safety for the 21st Century Act." N.d., https://www.epa.gov/assessing-and-managing-chemicals-under-tsca/highlights-key-provisions-frank-r-lautenberg-chemical (accessed November 28, 2025).

United States Environmental Protection Agency. "Understanding Global Warming Potentials." N.d., https://www.epa.gov/ghgemissions/understanding-global-warming-potentials (accessed November 28, 2025).

United States Environmental Protection Agency. "Technical Fact Sheet-Polybrominated Diphenyl Ethers." November 2017, https://nepis.epa.gov/Exe/ZyPDF.cgi/P100TLNI.PDF?Dockey=P100TLNI.PDF (accessed November 28, 2025).

United States Environmental Protection Agency. "What You Can Do to Protect Children from Environmental Risks." N.d., https://www.epa.gov/children/what-you-can-do-protect-children-environmental-risks (accessed November 28, 2025).

United States Fish and Wildlife Service. "Salmon: A Pacific Northwest Icon." June 7, 2022, https://www.fws.gov/story/2022-06/salmona-pacific-northwest-icon (accessed November 28, 2025).

Vacek, Edward Collins. *Love, Human and Divine: The Heart of Christian Ethics*. Washington, DC: Georgetown University Press, 1994.

Vatican Council II. *Gaudium et Spes*. December 7, 1965, https://www.vatican.va/archive/hist_councils/ii_vatican_council/documents/vat-ii_const_19651207_gaudium-et-spes_en.html (accessed November 28, 2025).

Vawter, Bruce. *On Genesis: A New Reading*. New York: Doubleday, 1977.

Ward, Peter D. *Under a Green Sky: Global Warming, the Mass Extinctions of the Past, and What They Can Tell Us about Our Future*. New York: Smithsonian Books/Collins, 2007.

Watnick, Valerie. "The Lautenberg Chemical Safety Act of 2016: Cancer, Industry Pressure, and A Proactive Approach." *Harvard Environmental Law Review* 43 (2) (2019): 101–60.

Westermann, Claus. *Genesis 1-11: A Continental Commentary*. Minneapolis, MN: Fortress Press, 1994.

White, Lynn. "The Historical Roots of Our Ecologic Crisis." *Science* 155 (3767) (1967): 1203–7.

Williams, Florence. "Toxic Breast Milk?" *The New York Times Magazine*. January 9, 2005, 21–4.

Wilson, Edward O. *Half-Earth: Our Planet's Fight for Life*. New York: Liveright, 2016.

Wohlleben, Peter. *The Hidden Life of Trees: What They Feel, How They Communicate*. Berkeley, CA: Greystone Books, 2016.

Wolff, M. S., P. G. Toniolo, E. W. Lee, M. Rivera, and N. Dubin. "Blood Levels of Organochlorine Residues and Risk of Breast Cancer." *Journal of the National Cancer Institute* 85 (8) (April 21, 1993): 648–52.

Wood, Matt. "How the microbiome affects human health, explained." *University of Chicago News*. January 2025, https://news.uchicago.edu/explainer/how-microbiome-affects-human-health-explained#health (accessed November 28, 2025).

World Health Organization. "Dioxins." November 29, 2023, https://www.who.int/news-room/fact-sheets/detail/dioxins-and-their-effects-on-human-health (accessed November 28, 2025).

Wu, Jiang-Ping, Xiao-Jun Luo, Ying Zhang, Mei Yu, She-Jun Chen, Bi-Xian Mai, and Zhong-Yi Yang. "Biomagnification of Polybrominated Diphenyl Ethers (PBDEs) and Polychlorinated Biphenyls in a Highly Contaminated Freshwater Food Web from South China." *Environmental Pollution* 157 (3) (March 2009): 904–9.

Yoffee, Norman, and George L. Cowgill. *The Collapse of Ancient States and Civilizations*. Tucson: University of Arizona Press, 1988.

Yong, Ed. "I Contain Multitides." *BBC Science Focus Magazine.* Aug. 3, 2017, https://www.sciencefocus.com/nature/i-contain-multitudes-by-ed-yong (accessed November 28, 2025).

Zhang, Jia, Paul Piff, Ravi Iyer, Sena Koleva, and Dacher Keltner. "An Occasion for Unselfing: Beautiful Nature Leads to Prosociality." *Journal of Environmental Psychology* 37 (March 1, 2014): 61–72.

Index